CHRISTIANITY AND THE MAKING OF THE MODERN FAMILY

Christianity and the Making of the Modern Family

Ruling Ideologies, Diverse Realities

ROSEMARY RADFORD RUETHER

Beacon Press

BOSTON

Beacon Press
25 Beacon Street
Boston, Massachusetts 02108-2892
www.beacon.org

Beacon Press books
are published under the auspices of
the Unitarian Universalist Association of Congregations.

05 04 03 02 01   8 7 6 5 4 3 2 1

This book is printed on acid-free paper that meets the uncoated paper
ANSI/NISO specifications for permanence as revised in 1992.

Composition by Wilsted & Taylor Publishing Services

Library of Congress Cataloging-in-Publication Data
  Ruether, Rosemary Radford.
    Christianity and the making of the modern family : ruling
  ideologies, diverse realities / Rosemary Radford Ruether.
      p.   cm.
    Includes bibliographical references.
    ISBN 0-8070-5404-6 (cloth)
    ISBN 0-8070-5407-0 (pbk.)
      1. Family—Religious aspects—Chrisitianity—History of
  doctrines.   2. Family—History.   I. Title.
  BT707.7 .R84   2000
  261.8'3585'09—dc21

                              00-008448

CONTENTS

ACKNOWLEDGMENTS

I dedicate this book to Rosemary Skinner Keller, my colleague at Garrett-Evangelical for twenty years and now dean at Union Theological Seminary in New York. This book grows out of the many seminars we taught together at Garrett-Evangelical in Christianity, Gender, and Family History. I also thank the students in the course in Gender, Family, and Religion in the spring of 1999 at Garrett-Evangelical, who read the first draft of this book and offered helpful feedback on its themes and thesis.

CHRISTIANITY AND THE MAKING OF THE MODERN FAMILY

> "[Focus on the Family] attempts to 'turn hearts toward home' by reason-
> able, biblical and empirical insights so people will be able to discover the
> founder of homes and the creator of families—Jesus Christ."
>
> —Focus on the Family

> "If anyone comes to me and can not hate his own father and mother and
> wife and children and brother and sisters, yes, and even his own life, he
> cannot be my disciple."
>
> —Jesus of Nazareth, according to Luke 14:25–26

Read together, these two statements must cause any reader to wonder,
What is going on here? How can the aims of Focus on the Family, a
group dedicated to strengthening "traditional values" by spreading
Christ's gospel, be so at odds with the vision of the biblical Jesus?

The answer is anything but simple. There is a deep conflict in
American society over the proper roles of men and women and over
the relationship of these roles to religious and moral values. This conflict has come to be known as the "family values" debate. However,
"family values" is a misleading and partisan term, used by groups that
champion a particular model of family—specifically, one based on
male headship and female subordination. These groups assume that
their model of the family is biblical. But actually there is little relationship between this model and the Bible: the historical Jesus in fact
appears quite often to have endorsed views that might be characterized as "antifamily."

This book engages in a historical excursus from the New Testament through Western Christian history and into American social
constructions of work, family, and gender. My goal has been to locate
and identify the basis for the current—and deeply ahistorical—ideology of "family values." To this end, my text focuses on three major
themes: the changing form and definition of family over the last two
millennia; the pattern of Christianity's volatile relationship, throughout its history, to the family; and the shifting nature of ideologies of

family, determined not only by changing family structures but also by the places where and the ways in which societies worship.

There has never, of course, been only one form of family. The very term in fact requires definition because it covers several distinguishable realities of human social and economic relations, of kin and non-kin, within households and also beyond them. These relations have been highly malleable in human societies through the centuries, changing to reflect different functions performed by kin and household groups in relation to the larger society.

To complicate things further, Christianity as a religion has varied in its stance toward the family as defined as a kinship group constituted by marriage and procreation. For much of its history Christianity took a negative or at least highly ambivalent view of the union of men and women in marriage, of sexual relations, and of procreation. The ideal Christian was seen as being unmarried, celibate, and childless—a profile that renders the Christian Right's effort to sanctify its concept of "the family" as normatively biblical quite simply untenable. There are several types of family in Hebrew scripture, none of which corresponds with the modern nuclear model. The New Testament, for its part, offers no single view of family. It is even, at times, frankly antifamily, though desires for alternative family structures and for the restoration of the patriarchal family are also expressed.

The negative view of marriage promoted by earlier Christian tradition was reformulated in the Protestant Reformation of the sixteenth century. At this time, celibacy was abolished as a higher Christian vocation and as a requirement for ordained ministry. Modern Christians think Christianity has always championed "the family," but this belief ignores three fourths of actual Christian history. It also fails to account for the conflicted views of sexuality and of women that continue to plague Protestant as well as Catholic forms of Christianity. (It is with these latter that this book is primarily concerned; Orthodox and other Eastern forms of Christianity are considered here only in reference to the Patristic period.)

There is yet another variable that affects ideologies of family: the changing location and role of religion. As I have noted, Christian family ideologies have been modified from largely antifamily to largely pro-family. But these changes conceal a multitude of differences. Earliest church practice, whereby the worship community was located within households but was in tension with marital relations, gradually gave way to liturgies conducted in separate edifices, headed increasingly by celibates who defined the married of the church as second-class Christians. When worship moves out of houses and into institutions run by clergy, it is no longer controlled by household members but is ruled instead from outside, by individuals who see themselves as members of a superior caste. The Reformation saw an attempt to make fathers (and then, in the eighteenth and nineteenth centuries, mothers) the primary inculcators of religious observance within the home. Today, in the United States, the norm, even among churchgoing Christians, is a secularized family, with very little religious practice actually going on in the home, despite the effort on the part of the Christian Right to turn "the family" into a religious symbol.

I intend to show that shifting ideologies involving the family and "family values" are generally coded messages about women and how they should behave in relation to men. Such messages are inspired by the assumption that women have departed from their proper role in the family through some recent corrupting influence, and must be persuaded and/or coerced back into that role by a combination of insistent propaganda (by religious and political leaders) and political policy.

Propaganda about women's misbehavior and corruption of society as causing a "decline" in the family is based on a misperception about the diverse work roles women actually have played in families in the past and still play today. This view sees women as either lesser or different, in ways that demand their confinement to supposedly unchanging and divinely ordained family duties such as housekeeping, child care, and care for the husband in his domestic and sexual needs, eschewing (paid) work.

I will try to relativize such perceptions of fixed family roles in Western Christian history by showing how changing economic configuratons have radically affected what is considered work, where work takes place, and who does what kind of work. I will also analyze the shifting messages about family propagated by religious and philosophical ideologues, in order to discern their purposes. It is my belief that this type of ideological message is typically *pre*scriptive, rather than truly *de*scriptive of what is actually happening in families.

In the first chapter I will locate the antifamily and alternative-family messages of the New Testament in the context of Greco-Roman and Jewish family patterns of the period. While both Roman and Jewish cultures connected religion with family, both also knew certain philosophical and ascetic models that negated the family in favor of "higher" forms of life. The New Testament's negation of the family is framed primarily in a context of eschatological expectation, but it also carries an implicit judgment regarding the family as an expression of worldly power. Moreover, its vision of the church as an alternative family was itself in profound tension with existing social constructions of the family in the Jewish and Greco-Roman worlds. This stance would be undermined by the later Pauline Epistles, which attempted to reinsert the church into existing patriarchal, slaveholding family ideologies.

In chapter 2 I will trace the continuing tension between the church, in its role as a new redemptive community in radical forms of Christianity, and existing social expectations. I will also show how asceticism was domesticated, within Greco-Roman Stoic views of family authority and disciplined sexuality, to become "orthodox" Christianity.

By the late fourth century, the effort either to create ascetic communities in the place of family or to integrate asceticism *into* the family had been reshaped into a hierarchical ordering of celibate elites, both male and female, over married people, who thenceforth became second-class citizens of the church. A vehement debate broke out in Latin Christianity over the relative status of marriage vis à vis celibacy. The proposal that both be accorded equal status was rejected by Ambrose, Jerome, and Augustine in favor of a position that allowed procreative sex within marriage, but only as a lesser spiritual option. Celibacy was seen as the normative expression of Christian life for all those living in the last age of world history and awaiting the heavenly kingdom, where there would be no more marrying or giving in marriage.

Chapter 2 also traces three major struggles that defined late Patristic Christianity in the West from their origins into the high Middle Ages: the effort to impose celibacy on the clergy, the push to Christianize marriage, and the attempt to control the ministries of celibate women.

The first stage of the effort to celibatize the clergy took the form of a decree that clergymen live as "brother and sister" with their wives. For their part, clergy wives were allowed a secondary ministry alongside their husbands. This effort ultimately failed because the church was unable to force clergy to live sexless lives within marriage. The next step was to forbid clergy to marry altogether, but that plan, too, had an inherent flaw: since day-to-day survival demanded the domestic work of women or servants, few men outside of monastic compounds could survive without women. In the twelfth-century reform movement, clergy wives were officially defined as concubines and their children as bastards, but that did not prevent most rural clergy from living in common-law marriages.

The effort to Christianize marriage required the imposition of the church's rules of monogamy, of sacramental indissolubility, and of forbidden degrees of consanguinity on Germanic forms of marriage that assumed polygamy, easy divorce, and marriage between kin, particularly among the nobility. This led to a continual power struggle over marriage between the church and the aristocracy through the Middle Ages. Yet the medieval church never clearly defined what constituted a valid marriage, nor did it tie marriage as a sacrament to a particular public church ceremony.

The control of celibate women and their cloistering in monastic compounds under male ecclesiastical control comprised a third area of church struggle that remained incompletely implemented by the medieval church. Women's desires to take up ministries of teaching and religious leadership often escaped the bounds of church control.

The Protestant and Catholic reformations are the subject of chapter 3. Here we see, on the Protestant side, a rejection of the celibate ideal that had shaped Christianity during its first fifteen hundred years, not only for the secular clergy but also for monks and nuns. Protestantism sought to unify church and family by insisting that marriage was a creational ordinance demanded of all, as well as a necessary means to control the lustful urges of fallen "man." Yet Protestantism also desacramentalized marriage and thus opened the way for divorce. On the Catholic side, the reforming Council of Trent attempted to succeed in the unfinished struggles to impose celibacy on priests and to strictly cloister nuns, and to define the marks of a valid and sacramentally indissoluble marriage.

The sixteenth century also saw a turning point in the gradual shifting of relationships between home and work, between private and public, between female and male spheres of life. In the early Middle Ages, the decentralized feudal and manorial system made for little difference between the work of the home and the public economy, between public and domestic administration. This enabled fluid gender relations across political and economic strata, together with a marked differentiation by class.

But with the redevelopment of market economies, local and interregional trade, and the state, these spheres of home and work, of domestic administration and public government, became increasingly separate. Urban political, merchant, and guild leaders sought to confine women to privatized roles in a domestic consumer economy and to forbid both their engagement in direct production for trade and their political self-representation. The urban middle class of the sixteenth-century cities of Germany and Italy thus became a key site of the redefinition of women's "place."

Chapter 4 traces the gradual construction of a pattern of family that modern American society would come to imagine as normative and "God-given": the "modern" or Victorian family. The product of a number of shifts in the relation of work, family, and gender, the first step in the creation of this model came with the burgeoning artisan economy, which located work in workshops attached to the home but sought to differentiate the auxiliary functions assigned to women from the primary production done by male guild members and journeymen.

This artisan economy was gradually undermined by merchant entrepreneurs who controlled all stages of production and marketing while subordinating the actual artisans to piece labor done for low wages by women, men, and children in the home. This system was eventually superseded by factories that integrated all stages of production in one site, transferring the labor of men, women, and children from the home into differentiated roles and wage scales within the factory. The assumption was still that the whole family—men, women, and children—would engage in productive labor for a family wage, but increasingly such families became redefined as proletarians who traded their labor for wages, rather than owners of the means of production.

The middle class shaped itself as an entrepreneurial elite over this worker population. In this new economy the apprentices of the artisan economy were expelled from the master's home and installed in their own workers' hovels. Over time, the duties involved in managing the business were also professionalized and expelled from the home: running the shops where the goods were sold, bookkeeping, collecting debts, and paying salaries were no longer the province of the entrepreneurs' wives, who were now relieved of the functions in which they had participated in the artisan and early factory economies. The office of the male business manager, doctor, or lawyer was removed from the home to a separate office building, and the home itself removed from proximity to the business and/or factory and relocated in a suburb. Gardens became places of leisure landscaped with ornamental flowers and lawns, no longer the kitchen gardens of vegetables and herbs that had once fed and cured the family. The architecture of the home was reshaped to create a refuge from the economic "world," with parlor, bedrooms, and nurseries clearly delineated by corridors. A series of changing relations of home and work redrew the boundaries that defined gendered spheres, setting off home, as the "nonworking" place of women, from office, the male world of paid work.

The hegemony of this model of the family for Americans in the post–Civil War period was more of an ideological triumph than a reflection of the actual predominance of this family form. Even for the white middle class, such a model often masked the contrary reality of continued economic production by the wife in the home, as she grew and preserved food, made soaps and medicines, and sewed clothes. The skills of home production and their economic role in family maintenance were only gradually lost in America in the twentieth century.

But in any event, the ideal of the male "breadwinner," in charge of the economic and political spheres and separated from the domesticated female world, was no sooner established as the ideological norm in the second half of the nineteenth century than white women themselves began to revolt against it, seeking education, political rights, and professional employment in order to liberate themselves from the domestic prison of the family. Chapter 5 traces the series of abrupt ideological shifts concerning gender and sexuality that took place between 1890 and 1940, as white women engaged in movements of emancipation into the larger worlds of professional employment and political participation from which they had been excluded by the men of their families.

At the turn of the century, white female suffragists masked their conflict with the family by adopting a social practice of celibacy and female bonding combined with a rhetoric of maternal family nurturance transferred from the privatized family to the larger society. This Victorian female reform culture characterized the generation that won women's rights to property, higher education, entrance into the professions, and, finally, the vote. The first generation of female professionals of 1900–1920 were typically single and often bonded with other women, while maintaining a demeanor of feminine moral transcendence of "animal" sexuality.

In the 1920s this Victorian female reform culture broke down when a new generation of white middle-class women "wanted it all": education, a job, sexual pleasure, and eventually marriage and children. Working wives and mothers were identified and debated as a social problem, though they had not been seen as a problem before, when black and immigrant women worked at low-wage jobs and also raised children. The newly discovered "problem" of working wives was primarily an ideological one relating to white middle-class women, who now posed a challenge to the separation of "spheres" that demarcated their wifely and maternal roles from the professional employment of their men.

Chapter 6 examines the shifting definitions of women's "proper" role from the end of the Depression to the rebirth of feminism. It is important to note, once again, that beneath the changing ideologies lay the very different realities of black and working-class wives who never stopped working. In addition, an increasing number of white middle-class women both married and worked. Mothers began to return to work when their children were younger and younger, often before preschool age. The proportion of working women grew steadily from 1900 to today, when women make up almost half the work force and most married women work.

In chapter 7 I discuss the rise of the Christian Right in the 1970s as a backlash against the civil-rights, feminist, student Left, antiwar, and gay-rights movements. Under the banner of "family values," the Christian Right has sought to reestablish as normative the Victorian model of working husband and full-time housewife, sanctifying this family form as both the revealed norm of the "Bible" and a reflection of the "order of Creation" established by God.

This concept of the family flies in the face of the economic need in most families for two wages, even as it flouts women's new legal and political autonomy. The policy expressions of the "family values" campaign are thus concerned as much with forcing women down as with forcing them out of the work force, and so exacerbate rather than relieve the conflicts experienced by women and men in families, and most particularly by single mothers, as they try to harmonize the demands of paid labor with those of child raising.

Chapter 8 surveys the economic realities of American society in the 1990s, when the rising cost of living and the need to work longer hours in order to earn an adequate wage created enormous tensions between family and work. A two-tiered wage system divided those who worked for hourly wages at or a few dollars above the minimum wage, often part-time and without benefits, from those with "full-time" job contracts with medical benefits and pensions.

Even two-earner families in the low-wage category barely rose above the poverty level in the last decade of the twentieth century. Those with better-paying full-time jobs also had to struggle to keep up with the demands of the middle-class American life-style, especially when raising children. The two-earner household thus became the predominant form of the American family in the 1990s. The poorest American families were predominantly those headed by single mothers seeking to support both their children and themselves with low-paid jobs.

In the concluding chapter I seek to reimagine families in several ways. First, I try to envision family policies that would fully accept diverse forms of the family and equal roles for men and women in both family and household care and paid labor. What kinds of policies would be genuinely supportive of women and men as equal partners in family care and paid work? What kinds of policies would promote an acceptable balance between these different but interconnected parts of people's lives? And what kinds of policies would adequately support those families which depend on the single wage of a woman?

Second, I distinguish between the role of the state in creating legal contracts for domestic-partner relations and that of the church in promoting covenanted communities and blessing their "holy unions." I suggest how the church's covenanting role could support diverse forms of family at different stages of a person's life.

Finally, I rethink the theology of marriage and family. The anti-family traditions of the gospels and early Christianity can in fact be understood as a critique of oppressive forms of family. In this light, theologies that sacralize family systems of "male headship" at the expense of women, children, and servants are not legitimate; they are forms of human sin, not divine mandate. This critique also opens up the theological space to reimagine family as a redemptive form of covenanted community, engaged in processes of mutual love and service that we might again be able to call sacramental.

In *Christianity and the Making of the Modern Family* I seek to play both a critical and a constructive role in the current discussion of family. I relativize the Victorian or "modern" family as a product of a particular social class and historical period and advocate an acceptance of a postmodern or pluralist understanding of family forms. I have tried to thoroughly deconstruct fallacious views about the "biblical" model of the family and to show the complexity of the ideologies of family in Christian history, as well as to reveal the many forms families have taken in different historical and socioeconomic contexts. I hope I have also been able to expose the negative consequences of current policies masquerading as "pro-family." But most important, I hope this history will inspire Americans, and specifically church people, to reimagine ethics, theology, liturgy, practices, and policies for the church and society that might actually promote good families— that is, families living in mutuality with one another in sustainable communities and environments. This is the task that still lies ahead of us.

Families in Jewish and Greco-Roman Worlds and Early Christianity

The worlds of the early Christians were the Jewish and Greco-Roman worlds. Early Christian ideas of family are therefore necessarily embedded in that context. Within the limits of this chapter I cannot do justice to the complexity of the data provided in the numerous recent studies done on Greek, Roman,[1] and Jewish[2] families in antiquity. I can only allude briefly to some of the major configurations of families in these two cultures which provided the backdrop for early Christian development, and the ideologies about family found in them, both positive and negative. I will then describe some of the peculiarities of the early Christian movement as a "fictive kin group"[3] awaiting eschatological transformation, and explain how this idea positioned the church in relation to marriage and procreation.

We must begin with some definition of terms. There was no word in the Greek, Roman, or Jewish worlds for what modern Americans take to be the central meaning of "family"—namely, the nuclear unit consisting of a married couple, man and woman, and their children, living, usually without other kin or non-kin, in a neolocal household. In antiquity it is necessary to distinguish the two different realities of *household*, as a residential unit for production, consumption, and service, and *kin*, as networks of people related by blood and marriage.[4] The core or nuclear family existed at the intersection of these two realities, not, as it is seen today, as a freestanding social and residential unit; hence its lack of a specific name in antiquity.

HOUSEHOLD AND KIN IN FIRST-CENTURY ROMAN CITIES
In Roman law and parlance the word *familia* meant something very different from the English word *family. Familia* referred to persons and

things under the sovereign control of the male head of household, or *paterfamilias*. This meant, first of all, his slaves, as well as any ex-slaves who owed him service. It could also include nonhuman property such as land, houses, and animals.

Children—even grown sons—remained under their father's *patria potestas* ("paternal power") until his death, unless the father emancipated them, at which point they were *sui iuris*, or under their own rule. Married daughters who had been given away in a form of marriage that did not put them under their husband's power (*sine manu*) also remained members of their birth family and under their father's authority, unless they had been given autonomy (*sui iuris*). The children's mother, meanwhile, if she herself had been married *sine manu*, might still be under her own father's *patria potestas*, unless she had been emancipated and gained autonomous control over her own property (*sui iuris*).[5]

This complex set of qualifications as to who was and was not included in the *familia* of the *paterfamilias* shows how markedly the Roman concept of the *familia* differed from modern assumptions about the meaning of the term *family*. The *familia* was further distinguished from the kin network (called the *domus* or "house" by the Romans), which consisted of the male lineage of blood descendants through the generations.[6]

Roman society was especially concerned with maintaining and reproducing this male lineage with all its rights of power and property. To this end, females needed to be exchanged between lineages for the purpose of producing legitimate sons. Increasingly, such transactions were effected without handing over to the husband the ownership of the property that a wife traditionally brought with her on marriage. By marrying *sine manu*, a woman retained the ownership of such property as a member of her own family, thus protecting it in case of divorce.[7]

Because Roman society and its law were also concerned with keeping the lineage of Roman families "pure" from admixture with foreigners, marriage to a person without Roman citizenship was illegal, and the offspring of such a marriage illegitimate. Slaves were also unable to contract legal marriages, nor could senators free and then marry them; hence the children of slaves (sometimes fathered by owners or their sons) could not pass into the paternal lineage.[8]

The Roman child, particularly of the wealthy upper class (comprising about 3 percent of the Roman population), grew up in a very different household from our own. The *familia* might consist of dozens or even hundreds of slaves, not including the thousands more that labored on estates owned by the *pater*. While the child's mother ideally supervised his or her early childhood development, he or she was usually nursed by a slave wet nurse and cared for by slave child-carers, often in the company of slave children (sometimes half-siblings) nursed and cared for by these same slaves.[9]

As a boy grew he would be handed over to slave tutors and then sent to school, sometimes also taught by educated slaves, to acquire those skills of public speaking that were seen as key to official life. A girl child usually was taught only the rudiments of reading before being trained in domestic skills in preparation for marriage. This latter typically took place shortly after puberty, joining her to a man who might be twice her age, chosen by her father from a lineage of one of his friends or political allies.[10]

Members of the Roman upper class married and divorced frequently with their shifting alliances and in their quest for legitimate male offspring. Many also adopted males of allied households, usually young adults, in order to gain suitable heirs.[11] A household might include stepmothers, stepbrothers and stepsisters, and other half-kin. Slaves did the manifold tasks of the household, including producing much of its consumer goods, managing the estates of the master, and supervising his business affairs. The master himself did not go out to "work" but instead oversaw his business and political affairs from an office behind the courtyard at the front of his house, assisted by slave or freedman secretaries.[12]

The front part of the Roman house was a quasi-public space where associates dropped in constantly to pay the paterfamilias honor, and where clients and former slaves congregated each morning to give him a morning salutation, run errands for him, or provide other services as demanded in return for food and monetary gifts.[13] In his daily rounds outside the house, the master might attend various social functions such as rites of passage for the sons of other lineages, or he might go to the baths, where he would knit together his political ties through assorted honorific formalities.

Poorer persons in Roman cities (the vast majority) had very different privileges from this upper class, though they lived within the orbit of the same system. Middle-level households with many fewer slaves and smaller houses would nonetheless seek to duplicate these patterns on more modest level. Slaves (who made up about a third of the population in Roman Italy in the first century) did not live in separate houses, but instead slept in the back areas of the same houses as their masters and their masters' children (few other than the master and his wife would have a separate bedroom).[14]

Poor freed or freeborn persons might live crowded together in rooms in apartment buildings (*insulae*), but these "apartments" were only sleeping shelters, without kitchens or toilet facilities.[15] Work, eating, and toiletry were all done on the street, in open plazas and public baths and in the eateries and workshops that were part of the extended households of the owning classes. The poorer person sought to attach himself to such a household for work, food, and contacts. Much as the poor man or woman might desire marriage and children, it was not easy to maintain continuity in such units, since slave unions could be broken up at any time by the master to sell spouse away from spouse or children away from parents. Moreover, the slave woman or boy was subject to sexual demands at any time from the master and his sons and friends.[16]

The poor urban freedman or freeborn man or woman, huddled with others in apartment rooms, could not afford to raise many children. Often such infants were put out to die or to be picked up by slave dealers. If poor parents wanted to keep a child, they might pay a neighbor woman to nurse or care for it, and at an early age seek to place him or her as an apprentice in a workshop.[17] This does not mean there was no sense of kin ties or affection between spouses or between parents and children; indeed, the efforts made to maintain such relations among slaves and poorer freedmen and the freeborn testify to the depth of feeling for these ties of blood and marriage.[18] But there were formidable obstacles to retaining such bonds in ongoing physical contiguity.

JEWISH FAMILIES IN ANTIQUITY

Much less extensive work has been done on the Jewish family than on the Roman in antiquity, but there have been significant recent studies. Carol Meyer, for example, has deduced from archaeological evidence the probable pattern of Jewish peasant family life prior to the rise of the monarchy in 1000 B.C.[19] It is likely that the kind of peasant family household she describes is similar to that of the Romans prior to the emergence of the slave economy in Italy in the third century B.C.

Meyer depicts a marginally self-sufficient agricultural society, grouped in villages of fifty to eighty inhabitants surrounded by a few acres of stony land on which they laboriously cultivated crops and raised animals. The villages themselves were composed of patrilocal households in which the adult males were mostly kin through patrilineal descent. These households, of which there were about six to ten per village, consisted of several small houses linked together by a common courtyard. These connected buildings typically housed a three-generational family of father and mother (while still alive), one or two grown sons, and the sons' children. When the father died, the head position passed to the elder son, who then continued the same pattern with his own children.

The houses themselves served mainly as shelters for work and animals in inclement weather, as well as providing storage for tools and food, with attached lean-tos used for cooking. The family probably slept in lofts above the ground floor. This household was both a core kin unit and a primary unit for production and consumption. All family members, excepting only the very young and the most feeble elderly, worked together for long hours to each day cultivate and process the food and to produce the clothes and other artifacts on which the family depended.

Mortality was high (as was the case generally in antiquity), with perhaps only one in four children growing to adulthood, though children were not exposed to die or be picked up as slaves, as was the Greek and Roman custom. Marriage was endogamous, favoring spouses within the kin group but outside of the immediate family (ideally cousins). Daughters were sent out as wives to related villages, and their daughters in turn returned to the family as daughters-in-law/wives. Enormous value was placed on retaining the family land and not selling it or allowing it to be alienated from the core paternal "house."

The village also practiced some communal sharing of tools and resources. This core paternal household/kin group and its village were, in turn, embedded in perceived larger networks of kin in nearby villages, constituting tribes, which in their turn saw themselves as being linked together as the "tribes of Israel," distinguished by their allegiance to the tribal god, Yahweh, and thereby separated from other "idolatrous" ethnic groups around them.[20]

The rise of the monarchy in A.D. 1000 threatened the self-sufficiency of these peasant households and villages, and the threat was aggravated by successive empires with their colonial occupying armies and administrations, from the Assyrians, Babyonians, and Persians from the eighth to sixth centuries B.C. to the Greeks and Romans from the third century B.C. The Jewish monarchy and then the occupying empires exploited the peasant-farmer economic base by imposing taxes and service requirements in the form of work corvées.[21]

When the surplus food produced by these peasants was confiscated through taxes, the peasants fell into debt, lost their land, and were forced into debtor servitude and slavery. Their indebted land was then taken over and turned into large estates for a new landed elite who exploited it for its monetary value in a trade economy, not for primary subsistence. Colonizing armies rounded up Jewish people and scattered them as settlers or slaves throughout their empires, then settled their own people in Palestine. Jewish tribal/religious identity tried to hold itself apart from these imperial cultures through customs relating to food, endogamy, and distinct cultic observances, but some assimilation was inevitable.

In the first century A.D., Jewish families in urban areas of Roman-controlled Palestine assumed a variety of forms. Wealthy, politically powerful households with many slaves functioned not unlike those of the Roman elite, with the exceptions that children were not exposed and polygamy was allowed.[22] Poorer Jewish families seem to have tried to reproduce in the city something of the paternal extended household of the rural village, with several related families' living together in apartments around common courtyards.[23] Eventually, however, economic destitution, migration, and enslavement scattered Jews across the cities of the empire, from Babylonia to Spain.

Jewish law allowed ready divorce and remarriage for men, but not for women,[24] as in Roman law. A divorced Jewish woman would find it hard to remarry, and would be forced into less repectable status if her natal family did not take her in. The Jewish woman who married

into the paternal household of her husband did not retain the economic autonomy afforded by the Roman provision of marriage *sine
manu*. But her dowry, and any money given to her by her husband at
the time of their marriage, were protected, to be returned to her in
case of divorce, by nuptial agreements (*ketubah*).[25]

JEWISH AND ROMAN FAMILIES AND RELIGION

For both Romans and Jews, the kin-household was the primary base
for religious identity and observance, and religion was closely connected with reproducing lineage and national identity. Religious
identity was integral to membership in a family. Roman households
honored the hearth (in the person of the goddess Vesta) and the *Pena-
tes*, deities concerned with family wellbeing and food supply. They
also venerated the *Lares*, or deified ancestors, represented by small
statues in household shrines associated with the *genius* ("spirit") of
the family, and specifically that of the paterfamilias. Prayers and liba-
tions were offered to these deities on a regular basis in the household,
and children thus grew up linked together with them through continual expressions of reverence (*pietas*).[26]

Religious observance was also deeply interwoven in Jewish family life. In the Diaspora, where the temple was not accessible, and after
its destruction in A.D. 76, holy days such as Passover, Tabernacles, and
the Day of Atonement were celebrated largely in domestic settings.
The rhythm of life was governed by the weekly alternation of work
and the observance of the sabbath, as well as by dietary laws, laws of
purity, and daily prayer. The socialization of children into observant
Judaism through both the practice of these laws and the careful explanation of their meaning was a primary obligation of fathers.[27] These
domestic religious practices set Jewish families and quarters apart
from their non-Jewish neighbors in multiethnic cities and sustained
Jewish identity from generation to generation.

Both the Jewish and the Greco-Roman worlds held strong cultural beliefs about the importance of family obligations. The Roman
upper class of the first century A.D. measured the contemporary decline of the family against an ideal of the archaic Roman family of
earlier centuries. The behavior of adulterous wives and disrespectful
children was contrasted with the ways of a purer, simpler time when
the word of the paterfamilias was law, children were obedient, and

women were hardworking and chaste. The family had been frugal, without the luxury of a slave economy; the head of the household had been a farmer-warrior ready to leave his plow in the field to respond to a call to arms, and then return to his plow without the temptations of great wealth and power.[28]

This idealized view of the ancient Roman family was elaborated by first-century idealogues to call the members of the Roman elite back to their original simple life as the source of their power and nobility. Augustus, the first emperor, promoted reforms of family law to encourage wives to bear many children (by giving them the privilege of *sui iuris*), and reinforced the power of the father over his grown offspring. Augustus's wife, Livia, demonstrated her return to more upright ways by spinning her own cloth.[29] But these reforms had little real impact because they did not reflect the economic realities of senatorial familes as the ruling class of a vast empire based on slave labor.

Educated Romans were also aware of Greek philosophical and literary traditions prescribing proper gender relations in family life. These precedents provided conflicting messages, however. The Peripatetics had held that women were inherently defective and inferior in their mental and moral capacities and should be strictly subservient. Peripatetic tracts on household management advised wives to be chaste, frugal, and hardworking while patiently tolerating sexual and other faults on the part of their husbands.[30] The Stoic tradition, by contrast, affirmed an equal humanity of women and men and advocated a partnership relation of spouses. The woman should be a chaste and frugal housekeeper, yes, but the man should also be faithful, engaging in sex with his wife alone and only for the sake of procreating legitimate children, not for sensual pleasure. Few ancient thinkers believed women should have any role in public life, yet Stoic teaching and changes in law encouraged a view of the couple as senior and junior partners, not as master and slave. Family business should be conducted with the advice of the wife.[31] The Greek custom of males' dining together with female entertainers was giving way among the Romans to a practice whereby wives were included in formal dining, either reclining on couches with their husbands or sitting on chairs beside them.[32] The Greek view that men could be friends only with other men—women being too inferior to be regarded as friends— was still cited among philosophers (to be repeated by Christians such as Augustine),[33] but this stance was belied by epitaphs that expressed deep affection between spouses.[34]

Jewish literature also puts great stress on the importance of the family. In the book of Proverbs we find standard advice on family life, with both mother and father charged with instructing their children in the ways of wisdom. The good wife is depicted as the competent manager of her household, setting her servants to work spinning and weaving the textiles for the house, and engaging in business transactions such as buying a field and setting out a vineyard. Her management of household production frees her husband to engage in public business "at the gates"—that is, judicial decision making.[35] Such a wise household manager is praised as a gift of God, and she provides the imagery for the figure of Wisdom, as God immanent in the management of the cosmos.[36]

Proverbs also reveals negative views of the "bad" wife, particularly the contentious one, who is described as being like dripping water on a rainy day.[37] The text strongly cautions against foreign wives, who pose a danger by bringing foreign religious customs into the household.[38]

Epigraphic evidence allows us to look beyond this prescriptive literature and recognize that Jewish women had by the end of the first century A.D. gained some independence in managing their property. Propertied Jewish women appear as patronesses of the synagogues, taking their place in the seats of the elders.[39] Moreover, education in rabbinic teachings for women, particularly for daughters of rabbis, was not unknown in this period.[40]

ANTIFAMILY TRADITIONS

Despite the centrality of the family to ethnic identity and social maintenance, both the Greco-Roman and the Jewish worlds of the first century knew of movements and ideologies that were antifamily. In the Greco-Roman world, for example, there was a misogynist tradition that saw wives as so great a burden that men were better off not marrying at all.

Philosophers also enjoined single life for other reasons. Cynic philosophers, as itinerant wise men who preached on street corners against corrupt social customs, demonstrated their freedom and their return to "nature" by sleeping outdoors and living on a bare minimum of food gathered from the wild or given them by supporters. Marriage and family were incompatible with such a life, so the Cynics counseled avoidance of acquiring a wife and children.[41]

A certain ascetic impulse also runs through Stoic and Platonic thought in this period, occasionally advising the philosopher not to marry but more frequently suggesting that sexual pleasure should be minimized and sex engaged in solely for procreation. There were no organized forms of philosophic celibate life among the Greeks and Romans of this era.[42]

Misogynist advice may be found in the Jewish tradition as well— for instance, the admonition that it is better not to marry than to have a contentious wife—but it did not prevent marriage from being the normal life-style for Jews. Jewish teaching also saw obedience to Yahweh as taking priority over family ties: a wife or blood relative could be disavowed or even killed to avert the risk of being drawn into idolatry.[43]

Among Jews of the first century we do find significant examples of organized celibate life, though our evidence for this leaves us with some doubts about how such celibate life was actually practiced in the first century A.D. One source is an idealized account by Philo, a Hellenistic Jewish philosopher from Alexandria (25 B.C.–A.D. 50). In his treatise "The Contemplative Life" Philo describes the Therapeutae, a group of Jewish celibates living a communal life, as the ideal expression of his philosophy.[44]

Those who adopted this life were evidently not necessarily unmarried: Philo speaks of them as giving up their possessions to their sons and daughters, to other relatives, or to friends. The first step in the contemplative life, for Philo, is to strip oneself of the property that ties one to the temptations of wealth and the tumult of cities. Thus the Therapeutae

> flee without ever turning their heads back again, deserting their brethren, their children, their wives, their parents, their numerous families, their affectionate bands of companions, their native lands . . . [to] take up their abode outside of walls . . . seeking a desert place,

wishing to disassociate themselves from the unwise and to associate solely with those seeking the contemplative life.[45]

According to Philo, the Therapeutae lived in the simplest houses grouped near one another, wore plain white garments, and consumed only bread (with hyssop and salt) and water, avoiding meat, sweets, and wine. They practiced long fasts, sometimes for several days, and ate only after nightfall. They kept no slaves and were served at table voluntarily by younger men of the order. These contemplatives studied the Torah through the week and came together on the sabbath for prayer, psalmody, sacred dance, and a shared meal.

Women as well as men could join the order. The women lived in separate houses and, when everyone came together on the sabbath, were separated from the men by a high partition that nonetheless allowed them to hear what was said. Women also participated in the sacred meal, being seated on the left side, once again separated from the men. The women were said to be old, and most of them virgins. Both sexes were celibates within the order, but it seemed significant to Philo that most of the women had never lost their virginity. This abstinence from sex was voluntary and undertaken for the sake of a higher life than that of family and children. They chose such a life

> out of admiration and love of wisdom, with which they are desirous to pass their lives, on account of which they are indifferent to the pleasures of the body, desiring not mortal but an immortal offspring which the soul that is attached to God alone is able to produce by itself and from itself, the Father having sown in it rays of light appreciable only by the intellect by means of which it will be able to perceive the doctrines of wisdom.[46]

Philo speaks of such celibate communities as being widespread in his time, to be found in all districts of Egypt. Both Greek and "barbarian" wisdom shared this quest for the higher life. Thus Philo places the Jewish ascetics within a larger movement that included all the wisdom traditions of the surrounding cultures. In the Jewish version of this life of wisdom, he links the Therapeutae with the Essenes.[47] This raises difficult questions about the nature of the Essenes as a Jewish movement in Palestine in this period, and whether they are correctly identified with the Therapeutae, on the one hand, and with the Dead Sea Scrolls sect, on the other.

The Essenes, as described by the first-century A.D. Jewish writer Josephus, were recognizably similar to Philo's Therapeutae. For Josephus, the Essenes represented one of the three schools of thought of

Judaism of his day. They were ascetic communitarians who eschewed pleasures of the flesh, scorned marriage, did not possess slaves, and lived under a strict regime of daily prayer and work, assembling twice a day for ablutions and a common meal. They wore white clothes drawn from a common store. They studied ancient Jewish wisdom both for soul-cure and for healing of the body. Josephus characterized this as a widespread movement existing in large colonies "everywhere."[48]

There are some differences between Philo's and Josephus' accounts. Josephus' Essenes pooled their property rather than giving it to relatives, and the celibate group consisted solely of males. Josephus knew nothing of Philo's double monastery that included celibate women. He ascribed the Essenes' scorn of marriage to a contempt for women as being incapable of sexual faithfulness,[49] while Philo wrote of both women and men as putting aside marriage for higher wisdom. Josephus also desribed a second Essene group that followed the same rules but consented to marry, though members were to have sex only for procreation and cease sexual relations at conception.[50] Josephus also depicted the Essenes as being parallel to the Greek philosophial ascetics in seeking release of the soul from the corruptible body.

The Dead Sea Scrolls sect at Qumran, near the Dead Sea, whose library was discovered in 1947 in nearby caves, corresponds in some aspects to Josephus' description of the Essenes. Members lived communally, assembled in a refectory for communal meals, practiced frequent ablutions, and appear to have been exclusively male.[51] Two major organizational documents of the group, the *Manual of Discipline* (or *Community Rule*) and the *Zadokite Document* (or *Damascus Rule*),[52] make no mention of celibacy, yet women and family life seem to be absent. But a third source, the *Manual of Discipline for the Future Congregation of Israel* (or *Messianic Rule*), says that women and children should be assembled to learn the rules of covenant. In this context, members of the order are referred to as "heads of families," and male youths from ten years of age are initiated into the order through a ten-year period of training and study.[53]

The worldview of the Dead Sea Scrolls sect was that of Jewish apocalypticists who were preparing themselves through strict observance of purity regulations, prayer, and study for a messianic advent and a final battle between "the Sons of Light and the Sons of Darkness." At that time they would be vindicated before their enemies within Israel, and before the larger, gentile world, as the true assembly of Israel. Thus the Qumran community seems to have had a totally different purpose and outlook from those of Josephus's Essenes, though this does not preclude the possibility that Josephus was describing the same group that is represented by the Dead Sea Scrolls sect.

Josephus, as a Hellenized Jew writing for a gentile audience, cast the Essenes' asceticism in philosophical terms. If he knew of any militant, apocalyptic orientation on their part, he would likely have concealed it from the gentile world.[54] Abstinence from marriage, or rather temporary abstinence from sexuality and the exclusion of women, might be practiced by such a Jewish apocalyptic sect, but with a different motivation from that embraced by philosophers.

Here, sexual abstinence and separation from women were necessary aspects of a period of intense purification in preparation for Holy War. By excluding women, the sect also removed the chief source of pollution via sexual intercourse, female menstruation, and childbirth. But sect members might well have married and produced children earlier in their lives, and if so, could bring their male children into the sect at an appropriate age. Thus family life was not permanently negated at Qumran, but rather was put aside for the period of preparation for messianic war.[55]

FAMILY AND ANTIFAMILY IN THE NEW TESTAMENT

The synoptic Gospels present the Jesus movement as a gathering of mostly marginal men and women out of their families and occupations into a countercultural community. This community is seen as a new eschatological family that negates the natural family. No one is worthy to be a disciple who prefers his family to Jesus—or, in Luke's words, "If anyone comes to me and does not hate his own father and mother and wife and children and brothers and sisters, . . . he cannot be my disciple" (Luke 14:26). Similar texts exalting homelessness and separation from the family may be found in the Gospel of Thomas, which reflects the same early Christian traditions.[56]

When a would-be disciple protests that he must first bury his father, Jesus tells him curtly, "Follow me and leave the dead to bury the dead" (Matt. 8:21–22), showing a shocking disregard for traditional family responsibilities to the dead father in Jewish culture. Matthew tells us that when James and John abandon their fishing to follow Jesus, they leave behind both their boat and their father, Zebedee, *in* the boat (Matt. 4:21–22). Jesus' mission causes enmity between family members: "I have come to set a man against his father, and a daughter aganst her mother and a daughter-in-law against her mother-in-law and a man's foes will be in his own household" (Matt. 10:35–36).

Jesus' own family, too, is negated in favor of his new family of disciples. His mother and brothers are described as believing that he is mad, and they come to seize him. As they stand outside asking to talk to him, Jesus repudiates them, saying, " 'Who are my mother and my brothers?' And looking around on those who sat about him, he said 'here are my mother and brothers! Whoever does the will of God is my brother and sister and mother' " (Mark 3:31, 33–35).

This enmity between family members is itself a foretaste of the apocalyptic troubles soon to come, when Jesus' disciples can expect those in political and religious authority to persecute them and family members to betray them: "Brother will deliver brother to death, and the father against his child, and the children will rise against the parents and have them put to death" (Mark 13:12). Marriage itself will cease to exist in the Kingdom of God. In the new age there will be no marrying or giving in marriage. Luke says that those accounted worthy to attain to this future age will not marry in the present age (Luke 20:35).

The parables of the synoptic Gospels are set in a Palestinian world where large households with many slaves are common. The relation of God to humans is often likened to that of a great ruler of a household (*oikodespotes*) to his slaves, tenant farmers, and hired wage laborers. Crafty slaves who know how to invest the wealth entrusted to them by their absent masters are praised as productive servants, while those who do not are condemned (Matt. 25:14–30).

Yet Jesus' followers are called not to emulate these wealthy householders, but rather to surrender their property, give their wealth to the poor, and follow Jesus with no thought as to where their food and clothes for the morrow are to come from. They are to live like birds of the air that do not reap or gather into barns, or like lilies of the field that neither toil nor spin (Matt. 6:25–32). When they set out to preach from town to town, they are to take no provisions with them—no bag, bread, or money, no extra cloak or sandals (Matt. 10:9–10; Mark 6:8–10).

They should not return evil by evil. If robbed of their coat, they should hand over their cloak also (Matt. 5:40). They should lay up spiritual treasure in Heaven, for earthy goods are fleeting (Matt. 6:19–21). Luke's version of the Sermon on the Mount blesses those who are poor and hungry—for they will be rewarded in the coming Kingdom—while calling down woes to come upon those who are rich (Luke 6:20–26). Those who have fed the hungry, taken in the stranger, clothed the naked, and visited the sick and the imprisoned will be on the right hand of Christ in his coming glory, while those who have not done so will be driven into eternal fire (Matt. 25:31–46).

Jesus and his followers are depicted as itinerants without means, who "have no place to lay their head," yet a variety of households host them in their travels. Mary Magdalene; Joanna, the wife of Chuza, Herod's steward (a highly placed person in the royal household); Susanna; and many others who travel with them are described as "providing for them out of their means" (Luke 8:1–3). Jesus is shown dining in the houses of leading Pharisees and staying with a wealthy tax collector—a scandal because of the presumed sinful nature of that occupation (Luke 14:1; 19:1–10).

Apparently his disciples have not given up all property and family ties. Simon Peter has a house in Capernaum, the main base of Jesus' movement in the Galilee, where Jesus heals Peter's mother-in-law—clearly an indication of his married status, though no wife is mentioned. Peter also has a boat into which Jesus can step to teach the crowds that press about him at the lake of Galilee. The mother of the sons of Zebedee shows up in Matthew's version of the story of Jesus' journey to Jerusalem to plead for a leadership role for her sons in the future kingdom (Matt. 20:20–21).

Jesus' relation to his own family is portrayed as hostile. He is repudiated by the people of his hometown (Nazareth) based on their knowledge of his family's lowly status: when he comes to preach in the synagogue there, they cry out, "Is this not the carpenter, the son of Mary, and the brother of James and Joses and Judas and Simon and are not his sisters with us?" (Mark 6:1–3). This naming of Jesus as the "son of Mary," and the absence of his father in the account of his confrontation with his mother and brothers, have raised questions for scholars about Jesus' possible illegitimacy.[57]

The virgin-birth stories may in fact have been created in part to cover the question of Jesus' lack of a father. Some have argued that Jesus was the son of a normal marriage between Mary and Joseph and that Joseph's absence can be explained by his earlier death.[58] But in a strongly patrilineal society, the son of a dead father is still called by his father's name. To be called the son of one's mother was the standard way of being characterized as illegitimate.

However this is understood, the antifamily patterns of the Gospels are underscored by tensions between Jesus and his own family and hometown folk. The Jesus movement appears to be made up of marginal people—landless laborers as well as wealthy but despised people such as tax collectors—in uprooted relations to their families, and critical of the religious and political authorities of their society. For these people, the Jesus movement becomes a new family. Bound together by ties of allegiance to their leader, they are assured that God is their loving father ("Abba") and that they will be blessed in the messianic age to come.[59]

As we turn from the Palestinian Jesus movement in the synoptic Gospels to the early Christian mission in the Diaspora, we find that the sense of the church as a "new family" continues in new forms. In this new family the members are united by their relation to Christ as their redeemer, through whom God is their father, and by their expectation of fulfilled redemption in a coming messianic age. This new family breaks down old kinship relations and separations.

People whom the kinship rules of the Greeks, Romans, and Jews were designed to distinguish from one another, and to prevent from intermarrying or eating at table together, now share a common table and spiritual kinship. In this new family in Christ, Jew and Greek, circumcised and uncircumcised, Scythian and barbarian, slave and free become brothers and sisters to each other.[60] But this new kinship in Christ also sets people in opposition to their natural kin and suggests to some that marriage itself is to be set aside.

Paul's letters are characterized by his constant address of the members of the churches he has founded as "brothers," as those who have been made siblings in a new family. (I use the term *brothers* here not only to translate literally the Greek *adelphoi* but to reflect Paul's androcentric thought. In using this term Paul thinks of males bonded as brothers and addresses the males primarily, though his communities consist also of females whom he occasionally refers to as sisters, *adelphai* [e.g., Rom. 16:1].)[61]

Paul argues in Romans and Galatians that these new brothers are the true sons or seed of Abraham, who will inherit the promise of redemption. With this argument Paul disinherits unbelieving Jews as the true descendants of their ancestor Abraham, even as he incorporates a new community of believers in Christ, both Jews and gentiles, as the true descendants of Abraham and the heirs to God's promise to him of redemption. This argument turns on dualisms of flesh and spirit, law and faith.

Mere genealogical descent and external marks of obedience to the law—that is, circumcision—do not, Paul insists, make a man a son of Abraham and heir to his promise. Instead, Paul cites the fact that the promise was given to Abraham by faith *before* circumcision to argue that it is believers, not blood descendants who obey the law through circumcision of the males, who are Abraham's true sons and heirs (Rom. 4; Gal. 3:6–9, 15–18). Indeed, circumcision annuls faith, he says, because it means one no longer believes spiritually but demands external signs of descent and obedience to the law in the flesh (Gal. 5:2–5).

Paul also points to the two wives of Abraham, Sarah and Hagar, and their children to argue that Christians are the sons of the free woman, not the slave woman. Their mother is not the fleshly Jerusalem that bears children in bondage to the law, but the eschatological new Jerusalem of freedom in the spirit (Gal. 4:21–31). In this way Paul anuls as fleshly the Jewish claims of familial relationship to God marked by circumcision, and transfers these claims to the church as the true spiritual sons of Abraham inwardly circumcised, hence the children of God and heirs to the promise of salvation.

Paul's letters are larded with family analogies designed to negate inferior forms of household relations and to elevate the higher form of such relations enjoyed by this new family of God. The inferior *familiae* of the household are the slaves under the master, while the Christians are those released from slavery and adopted as sons and thus as true heirs, who can call God Abba, "Father" (Rom. 6:16–19; 8:12–17). Paul here draws on the familiar adoption practices of Roman families to imagine a similar adoption by God, through which former slaves may be made sons of God.[62]

Young children also are like slaves, taught by slave tutors (*paidago-goi*) and governed by trustees and managers (*epitrophoi* and *oikonomoi*) until they come of age. So, too, Jews under the Law and gentiles ruled by lower cosmic spirits were like children ruled by slaves and managers. But now they have been freed from these lower rulers and have become true children of God who can call God Father, "Abba" (Gal. 3:23–26).

Likewise, a Christian is like a wife who is bound to her husband while he is alive, but who after his death is free and can bind herself to another. So former Jews were once bonded to the Law, but now in Christ the Law is dead and they can bond themselves to Christ in whom is freedom from the Law and from the sinful passions aroused by the Law (Rom. 7:1–6).

The members of this true family of God are to love each other like true brothers. They are not to quarrel or be in dissension. They are not to fall back into old fleshly practices such as circumcision, nor into the polluting ways of the Gentiles through indulgence of the flesh in lust and bodily pleasure. Paul praises the Thessalonian Christian men because they know how to possess their vessels (i.e., wives) chastely, having sex abstemiously without seeking sensual pleasure (1 Thess. 4:4–5).[63]

Paul calls these communities of brothers to live in imminent anticipation of a coming eschatological age. It is through their baptismal rebirth in the death and resurrection of Christ that they are adopted as members of the eschatological body of Christ. Having died to the sinful old age of flesh and the Law and already participating in the age to come, they must live in strict spiritual discipline, not indulging the flesh. They must also cultivate love for and harmony with one another.

Although this new identity has been given to them in baptism, Paul sees it as being highly insecure, threatened by active demonic powers that have not yet been conquered. These are to be conquered in the messianic advent, which, though soon to come, has not yet happened. Any dissension, bodily indulgence (for gentiles), or acquiesence to the Law (for Jews) suggests for Paul a retrogression to old identities and hence a loss of the new identity as God's eschatological family.

Paul's view of sexual abstinence in relation to Christian eschatological identity is ambivalent. For himself, not marrying and abstaining from sex altogether express his readiness for the age to come.[64] But Paul is dubious of the ability of some of the other brothers to attain the same level of purity, and he fears that those of strong passions will commit a worse sin—fornication—if they are not constrained by marriage. Within marriage, spouses should not deprive each other of sexual relations permanently; they may set aside times for prayer when they abstain from sex, but they should then come together again lest they be tempted to fornication (1 Cor. 7:1–5).

In a convoluted section of his first letter to the Corinthians, Paul advises virgins (i.e., not-yet-married men and women) to remain as they are, "in view of the impending crisis" (the nearness of the apocalyptic events). But he shifts quickly to the idea that both the married and the unmarried should stay as they are—that is, virgins should not marry, and the married should not discard their spouses. It is not a sin to marry, he asserts, but it is better not to, due to the distress that will be experienced in marriage, and also because "the appointed time has grown very short." In this time of impending apocalypse, even those who have wives should act as if they had none—meaning, they should practice sexual abstinence (1 Cor. 7:25–35).

Paul states his own preference for celibacy by saying, "I wish that all were as I am" (1 Cor. 7:7), but he allows that it is better to marry than to be aflame with unsatisfied sexual passion (7:9). Significantly, Paul never mentions children as a purpose of sexual relations in marriage. Sex is discussed only in terms of the satisfaction or restraint of (male) sexual desires.[65]

In general, children are strikingly absent from the Epistles of the New Testament. This is not to say they are not there, but there is no interest in how to pass down the faith through the education of the young, a concept so central to the Jewish tradition. This reflects the eschatological orientation of the early church, which did not expect to continue within history but instead imagined it would be caught up into the eschaton within a generation, obviating the need to produce children. The annulling of the Law thus included the annulling of the commandment to produce children.[66]

A Christian community of this type would have appeared deeply subversive of family life as that was understood by both Jews and Romans. For Jews the Christian community violated the basic commandments of producing and educating children, as well as the circumcision and purity laws that separated Jews from gentiles in table fellowship. Their very identity as God's family was revoked by a Christianity that claimed to be the new family of God, the spiritual offspring of Abraham and heir to the promise, in a way that discarded them while gathering a new people together across all barriers of separation.

For Jews, Greeks, and Romans, Christianity subverted the notion of family by drawing converts into a new and "promiscuous" order while at the same time forbidding these new Christians to offer reverence to the religions of their natal or marital households. In antiquity, as we have seen, religion was primarily familial (and civic by way of extension of family cults), not personal or individual. A youth, wife, or slave who converted to Christianity adopted an identity that annulled this household religion and despised it as idolatrous and superseded. Such a new identity thus subverted the fidelity and reverence of the convert to his or her household and kin group of origin and its collective *genius*.

Even when a head of household converted and brought his whole household with him (children, wives, and slaves), that conversion to Christianity still subverted the relation of that household to the piety due the larger kin network. The Christian paterfamilias would, for example, presumably no longer gather with his kin at the family tomb to pay respect to their ancestors.[67] He would also now claim brotherhood with people whom the rules of his family excluded from kinship. Paul expected such familial alienation and even praised his new converts for being persecuted by their relatives even as the church in Judaea was persecuted by their Jewish compatriots, taking this as evidence that they shared the same prophetic identity (1 Thess. 1:4).

The subversion of family allegiance and hierarchical order by Christian conversion, particularly when the convert was a subjugated person in the family—that is, a wife, youth, or slave—invoked great hostility toward Christianity in the gentile world, which typically saw it as undermining the order of the family and of the state. It suggested a new freedom of women, young people, and slaves to disobey their husbands, fathers, and masters and make their own choices about their lives.

As we move to the second generation of the Pauline Christian churches, we find a split opening up in church practice over questions of marriage and family hierarchy. A leadership group that would come to dominate the shaping of the Christian tradition sought to shore up Christian respectability by mandating a traditional patriarchal ordering of family members: wives were to obey their husbands, slaves their masters, children their parents.[68] The new freedom in Christ that brought people together in a new family across ethnic lines was still proclaimed, but now in a spiritualized way that did not threaten the subordination owed by wives, children, and slaves to the paterfamilias.

But it is doubtful that this shoring-up of internal order in Christian families would have done much to assure the Greco-Roman world of Christian acceptability. That world would still see a group that defied ethnic and class separations and told its members to shun the expressions of piety toward family and civic deities upon which the flourishing of society and the state was thought to depend. This view of Christianity as a lower-class movement that subverted all family and social authority was well expressed by Celsus in an attack written in the second century (ca. A.D. 189):

> In private houses we also see wool-workers, cobblers, and laundry workers, and the most illiterate and bucolic yokels, who would not dare to say anything in front of their elders and more intelligent masters. But when they get hold of children in private and some stupid women with them, they let out some astounding statements as, for example, they must not pay any attention to their father and schoolteachers but must obey them; they say that these talk nonsense and have no understanding . . . they alone know the right way to live. . . . And if just as they are speaking they see one of the schoolteachers coming or some intelligent person, or even the father himself, the more cautious of them flee in all directions; but the more reckless urge the children on to rebel. . . . They whisper to them that in the presence of the father and their schoolteachers they do not feel able to explain anything to the children . . . but if they like they should leave the father and their schoolmasters and go along with the women and little children who are their playfellows to the wooldresser's shop or the cobbler's or the washerwoman's shop, that they may learn perfection. And by saying this they persuade them.[69]

Many Christians in the first and second centuries believed that conversion transferred the individual into an eschatological identity set in opposition to family structures that reproduced a fallen history. For them becoming Christian meant renouncing sexual relations and family ties. In apocryphal Gospels, in the Acts of the Apostles, and in martyr literature the motif of rejecting family and parental authority to pursue Christian perfection is a typical one.

In the mid–second–century Passion of Saints Perpetua and Felicitas, two women, one nobly born and the other a slave of her household, are united as sisters in their common determination to die for their faith. Perpetua has just had a child, while Felicitas delivers a child in prison. Perpetua is begged by her aged father to consider her duty to her infant son, but she spurns the demands of motherhood, surrendering her child to be cared for by others, in order to express her ultimate loyalty to Christ in martyrdom.[70]

In the apocryphal Acts of Paul and Thecla, also from the mid–second century, a young women from Iconium, engaged to be married, is converted by Paul. She straightaway rejects the claims of her fiancé and family and leaves home to follow Paul. Her enraged fiancé complains to the governor that the Christian faith has subverted his marriage rights. For the rest of the narrative, Thecla's mother, her fiancé, and the agents of the state pursue her and try to punish her for her rebellion against family and society. She is twice thrown to the lions and miraculously escapes both times unharmed. At the conclusion of the narrative she is commissioned by Paul to preach in her hometown.[71]

In this and other narratives in apocryphal Acts, conversion to Christianity is equated with the rejection of marriage in favor of celibacy.[72] This choice is seen as freeing women from their subordination to the family and enabling them to preach as itinerant missionaries. A similar motif may be found in the accounts of the Montanist movement, where two women leaders, Priscilla and Maximilla, travel as spirit-possessed prophets, having rejected husbands and family.[73]

The identification of Christianity with celibacy and autonomy from the family is hotly contested by the second-century author of the pastoral Epistles. The author of 1 Timothy denounces those who "pay attention to the deceitful spirits and teachings of demons through the hypocrisy of liars whose consciences are seared with a hot iron. They forbid marriage . . ." (4:1–3). Timothy defends the patriarchal ordering of the family as the model for the Christian church. Bishops and elders are to be selected from proven *patresfamilias*. Women are to keep silence in church; they are inherently subordinate due to their secondary status in creation and their primacy in sin. They will be saved by accepting their subordination and "through childbearing, provided they continue in faith and love and holiness, with modesty" (2:11–15).[74]

The mid-second-century Christian church saw a battle between those who endorsed a countercultural, eschatological Christianity subversive of the family and those who sought to reintegrate Christianity into patriarchal family and social patterns. This conflict would never be completely resolved, for the reading of the New Testament, the normative Christian Scriptures, would constantly revive the question of the meaning of the antifamily teachings of the early church. But the conflict would gradually be mediated by the definition of celibacy as a internal, "higher" choice of Christian perfection for a spiritual elite of men and women, ranked above a normatively married laity.

Celibacy for men would be identified with clerical leadership, while female celibacy would be privatized in monastic enclosures. Celibacy would be Hellenized as a choice of a mystical ascent to perfection, similar to Philo's Therapeutae, rather than being understood apocalyptically as an anticipation of the imminent eschaton. Yet even this institutionalization of celibacy in clericalism and monastic life would continue to carry the message for fifteen hundred years (and still does today for Catholic and Orthodox Christians) that marriage is a second-class choice for Christians. Those who aspire to perfection should renounce sex, marriage, and reproduction for a chaste single life.

CHAPTER 2

Asceticism, Sex, and Marriage in Patristic and Medieval Christianities

The world of early Christianities is not only alien to our own presuppositions about sex and family, shaped as they are by the Reformation revolt against celibate clericalism, but also quite different from the medieval world with its ordered hierarchy of celibate over married. The medieval Latin system itself emerged only through many centuries, during which some of the wilder movements of Christian world renunciation were tamed. Even so, the impulse would continue to linger in Eastern Christianity in the form of hermit holy men lodged in remote caves of desert wilderness.

SECOND-CENTURY CHRISTIANITIES

The Christianity of the second century must be spoken of in the plural, for from the beginning, a number of very different visions arose from a common allegiance to Christ as the risen Lord. For many Christians of that time—probably the majority of its creative visionaries, if not its humbler practitioners—Christianity embodied a radical message about the end of the present age and the possibility not only of overcoming sin but of dissolving the limits of finitude of the visible cosmos that held the body hostage at death.[1]

As Peter Brown has shown in his masterful work on sexual renunciation in early Christianity,[2] Christians came to focus much more insistently on the body and the repression of its needs for food, sleep, and sexual urges than had pagan ascetics, because they had a more radical vision of its potential for transformation. Males of the pagan classical world looked on the body as an inferior element, much as they regarded slaves and women. They believed that the philosopher, as a respectable paterfamilias, should discipline these inferiors to serve the patriarchal household, kinship group, and civic society. But he should also give them their due.

Thus there was a place for the delights of marriage and the table, though excesses should be curbed. Well-tempered sexual intercourse undertaken to produce well-formed, legitimate children was a responsibility of every householder and the prime purpose of women's existence. But in due time the philosophically inclined should reduce these pleasures to a minimum, even letting sexual intercourse go altogether, in preparation for that separation of soul from body in which the intellect would soar free to the stars unencumbered by mortal clay.

Christians entertained a more unthinkable notion: that of the resurrected body. Far from being doffed at death to allow an immortal life of the soul alone, the Christian expected the body to be transformed, and in so doing to lose the urges for sex, food, and sleep that signaled its fall into mortality. This immortalized body, the companion of the soul, would be exalted with it into a new redeemed world of the "New Creation." The urges of the body must thus be more severely suppressed during life to anticipate this transformation in which the body's finitude would be discarded in a redemptive transmutation.

For ancient Christianity, the incarnation of the *Logos* of God in the body meant something very different from the modern Christian use of that doctrine to claim an embrace of mortal physicality.[3] Rather, the incarnation of God into the human body meant that the immortal, unchangeable substance of God has descended into mortal flesh in order to transmute it into an immortalized form, free from death and decay. God became human to make us divine—that was the ancient Christian understanding of incarnation: not to celebrate but to overcome the frailties of the flesh that tied it to corruptibilty and death.[4]

Many of the forms of Christianity of the second century sought to live out that vision as one that was already transforming daily life, through a deep renunciation of all the ways the finite body reproduced itself through temporal processes. By such practices as sexual continence, fasting, and vigils, Christians anticipated the definitive transformation of the bodily in a redeemed cosmos whose imminent arrival they expected. These practices became a sign that they had already shifted their allegiance from the present world to the world to come.

The renunciation of sex was seen as a key expression of world renunciation, but not necessarily because sex was the most urgent need of the body; for many monks, hunger, the craving of the belly, was a more insistent bodily demand, and less easy to control.[5] Rather, sex tied a person to marriage and family, to the pride and avarice of the kinship group that desired to reproduce the large houses, the great landholdings with their crowds of slaves and clients, the demand for power and status in the civil and imperial world. Through sex and marriage, "the world" as a social system of power and possessions was reproduced. To renounce marriage was to renounce that "world" in all its social, economic, and political implications.

In the second century, many of the forms of Christianity that arose in the Christian heartlands of Asia and made their way to Rome, the governing city of the empire, burned with versions of this kind of fervor. For Encratites ("Self-controllers") such as Tatian, a Syrian disciple of Justin Martyr who authored, in the third quarter of the second century, the *Diatessaron,* the first effort to harmonize the four Gospels, being a Christian meant giving up sex, meat, and wine.[6] Syriac Christianity generally saw conversion to celibacy as a condition for baptism. Not just a "higher" calling for an elite of holy men and women, it was the normal state for all who had definitively committed themselves to follow Christ and were living now in anticipation of the end of the present age and the resurrected body.[7]

Marcion, reputedly the son of a bishop of Pontus, was another Eastern Christian radical. He appeared in Rome in about A.D. 139, claiming to renew the vision of Paul, only to be rejected by a Roman Christianity that was solidly rooted in households. Marcion took his message back, with great success, to an Eastern Christian world where such radicalism was seen as less strange, indeed as normal Christianity.[8] For Marcion, to be a Christian was to be freed by the higher God of love, the father of Jesus Christ, from the demonic creator and ruler of this world, the God of the Old Testament Law.

The renunciation of marriage in favor of celibacy meant the annulment of all the laws of the creator God that divided man from woman, Jew from gentile, Greek from barbarian, free from slave, rich from poor, healthy from diseased. The Christian church was a new family where all bonds of exclusivity peculiar to Jewish, Greek, and Roman societies, with their concomitant social divisions, were overcome. All strangers became kin, equal recipients of love and service. This new family radically disrupted existing social ties, dividing child from parent, slave from master, in order to knit together a new acosmic family of the God of love that had transcended this world, dissolving its separations.[9]

Other bands of second-century Christians, such the followers of the New Prophecy, renewed the apocalyptic expectation of apostolic Christianity. The end of the present age, when the current social order would be dissolved and the New Jerusalem would descend to Earth, was fast approaching. Women and men spoke as prophets of the Holy Spirit manifest in the church. At such a time marriage, reproduction, and the cultivation of fields were all out of place. Christians must put aside such distracting means of reproducing daily life and ready themselves for martyrdom in the final convulsion that would transform the evil world into the Kingdom of God.[10]

Other Christians spoke a language of mystical transcendence of the visible cosmos through the eschewal of lower physical processes such as sexual union, only to capture their promise of unity on a higher spiritual plane. The followers of the gnostic teacher Valentinus, who taught in Rome in A.D. 138–166, learned to interpret the facts of finitude through a story of the origins of this fallen world.

In the beginning, they were told, a higher spiritual cosmos had emerged from "depth" and "silence" to generate an expanding spiritual universe through the union of male and female spiritual principles.[11] But one lesser expression of these female beings, Sophia, played the cosmic Eve, stepping out of place and causing the eruption of an abortive lower world of fallen matter. The task of the gnostic, the quester for liberating knowledge, was to wean himself or herself from the illusions of this lower cosmos and return to the higher spiritual fullness. Putting aside physical sex for the spiritual union of male and female principles in the self was key to this process of reascent from the fallen temporal world of lies and bondage to the higher world of true spiritual being.[12]

An emerging Christian leadership in the great cities of the empire—Alexandria, Carthage, and Rome—which was closer to Christianized synagogues in its Jewish respect for disciplined families, set itself against the radical world renouncers. Like Paul, these defenders of Christian households did not so much deny the value of continence over sexuality, or the vision of a transformed body and cosmos in the age to come, as they rejected the claim that such a change could be lived out fully in the here and now.

For Clement of Alexandria, writing in the early third century, the gnostic search for perfection was to be reintegrated into a Christianized version of the Stoic philosopher-householder. The pleasures of the table and the marriage bed had their humble place in created goodness and should be given their due, but also tamed and limited. Thus chaste intercourse, carried out with dignified motions and solely for the purpose of procreation in the earlier years of a marriage, could be gradually given up altogether in later years as the householder devoted himself to the higher joys of intellectual wisdom.

All these goods ultimately come from Christ, the cosmic creator through whom the Creation was being renewed and transmuted into higher spiritual union with God. Ordered continuity from lower to higher, rather than abrupt disaffiliation from a demonized lower world for the sake of the higher, was Clement's vision.[13]

Tertullian, writing in Carthage during the same period as Clement, also sought to defeat the Marcionite and Valentinian despisers of creation. Marriage and sex for procreation were not to be rejected but rather placed in an austere discipline within marriage and the ordered patriarchal household. Youths were to discipline their sexual urges by cleaving to one wife and giving themselves only periodically to procreative sex, taking much time out for prayer. Later in life this "chaste" sex could be given up altogether, in a church community run by elders who served as both *patresfamilias* and exemplars of postmarital continence.[14]

Yet the call of a virginity embraced at puberty, excluding any period of marriage—a virginity tied to a vision of transcendance and transformation of the limits of the body itself—was not to disappear from Christianity. In the third century it was renewed by the Alexandrian teacher Origen, whose biblical terminology veiled the similarity between his thought and that of Valentinus.[15] Like Valentinus, but in the more acceptable language of the triune God, Origen saw the divine One emanating forth into an original fullness of Father, Word, and Spirit, together with a community of spirits, or *logikai,* that mirrored the divine Word.[16]

These created spirits then misused their free will to detach themselves from union with God. In their fall they took on various levels of visible materiality, from the shining matter of the stars to the dark bodies of demonic powers. The frail flesh of humans was but one manifestation of this potential of created substance to descend into variable permutations, expressing levels of alienation from God. Physical differences, including gendered bodies of male and female, were but transient expressions of this malleable matter.[17]

Those who desired reunion with God should avoid sexual coupling, not waiting for old age but beginning when puberty first stirred the sexual urges, in order to commence the long process, which would go on through successive incarnations, of reascending from more dense and temporal to more spiritual and immortal forms of the created substance. As the soul reascended to God, its sustaining material body would lose the characteristics of mortality and come to approximate the fiery bodies of the stars and ultimately the spiritual body of the risen Christ, the exemplar of Christian redemptive hope.[18]

Origen's brilliant mind led him to explore some of the consequences of this radical Platonic Christianity, from an acceptance of reincarnation to the possibility of a succession of cosmic falls and reascents. While these suggestions would be repudiated by later Christian orthodoxy, the core of Origen's vision of the fallen body and the promise of its transmutation into the glorified body would inspire new generations of Eastern Christians who sought to unify asceticism and philosophical contemplation.

FOURTH-CENTURY ASCETICISM, EAST AND WEST

One such mystical theologian was the Cappadocian church father Gregory of Nyssa, writing in the last quarter of the fourth century. For him, sex, physical procreation, and the temporal corruptibility of the body were no part of God's original intention regarding Creation. Rather, humans had been created with spiritual bodies and would have reproduced by some "angelic" means if they had not fallen. Maleness and femaleness had existed only potentially, in anticipation of the fallen state to come.[19]

With the fall from God, the body had taken on "coats of skin," the attributes of corruptible finitude.[20] Physical sex for procreation had then become necessary in order to compensate for the loss of the original immortality of the spiritual body. Nyssa saw the reascent of the embodied self from the fallen state as a long process of reawakened communion with God, reflected in the inner spiritual nature of the mind or soul. It was the attachment to temporal needs—pride, avarice, bondage to sexual pleasure—that must be given up through the disciplines of ascetic renunciation and contemplative thought.

Thereby, he believed, the self also could free itself from the anxieties associated with those needs—for example, the fear that wealth, once accumulated, would be taken away, or the attachment to a spouse, or the pride of progeny dashed by early death. Virginity, for Nyssa, epitomized this inner spiritual process of freeing the self from the greed and fear associated with attachment to transient material things. Marriage and sex were one expression of this attachment, but not the most insistent. Nyssa, himself married in his youth, could envision a form of chaste wedlock gradually given up for higher philosophical pleasures. In this he was not unlike Clement.[21]

Nyssa's focus was on the deeper process of self-transmutation of body/soul by which the Christian anticipates a final transformation in which the material body will be changed into the spiritual body of the resurrection. Then the body will lose its temporal accretions, or the "coats of skin" that tie it to eating, evacuation, procreation, sleeping, and decay, and become the immortalized body that can share in the endless ascent of the soul to fuller and fuller communion with God, going on "from glory to glory."[22]

In the late third and the fourth centuries, new waves of Encratites emerged from the Eastern Christian towns of Egypt and Syria to take up residence in the desert wildernesses beyond the settled regions. These monks claimed that through radical renunciation of the needs of the body, they had already attained the redeemed body and lived like the angels of the future heavenly age.[23] Holy men living as solitaries, of the type of Saint Anthony in his desert tomb in upper Egypt, in small groups or even in larger communities that "made the desert a city," became heroes to a new generation of Christians in an era when Christianity itself was being incorporated as the religion of the Roman empire.[24]

These holy men, whose feats of fasting, going without sleep, and abstaining from sex fascinated the new upper-class Christian elites, no longer seemed to threaten the very structures of political and economic power or of daily life, as had the Encratites of the second century. A new entente was reached between ascetic holy men (and women) and settled householders, which made each dependent on the other.

The wealth of the householders fed and supported the ascetics, while the ascetics assured the householders of the healing touch of the holy. The holy ones mediated not only between Heaven and Earth but between angry government officials and hapless citizens. The humble needs of reproducing daily life were served as well: if fields or wombs were barren, if a sick child was in danger of early death, such insufficiencies of nature could be healed by the saving touch of the holy man or woman.[25] Through their prayer and example, the monks also assured the householders that they, too, would finally be delivered from the vicious circle of birth and death, without having to renounce its work here and now.

But for many Christians, as for the larger pagan world, relations between the married and the celibate in the church, between householders and world renouncers, remained tense, particularly when the virginal included both young girls and mature matrons of no small influence. Asceticism continued to imply a leveling of the hierarchies of the household and society, of wealth and poverty, of slaves and the governing classes, of male and female. At the same time, increasing efforts were made to impose sexual continence on the clergy. The debate over celibacy and marriage that erupted in late-fourth-century Christianity reflected a deepening conflict over an asceticism that seemed to denigrate the honored functions of marriage within society.

In about 382, a Latin cleric named Helvidius wrote a treatise in which he defended the equal status of virginity and marriage through the story of Mary, the mother of Jesus.[26] Helvidius claimed that Mary had conceived Jesus virginally but after Jesus' birth had had normal sexual relations with Joseph and had borne him the several children referred to in the Gospels as Jesus' sisters and brothers. Thus virginity and marital sexuality received equal honor from her example. This interpretation conflicted with popular church traditions that made these brothers and sisters half-siblings to Jesus—as children of Joseph but not of Mary—and held that Mary had remained virginal not only in the conception but in the birth of Jesus and thereafter (*in partum* and *post partum*), having taken a vow of virginity in childhood.[27]

Jerome took up the cudgels against Helvidius, using strained exegesis to insist that the brothers and sisters of the Lord mentioned in the gospels were cousins, children of a sister of Mary (also named Mary). Both Mary, Jesus' mother, and her guardian, Joseph, remained lifelong virgins. Jerome waxed particularly indignant at the suggestion that faithful marriage and virginity could be judged equally holy. Painting a repellent picture of married life as being filled with the "prattling of infants, noisy clamoring of the whole household, the clinging of children to [the wife's] neck, the computing of expenses," and the flagrant lust of the husband's parties, Jerome insisted that holiness was possible only when marital sex, together with all such involvements, were given up. Women, for their part, could be holy only when they "ceased to be married women, who imitate the chastity of virgins within the very intimacy of marriage."[28]

A second opportunity more fully to define these views arose when one Jovinian, himself a monk, questioned the excesses of the new ascetic enthusiasm as a form of Manichaeanism.[29] Jovinian saw all Christians as sharing equally in the saving efficacy of baptism into Christ. He attacked those who regarded the sexually continent as having a higher status in Heaven than faithful, baptized married people. Virgins, widows, and married women who had been reborn in Christ would all receive the same reward in Heaven if they had been equally faithful.[30]

A common proof text for the view that virgins and widows would have a higher status in Heaven than the married was Mark 4:20: "These are the ones sown on good soil: they hear the word and accept it and bear fruit, thirty, sixty and a hundred fold." Ambrose, Jerome, and Augustine all interpreted this text as referring to the three states of Christian life: married, widowed, and virginal. Virgins would bear fruit a hundredfold and continent widows sixtyfold, while chaste wives and husbands could expect at best only thirtyfold.[31]

Jovinian, in claiming that there was no difference in the rewards for virgins, widows, and married people if all were equally baptized and faithful, launched a frontal attack on this antisexual hierarchy of holiness. He was roundly rebuked by the three church leaders, who saw to it that his views were condemned at synods in Rome and in Milan, where Ambrose was bishop.[32] Jerome wrote a vehement rebuttal of Jovinian's treatise that became an embarrassment to his colleagues due to its satiric denigration of marriage. Responding to Jovinian's use of 1 Corinthians 7 to defend the equal status of marriage, Jerome turned Paul's cautious allowance of marital sexuality into a flat negation: "If it is good not to touch a woman, it is bad to touch one, for there is no opposite of goodness but badness."[33]

Although Jerome conceded that marriage was still permitted in the Christian era, he insisted it had been superseded by the higher glory of virginity, which anticipated the heavenly state "where there will be no more marriage or giving in marriage." Thus Jerome left the reader with the impression that a fully committed Christian life was impossible for those who did not abstain from marital sex. It was best of all not ever to marry, and second best to dedicate oneself to celibacy after one's spouse died. The married were ranked lowest and should abstain as much as possible, preferably altogether. In Jerome, even "chaste sex" in marriage—that is, sex solely for the purpose of procreation—came perilously close to being condemned as incompatible with Christian virtue.

Augustine sought to repair the negative impression created by Jerome's intemperate defense of the superiority of virginity and continent widowhood over marriage. In his treatise "On the Good of Marriage," he tried a more measured approach, defending marriage as imbued with three "goods": progeny, fidelity, and sacrament. Marriage had its benefits in producing children and channeling the sexual urge into faithful wedlock, thus guarding against the worse evil of fornication. In addition, marriage symbolizes the union of Christ and the church, and thus it expresses the sacramental bond of Christian community.[34]

Augustine would gradually back away from his earlier Origenist view of the original Creation, rejecting the common Eastern Christian notion that there would have been no sexual differentiation or reproduction in Paradise.[35] In his later exegesis of Genesis 1, Augustine would come to accept the idea that sexual reproduction would have taken place in the original Creation. Gender differentiation, marriage, and sexual coupling for the sake of reproduction had all been part of God's original plan, not things added only after or with a view to the Fall.[36]

Yet Augustine would also limit this affirmation in ways that made marital sex seem distinctly third-rate, bordering on sinfulness. In Augustine's view, while physical sex and reproduction might have figured in God's original plan, sex in Paradise would have been devoid of the hot pleasure of male sexual ejaculation. Concupiscence, Augustine believed, had come about only through the Fall and expressed the loss of control of mind over body, the division in the self that made manifest the division from God. Thus in our present, fallen state, sex, even within marriage, carried with it sin, and through it the original sin of Adam was passed on to the next generation.[37]

Augustine's view of sex, even in a chaste marriage, was thus more than a little ambiguous. Although the result—children—was good and continued to be blessed by God, reproduction could not take place without sinful "lust." The sexual act was itself the means of generating sinful offspring, who could become children of God only through baptism. This sinful act of sex was allowed for the good end of reproduction (hence forgiven), and yet it was still sinful in its objective nature and consequences.

Paradisal sex also differed from present, fallen sex in other ways. Women would not have been "deflowered" by it but would have retained their "virginal integrity," like Mary, in both the sexual act and parturition, suffering no labor pains—a view that suggests something less than fully embodied sexual penetration and childbirth. This view would also be expanded to claim that women in Paradise would not have menstruated; monthly bleeding was seen as an expression of women's "cursed," fallen state.[38]

Moreover, Augustine, like Jerome, was convinced that marital sex and procreation were no longer commmanded by God, though they were still allowed in the Christian era. In creating humanity, God had blessed reproduction in order to produce a certain number of humans from which the elect would be drawn. The patriarchs of the Old Testament had even been permitted multiple wives so as to hasten the process by which the generations of humanity would be born to the time of Christ.[39]

But with the birth of Christ, the new era of the virginal had begun in human history, anticipating the culmination of the present world and the dawn of the "New Creation," when marriage would no longer be necessary. It was virgins who represented this redeemed era: to be fully dedicated to Christ was to put aside reproductive sex.[40] Augustine thus suggests that marriage was in some sense sub-Christian. Although still retaining the "goods" from its creational mandate, it had been essentially flawed by the Fall and would have no place in the age to come, which the Christian life should both mirror and anticipate.

THE DEVELOPMENT OF CLERICAL CELIBACY

The fourth century saw a major effort to clericalize sexual continence. As we have seen, sexual renunciation in earlier centuries of Christianity had not been linked to ordination. Many movements that exalted sexual renunication saw it as a leveling choice that overcame hierarchies of gender, class, and ethnic identity, as well as a means of standing against systems of social dominance. Sexual renouncers, male and female, were a charismatic, prophetic leadership of the "holy," not part of a clerical system.

By contrast, the ordained leadership of the church was mostly married. I Timothy advises that priests and bishops should be *patresfamilias,* and in the fourth century most priests and bishops were married and the fathers of children. It was expected that they have sex only for procreation, abstain in preparation for festivals and during their wives' menstruation and pregnancy, and ease into continence in their older years. But this was no more than what was asked of a good Christian paterfamilias generally.

With the Council of Elvira in Spain (A.D. 309), however, a new note was sounded. Now all bishops, presbyters, and deacons were called to give up sex with their wives as a condition of their ordination. It was still assumed that the leadership would be drawn from married householders, but once ordained, the clergy must abstain permanently from sex in order to possess the requisite "purity" to stand before the altar as priests.[41] Those who did not abstain and so produced children were to be "expelled from the dignity of the clerical office."[42]

The fourth century saw a new advent of monastic bishops, men of great talent such as Ambrose and Basil the Great. In the fusion of church and empire that evolved under Constantine and his sons, a practice of delaying baptism developed. In order to avoid backsliding from baptismal purity, baptism was postponed until one was either on the point of death or else ready to renounce the world for the ascetic life.[43] Those who, like Augustine, sought baptism after adult conversion expected to retire to a monastic life. But church leaders did not long allow such talented men monastic retirement, instead tapping them to become priests and bishops.[44]

The monastic bishops gathered around them celibate priests who would live together in monastic community, while also making the bishop's seat the base for new administrative power that would rival and, in the West, replace Roman governors and the emperor. This increased the pressure on married priests to imitate the continent by putting aside sexual relations with their wives. Western synods and episcopal decrees at Rome (in 386), Milan (in 390), and Carthage (in 401) reiterated the demand that the ordained, including deacons, give up sexual relations with their wives.[45]

The Eastern church followed a different path of development from the Western, allowing celibate and married priests to coexist. In 692 the Trullan Synod, dominated by Eastern bishops, would rule that deacons and priests who were already married before their ordination could—indeed must—continue to live with their wives. The unmarried who sought ordination should, in contrast, embrace monastic celibacy and could not later marry. In the Eastern tradition, bishops were drawn from the monastic clergy.[46] The Western church rejected the canon of this council that allowed clerical marriage, and thus began a division between East and West that was to widen into a final split in 1054.[47]

In the West, the sixth century saw stepped-up efforts to impose postordination celibacy on a still largely married clergy. Recognizing the need to involve wives in this decision, church leaders developed a practice of having the wife also take a vow of continence at the priest's ordination and in turn receive a special vestment. She could be addressed by female forms of the honorific titles—*deaconissa, presbytera, episcopa*—and function as a kind of assistant to her husband in caring for the church and undertaking a pastoral ministry with women.[48]

But this solution conflicted with the insistence that other women's ministries, such as the female deaconate and orders of virgins and widows, could not be ordained.[49] It also did nothing to allay the suspicion that the presence of the wife would "tempt" the husband to return to sexual relations with her. New rules were devised to demand that the wife sleep in a separate room from the husband and that she always be accompanied by an attendant.[50]

The meaning of sexual continence itself changed during this period. In earlier Christianity it had been linked to a countercultural transcendence of the "world" that was open to all Christians, men and women. But this radical vision did not fit well with clerical institutionalization. Instead, ideas of cultic purity were revived from the Levitical laws and applied in a totalizing way to a Christian temple priesthood. Not just sexual relations, but all contact with women's bodies was seen as inherently polluting. The example of the priests of the Old Testament who abstained from their wives when offering sacrifices was cited to claim that Christian priests, who continually offered sacrifice at the altar, must be in a permanent state of ritual purity, free from contact with women's polluting bodies.[51]

This emphasis on cultic purity as the primary rationale for priestly celibacy discouraged the possibility of associating even a continent wife with her husband in ministry. It also threw a pall over any association between other continent women, whether deaconesses or widows, and priests in liturgical functions—a proscription reflected in the demands that women be veiled and cover their hands when they received the Eucharist and that even women who cleaned the altar linens must receive them with covered hands outside the sanctuary.[52] Only an aged female relative, such as a mother, could live with a priest as his housekeeper. None of the legislation expressed any concern for the fate of the wife and children who were to be discarded; in fact, they were threatened with slavery and punitive abuse.[53]

In the chaotic conditions of the seventh century in Merovingian Gaul, this effort to enforce continence in the married clergy was largely abandoned and forgotten, though it remained in place in the canonic tradition for later revival. Here the main concern was instead with a clergy that sank to the level of "barbarian" secular society, living with several concubines and sharing in unruly feasting and violence. In 742, when Boniface, the Anglo-Saxon missionary to the Germans, sought to restore the canonical demands that priests separate from their wives and live in permanent continence, Pope Zachary appeared unaware of any such tradition. He replied that priests indeed should not be adulterers, citing 1 Timothy that priests should be husbands of only one wife.[54]

Boniface, needless to say, was not satisfied with this answer drawn from the New Testament, and sought to enforce the canons that dictated complete continence for the ordained, including deacons, priests, and bishops. He presided over a Frankish reform synod that prescribed imprisonment, flogging, and a diet of bread and water for two years for clergy who lived with women. Wives were not distinguished from concubines, with both being dubbed "whores," and sexual union with any woman defined as "carnal sin."[55]

But these decrees seem to have had little effect. Even the demand that "concubinous" clergy be deposed was seldom enforced. From the ninth to the eleventh centuries most priests continued to marry and have children, often making their sons heirs of church property and offices. Indeed, unless a man lived in a monastic community where the household work was done by either the monks themselves or servants, he could scarcely survive without the services of a woman who could cook, clean, spin, weave, make candles, and grow vegetables and herbs. Women provided the domestic economy upon which the household depended. With an average life expectancy for women somewhere around thirty-five, few adult men would have had able mothers alive to do such work for them. The most feasible solution for most men, then, was a wife.

Although such priests might concede that celibacy was a higher way of life, it was assumed to be an unrealistic constraint to impose on ordinary priests. The best that could be expected was that they be faithful to one wife, not sexually promiscuous. Yet the struggle to impose continence on the clergy had done its work. Priestly marriage, even if tolerated, was presumed to be illicit. Vituperation against fornication, combined with the demand for ritual purity, tainted all such relations, regardless of their fidelity, as sinful and polluting. The sanctity of marriage was denied to priests, and the status of their children was uncertain, even though many went on to illustrious careers in the church. Even at the time of the Reformation it was common for clerical families to intermarry.[56]

THE CHRISTIANIZING OF MARRIAGE

Before we trace the renewed effort to enforce celibacy on all priests in the reform movement of the eleventh century, it may be instructive to examine the parallel movement to christianize marriage in the seventh to ninth centuries. The Christian church had grown up in the shadow of two systems of family law, Roman and Jewish, details of which were described in chapter 1. The evolution of the church from persecuted sect to established religion in the fourth century had little impact on secular Roman or Germanic laws regarding marriage.

Christians had their particular marriage codes, including strict monogamy, no divorce or remarriage, and continence for prescribed periods within marriage, which were enforced through internal church discipline, increasingly expressed in canon law. The canons of the Council of Elvira, which prescribed clerical continence, also bore witness to the codes of Christian family life enforced through the church. Standing at the back of the church in the stance of a penitent for a set period of time and having communion withheld were the sanctions imposed on those who had sexual affairs yet wished to continue in communion with the church.[57]

In the fourth century, the Christian church in the Western empire was confronted by Germanic and Celtic tribes that were moving into partly Christianized regions. Many of the Germanic tribes initially were converted to an Arian Christianity, and so the struggles of Ambrose and others were to prevent the legitimization of this "heretical" form of Christianity by the emperors.[58] In 496 Clovis, the king of the Salic Franks, who was rapidly expanding his power in Gaul, was baptized a Catholic Christian along with three thousand followers in the cathedral at Rheims, having been influenced by his wife, Clotilda, a Burgundian of Catholic faith.[59]

This mass conversion allowed Catholic churchmen to leapfrog over the Arian German groups that had come into Italy earlier, and enabled them to enter into an alliance with the Franks to control church and state in the crumbling Western empire. The alliance of Gallo-Roman women from old ruling-class families with German men of warrior nobility was a major means of fusion of the two cultures, Roman and "barbarian," during this period. Catholic churchmen played a key role in linking this alliance with orthodox Christianity.[60]

The marriage customs of the Celtic and German "barbarians" were, however, very different from those of the Romans, as well as from those favored by the church. Specifically, the Celts and Germans practiced a "resource polygyny" that allowed powerful chiefs to accumulate a plurality of wives and concubines. These many women not only afforded such chiefs a variety of sexual relations and many children, but also offered the skills to run large household economies, including doing much of the agricultural work.[61]

Such a chief could have several wives at once—sometimes even marrying sisters—as well as multiple concubines. The distinction between wives and concubines was fluid. The wife was secured through a more formal arrangement with her kin, which might include a wedding gift or dowry of extensive lands as well as moveable wealth. Divorce was by mutual consent, with the wife expected to take her wedding gifts with her.

Alongside his wife or wives, the chief could have "freelove" relations with concubines of lower-class families. If she was able to hold his affections, a concubine, too, might gain from a powerful lover valuable gifts that she could control. Thus marriage and concubinage were a perilous but potentially lucrative means for women to rise in status, to accumulate wealth, and, in the case of a wife, to exercise political influence through the network of her own kin and that of her husband and children.

This plurality of women was one of the perquisites of chiefly power and wealth. Poorer men could afford only one wife; some who could afford none became bandits or attached themselves to great households in hopes of gaining the power to seize a wife or the wealth to merit receiving one from her kin. Women as wives, concubines, servants, and slaves were concentrated in the great households, leaving other men bereft of female sexual and domestic service. Bishops in Merovingian Gaul (in the sixth and seventh centuries) railed at the immorality of these practices but had little actual impact on them, and often conformed to similar ways of life themselves.

This was all to change radically, at least in theory, in the mid–eighth century with the advent of the Carolingian dynasty in alliance with reforming monks such as Boniface. Boniface's vision of a Christian society required both the removal of wives from the households of priests and the banishment of plural wives from the households of the nobility. Two key ideas guided the effort to Christianize marriage: indissoluble monogamy and prohibition of incest with kin.

Indissoluble monogamy meant that a man could be married only once and could not divorce and remarry even if his wife committed adultery, a standard drawn from the stricter version of the proscription against divorce in the Gospels. Incest taboos were extended to the seventh degree of relationship, including not only blood kin but also in–laws and spiritual relatives (i.e., godparents and their kin).[62] The reasons behind the broad definition of forbidden relations for marriage in this period are somewhat mysterious; the Romans had, after all, traditionally proscribed marriage only to the third degree of kinship, while the Jews had permitted marriage between first cousins.

The net effect of the enforcement of these two laws—of indissoluble monogamy and incest prohibition through the seventh degree of kinship—was to create a greatly widened exogamy. Nobles had to search for women among more remote households to find suitable mates with whom they shared no bonds of kinship through blood, marriage, or baptism. Since a nobleman would want his one legitimate wife to be of equal or greater status, such a wife must be chosen carefully. She must combine sexual attractiveness (to gain the affections of her husband) and a pleasant personality (to hold them) with good health and fertility, extensive household-management skills, and strong connections with a powerful and wealthy but suitably distant family.

Such a jewel was hard to find, and Western Christian history from the eighth century on was filled with wrangles between churchmen and nobles over marriage and divorce. The churchmen insisted that a noble keep a wife even if she did not provide affection, sons, or good connections, while the nobles themselves argued they should be able to seek another wife to supplant the one who had failed to supply these. Many areas of contention arose through the church's legislation. Perhaps, for example, the first relation might not really have been a valid marriage, due to some hitherto unsuspected kinship, and could be declared null, thus allowing the noble to marry a second, more desirable wife?

Few men actually knew all their relations through the many degrees of kinship by blood, marriage, and baptism—hence the possibility of a noble's claiming impediments to a marriage that he now wanted annulled. Depending on his temperament or his political alliances, a churchman might or might not accept such a "reason" for annulment. If the answer was no, the prince and the churchman might engage in a long duel of strength as the prince sought to cast off one wife, often using a convent as a place to deposit her, and marry another, while the churchman insisted that he remain faithful to the first wife.[63] The contest of Henry VIII and Pope Clement VII in the sixteenth century was only one of many battles in the war between church and nobility over marriage and remarriage.

Precisely what distinguished a valid, binding marriage from a casual affair was also unclear. The medieval church had developed little in the way of a marriage ritual, despite its definition of marriage as a sacrament.[64] A blessing at the church door (or even in the marriage bed) by a priest was deemed good, but it was not required to define a valid marriage. Mutual consent became the dominant church definition of binding marriage, even if the marriage was unconsummated, though other canonists maintained that a marriage was not complete until it had been consummated.[65]

This question was complicated by the need to affirm that Mary and Joseph had had a true marriage, even though an unconsummated one. The emphasis on the consent of the couple, rather than parental approval, as the key to marriage opened the way for a clandestine elopement of young lovers to be declared a binding marriage, even against the wishes of their parents for a more suitable spouse. It also allowed a girl to resist a match forced upon her by her parents—a resistance the church tended to support, particularly if the girl claimed she had a higher calling to chastity.

Many popular lives of saints turned on this drama of a precociously celibate girl in her early teens (still the typical age of marriage for girls of the upper class) resisting pressure and abuse from parents and fiancé and defending her vocation to virginity. In the end she was usually vindicated and allowed to leave triumphantly for the convent, with churchmen rewarding her tenacity and her parents persuaded to relinquish her.[66]

The church's ideal for Christian marriage, which it sought to enforce primarily in a power struggle with the nobility (not until much later would lower-class unions come under such regulations),[67] called for a single moral standard for both men and women. Women had long been asked to be virginal at the time of their marriage and faithful to one man all their life long; now men were asked to conform to the same standards.

But the princely class did not readily give up its desire for a succession of wives to meet dynastic needs, as well as for a diversity of sexual relations to satisfy its sexual and affective appetites. Nobles continued to keep concubines and to have casual affairs, though these were now clearly distinguished from the one legitimate wife. The church tacitly conceded this double standard, instead spending most of its moral energy to secure the indissolubility of the one "valid" marriage.

The result of this definition of monogamy was, as Susan Wemple has shown, an ambiguous one for women. The one legitimate wife was more secure against rivals, and at best could be greatly honored if she could manage the many demands upon her. Rivals for her husband's affections might abound, but they could not become the wife, or mother of his legitimate children.[68] Most "sensible" upper-class women learned to acquiesce to this arrangement (unlike, in our own day, the late Princess Diana of England). A sharp distinction between wife and concubine, between legitimate children and bastards, was now drawn. Other women could seldom hope to rise to favor and gain the status of wife, once a marriage had been confirmed.

CONTROLLING CELIBATE WOMEN'S MINISTRIES

A third line of development in Western Christianity, that of women's ministry and monastic life, must be sketched to complete this picture of the emerging Latin Christian society of the high Middle Ages. In the early centuries of Christianity, female vocation to celibacy had been lived out primarily within the family itself, not in separate institutions of female monasticism. The young girl vowed to virginity would withdraw into a room within her own home, there to be cherished as a sacred being by her family.[69]

Older women who claimed such a vocation, particularly widows with property, might turn their houses into monasteries, gathering female relatives and servants into a community of pious study, prayer, and fasting. In the fourth century some of these upper-class women ascetics journeyed to the Holy Land, there to found extensive monastic settlements for hundreds of women, together with hospitals, hospices, and parallel male monastic institutions led by male associates.[70]

Already by the late first century, female renunciates had served and been supported by the local church. Some of these were simply needy elderly widows, but others were young widows and virgins who played roles in liturgical and pastoral ministries, whether in choirs, as catechists and assistants in the baptism of women, or as distributors of communion to women at home. The female deaconate also played such roles.[71] Conflict eventually arose as to whether these women enjoyed a type of ordination or not. The Eastern church conceded an ordained deaconate to women for many centuries. Powerful patronesses, such as Olympias of Constantinople, were ordained to the deaconate and presided over extensive communities of women that were attached to city churches.[72]

In the sixth century, Western church synods decided against any ordained status for such groups of continent women, and also sought to marginalize clergy wives as potential clergy.[73] But these decisions remained ambiguous. Radegund, a Thuringian princess who revolted against her Merovingian husband, Clothar, to found a monastic community in the fifth century, was ordained a deaconess by Bishop Medard of Noyon,[74] and quasi-clerical roles and titles reappeared in the ninth century to designate powerful abbesses.[75] As the female pastoral ministry was marginalized, remnants of it became fused with female monasticism.

Two different perspectives on female monasticism must be distinguished. Many female monasteries were founded by women who sought a place for their own vocation and then gathered communities of women around them. In Britain, Ireland, and Germany in the sixth to tenth centuries, these were generally noblewomen, some in search of refuge from violence or forced marriage, though the convent might also be open to lower-class women, often former servants associated with the foundress. These noblewomen gave over large tracts of inherited land to their foundations, which effectively became female-ruled kingdoms. Some had a standard of learning comparable to that in male monasteries of the period, complete with libraries, schools, and scriptoria.[76]

But such elite monastic foundresses did not eschew all family relations when they embraced celibacy. They often took female relatives with them and passed on their foundations to sisters or daughters. The female monastery was seen by kin as an extension of the family, a place for prayer, memorial, and burial for relatives. Talented ruling-class women could chose the convent, with its extensive lands and serfs, as a sphere of power and leadership. Convents were interdependent with other family holdings, performing functions that supported family ambitions and needs.[77]

This also meant that family monasteries became places to discard (or even imprison) unwanted women and children, regardless of their real vocation (or lack of one) to such a life. This ambiguity—between the female monastery as an alternative community to the family on the one hand and as an extension of the family's economic and social needs on the other—dogs the history of female conventual life, as indeed it does monastic life as a whole during this period.

THE REFORM MOVEMENT

The eleventh-century reform movement, led by popes such as Gregory VII, would seek to cut through the tangled skein of relations between church and family and between celibacy and marriage to create clear divisions. Two main expressions of this struggle were the crusades against simony—that is, lay control of church lands and offices—and clerical marriage.

First, the church sought to place all church offices, with their attendant lands and income, wholly under the control of the church. No longer could noble or royal families regard the offices of bishop, abbot, or priest, with their benefices, as extensions of family holdings, appointing to them family members and clients. Church property and leadership were to be strictly separated from secular nobility. Appointments were to be made by the church alone, according to a system of ecclesiastical rule culminating with the pope.

Second, clerical marriages were to be once and for all broken up, in order both to create a pure priesthood worthy to offer the sacrament of Christ's body, unpolluted by female contact, and to prevent clergy dynasties from perpetuating themselves by passing on church land and offices to children. Victory in this struggle did not come easily. From the mid–eleventh century to the mid-twelfth, popes and other reformers dueled with representatives of the imperial nobility who defended lay investiture, and with defenders of clergy marriage who allied themselves with the imperial party.[78]

The rhetoric grew vehement on both sides. The reformers characterized the simoniacs and married priests as fornicators and heretics who were prostituting the church, while their opponents charged that the reformers were simply out for wealth and power themselves, suggesting that they were sodomites whose preference for sexual relations with other men gave them no sympathy for the plight of the married.[79]

By the mid–twelfth century the battle was largely won for the reform side. The lay nobility had to withdraw from former claims to control church land and offices. The nobles now sought more consolidated control over their own lands and family systems through a heightened system of male primogeniture and patrilineage, rather than the dispersed network of kin drawn from paternal and maternal relations characteristic of earlier times.[80]

The first Lateran Council (1139) defined the sacrament of ordination as an impediment to marriage, rendering any marriage of the ordained invalid by nature. Priests were declared unable to contract a valid marriage; their sexual relations could thus be only sinful fornication and their children "sacrilegious bastards."[81] Bastardy itself was also made an impediment to ordination, so the sons of such unions could not themselves become priests.[82] This reform did not, of course, actually prevent many priests from seeking sexual solace, anymore than earlier reforms had done. Not a few, particularly rural curates, continued to form committed relations and raise children. But these unions were deprived of any official validity or moral dignity.

The victory of this reform movement shaped Christian society and culture of the high Middle Ages in a specfic mold. The celibate male clergy, both secular and regular, was sharply distinguished from the married laity. Their celibacy made priests innately superior to married laypeople, whose sexual relations were tarred by the suspicion of sin. This hierarchy of celibate over married undermined the early Christian sense of the church as a whole constituting a "new family." The metaphor of church as new spiritual family over against the "world" would now be transferred to celibate monastic communities. The married laity was meanwhile demoted to being itself a part of the profane "world," rather than part of the new spiritual family of the church.

The medieval church developed no spirituality tailored to married laypeople, offering them only the option of sexual continence if they would be truly holy.[83] Unlike the Greco-Roman culture, which had allowed the married to see the procreative fire in their bodies as an expression of the same divine energy that sustained the cosmos,[84] the medieval church taught Christians to see only shame in their sexual coupling, separating them from God.

The degradation of married sexuality in the light of antisexual purity also shaped a mystical spirituality for men and women built on sexual sublimation. The man taught to abhor attraction for real women could instead meditate on vivid visions of being joined in marriage with a beautiful young virgin Mary.[85] Christian women, warned against all the sexual feelings that lurked in their own bodies and in those of men, could yet be admired as saints when they had visions of being espoused to Christ as their celestial lover, and of birthing and suckling the baby Jesus.[86]

Thus the powerful urge for a sexuality united with affective love for spouse and children, rigorously repressed on the physical level, reappeared as spiritual visions, but in a way that despised rather than rehabilitated those visions' negated physical counterpart. The sixteenth-century reformers revolted against this system of male celibate clericalism triumphant over sex and marriage. We will ask in the next chapter whether they deeply transformed it or merely tinkered with some of its trappings.

CHAPTER 3

Family, Work, Gender, and Church in the Reformation Era

There is broad agreement among family historians that the late-medieval and early-modern periods saw a significant realignment of gender in relation to family, work, and the state. The first half of the sixteenth century was a crucial turning point in this process.[1] But exact definitions become ever more complex as more regions of central and western Europe are studied in detail. Differences of class among royalty, feudal nobility, urban patricians, merchants, guilds, journeymen, urban proletariats, and peasantry, both urban and rural, must be recognized, as must regional variations. Gender differences have to be seen in these many contexts.

THE REALIGNMENT OF GENDER ROLES, 900–1500: AN OVERVIEW

Even among cities that espoused the Reformation within the same region, such as southern Germany, different patterns were exhibited, depending, for example, on whether the town council came to include a representation of guild leadership, as in Augsburg,[2] or rejected this reform for a closed merchant and patrician oligarchy, as in Zwickau.[3] Descriptions of general trends become ever more qualified as comparative studies of different classes and groups in distinct towns and regions are undertaken. Attempting to generalize about these patterns of change in the space of one chapter is a perilous challenge, but it is nevertheless crucial if we wish to understand the legacy of this era in the definition of family and gender roles of Western society in the modern era.

Broadly, we can see in these centuries trends that gradually shifted the boundaries between households, political power, and economic production for trade. These shifts redefined the functions and relations of members of the household and their roles. Conceptualizing such shifts in terms of changing definitions of "public" and "private" has been useful, but it may be misleading to the extent that it suggests a fixed boundary separating these spheres.[4] Rather, we should imagine a process of expansion and differentiation of political and economic activities in relation to work done in the households. The work done by women that once encompassed these activities in simpler societies became marginalized and set in opposition to expanding arenas reserved for men. The process began inside the household itself, with certain work done by men in certain areas of the house separated from the work roles and places of women. Men monopolized these expanding roles while women became confined within other roles defined by their exclusion from the developing political and economic arenas of men.

All of this needs to be seen in terms of a long process of redevelopment of the state and of the urban productive and trade economies from their most decentralized point in the ninth and tenth centuries. The collapse of the Roman Empire and the disintegration of its state system of government, army, urban life, and market economy took shape as a long process of devolution to a localized form of political, economic, and military organization. In its most decentralized form, manorialism, economic production was focused primarily on consumption and local exchange in related villages centered in the estates of the lord of the manor, who commanded political relations, defense, and a portion of the villagers' labor for work on his lands.

In this context of decentralization, political and economic relations, for the landed nobility, were household relations. The role of the wife of the lord in administering the economic and financial affairs of the estate was coterminous with administration of the realm. Productive activities such as the weaving of cloth were done by women servants, slaves, and girls in workshops attached to the estate and available for local use by nobles and churchmen.[5] Access to political power came through the inheritance of land and title. Women as wives, daughters, or mothers might rule in the absence of a husband, for lack of male heir, or as regents for a son not yet of age.

In relation to this situation of decentralization in the ninth and tenth centuries, the later Middle Ages and the early modern period were times of state formation by national and territorial kings and saw the redevelopment of urban life. Local nobilities were gradually shorn of their autonomous political power and subordinated to a centralizing national state, as in early modern England and France. As state bureaucracies developed to administer this expanded state, the queen's administrative role became increasingly distinct from that of the realm and was eventually confined to oversight of household work. While extensive, this role was nonetheless separated from state administration.

The fourteenth and fifteenth centuries brought the revival of classical doctrines such as that of Aristotle, which forbade women political rule on the basis of their inherent incompetence as irrational beings. In the self-governing cities that grew up first in Italy and then in areas such as Germany, governed by town councils drawn from the urban propertied classes, women were strictly excluded from election to or inheritance of political office—even though women were defined as citizens, paying taxes and contributing soldiers to the city defense on the basis of their wealth in property and production.[6]

This definition of women as excluded from political office by nature was seconded by almost all male thinkers (with a few notable exceptions) in the sixteenth century, and would continue to influence Western political organization through the liberal revolutions of the late eighteenth and nineteenth centuries, when women are excluded from the new definitions of the political rights of citizens. In the early modern era the chief contradictions to this dogma were female members of the nobility and royalty, who continued to enjoy the possibility of inheritance of political rule and administration of territories through kinship.

Debate about women's rule focused on these royal and noble women and often turned on whether or not the male debater saw his own cause as being supported by a woman ruler. Thus John Knox assailed women's rule in his treatise "First Blast against the Monstrous Regiment of Women" (1558), an attack on Mary Tudor, who sought to undo the English Reformation begun by her father, Henry VIII, and restore Catholicism; but he grew silent on the subject when Mary was succeeded by a Protestant queen, Elizabeth I.[7]

Likewise, Sir Thomas Elyot's treatise defending women's rule

(1540) may actually have been written to support the deposition of Henry VIII in favor of his former divorced wife Catherine of Aragon, as regent for her daughter, Mary.[8] For its part, Agrippa von Nettesheim's exceptional defense of women's equality in political affairs was originally inspired by a queen patroness of the university where he lectured.[9] And when dealing with noble Protestant women patrons, even leading reformers such as Calvin muted their teaching that women must always be subject to their husbands and play no public leadership roles.[10]

If family remained a potential source of political power for women of noble or royal lineage, where rule was still linked with inheritance through kinship, the same could not be said for propertied women of the cities, where civic responsibility was split by gender from political leadership. None of the (few) humanist defenses of women's political rule addressed bourgeois women, who had been excluded from the beginning from office in town councils.

It is in the context of urban life that we can see most clearly the development of the new work relations that would exclude women from more advantageous forms of productive work and redefine male-female relations in the household. As cities grew in the thirteenth century, regulated crafts or guilds that monopolized particular products developed. In the fourteenth century these began to vie for a share of political power with the merchant and patrician elites, with differing results—sometimes taking over town councils, sharing power with older elites, and sometimes being excluded altogether.

Guilds regulated the prices and quality of their products and prevented those who were not guild members from producing their crafts. There remained areas of free or unregulated production in small, low-cost items such as brushes, combs, and wooden spoons and bowls. Both regulated and free production took place in households, but regulated craft work was increasingly differentiated from women's work.

The guild system brought together a household-based work force that included the master, his wife, younger and older children, maids, apprentices, and journeymen. Crafts such as shoemaking demanded seven years as an apprentice followed by another seven years as a journeyman, during which the craftsman-in-training traveled and learned by working with several master craftsmen. At the end of this period, he produced his "masterpiece." If this was approved by the guildmasters, and there was room for another shop in town, he would become a master with his own workshop. The guilds generally did not allow journeymen to marry, but they required it of masters, for a wife was seen as an integral and necessary part of the household production system.

The guilds also regulated the morals of their members. Both the master and his wife must be of good moral reputation, and neither could be illegitimate (a rule that excluded the children of priests, among others). The wife played an extensive role in such a household economy, washing, cooking, and providing heat, light, food, drink, and clothes for the whole household work force, with help from her children and maids. She shared in the actual productive labor and often sold the wares from a shop at the front of the house or from a stand in the marketplace. She often kept the books for the household shop and collected debts.[11] Thus she shared the skills of production and management and ran the business's supportive services; in return she was allowed to carry on the workshop if her husband died.

In the beginning, none of the guilds explicitly excluded or limited women's work, and certain guilds, such as those concerned with silk production, linen weaving and candle-making, were predominantly female in some cities.[12] However, from the mid–fifteenth century the guilds began to curtail women's work. A widow was no longer allowed to carry on the work of the shop for more than a few months after her husband's death, or to take on new apprentices and journeymen.[13] As the market for goods tightened, the guilds were closed to new shops. Widows were encouraged to marry journeymen to replace their dead husbands, and sons of masters were given privileged rights to succeed their fathers. Thus fewer journeymen could hope ever to become masters of their own shops.

Journeymen responded to these narrowed opportunities by organizing their own associations, living in journeymen's hostels rather than in masters' households, forming their own drinking clubs, and shaping a male camaraderie that networked between cities. They also pushed to further limit the work of women in the shop, excluding first maids and then daughters and wives from doing the same work as the craftsmen. This was a matter of both work opportunity and male "honor." By preventing the maids and then the daughters and wives of the master's family from sitting beside them and doing the same craftwork as a jeweler, shoemaker, or weaver, they kept more workplaces for themselves and also separated the skilled, superior work reserved for men from the inferior work done by women.[14]

Women of the household were now relegated to supportive services and auxiliary work—for example, washing and carding wool or spinning thread to be supplied to the weavers—and no longer allowed to take part in the productive labor. They were thereby also excluded from learning the craft and being able to do its work on their own. They might be forbidden even small tasks, such as weaving dishcloths, if the resulting products were to be sold. Women's work for household consumption was thus increasingly separated from production for sale. Women might still monopolize the minor areas of free production—usually done part-time and seen as unskilled labor—but the sale of such products did not bring in enough to support a household.[15]

The increasing exclusion of women from skilled production demoted women to low-paid and unpaid work. Women baked for their families but could not sell baked goods in the market, except for small items such as cookies or pretzels. They were forbidden to butcher or sell meat but might make and sell sausages from the entrails. They could peddle locally grown fruits, vegetables, and herbs, but were generally kept from long-distance trade. They could sell used clothes and household items but were not allowed to repair clothes for sale, lest they impinge on the tailor's craft.

Similar trends emerged in arts traditionally associated with women in the family, such as healing. Women might still grow herbs and concoct remedies for their families, but professionalized doctors and apothecaries increasingly prevented them from offering their medical services to others for a fee.[16] As educational and licensing requirements were developed, women were excluded from the education and forbidden the license. Only midwifery hung on longer as a female skill inappropriate for men: not until the nineteenth century did men take over birthing, marginalizing midwives as dangerous quacks while denying women access to medical schools.[17]

Women still did the low-paid work of feeding, washing, and caring for the poor, the sick, and the elderly in city hospitals, pesthouses, and orphanages. Domestic service in the households of others was a major area of female employment, with maids' receiving a pittance beside their room and board.[18] Agricultural work continued largely unchanged, as the sphere in which the majority of men and women were employed. There women went on raising fruits, vegetables, and poultry and helping with the harvests, peddling their produce in local markets.[19] Women's workload did not lessen, but it was increasingly unrecognized, relegated as it was to low-paid and unpaid supportive labor for male-monopolized production and professions.

CONFLICTS OVER CELIBACY, MARRIAGE, AND SEXUAL MORALITY

Many recent studies on the Reformation in German cities have shown the importance of the guilds and their ideal of the patriarchal household for Reformation marital ideology. Ideally the guildmaster was the model paterfamilias, himself dutifully monogamous and keeping his household of maids, sons and daughters, apprentices and journeymen under strict control. But as Lyndal Roper has demonstrated in her detailed microstudy of the Reformation in Augsburg in the crucial years from 1525 to 1550, this was an ideal fraught with anxieties and contradictions.[20]

In Augsburg the guilds had secured shared representation on the town council with the patrician and rich merchant families; they thus joined with the town's elite in control of what was seen as a potentially disruptive population of journeymen and day laborers who had little hope of attaining the status of masters themselves. Wealthy merchants such as the Fugger family challenged the guilds' householder ideal with their luxury and their promotion of a form of mercantile capitalism that undermined the autonomous household economy.[21]

On the eve of the Reformation, Augsburg, with its population of thirty thousand, had a cathedral and six parish churches with attached celibate clergy. There were male and female houses of religious orders: Dominicans, Benedictines, Carmelites, Franciscans, and Augustinians. These houses, whose members were drawn mostly from the upper classes and which owned extensive properties beyond the walls of the city, bespoke the leisured privilege of a celibate class of men and women that conflicted with the frugal married-householder ideal of the guildmasters. The guildmaster also suspected that his control over his own wife might be subverted by the intimate confidences she shared with her confessor.[22]

The ecclesiastical establishment moreover defied control by the town council, as it paid no taxes and was linked to a system of church power independent of city government. Already in the fifteenth century, city governments had vied with church-owned institutions, seeking to take over hospitals, schools, and orphanages and putting their endowments into the city treasuries. A key aspect of the Reformation must be seen as a vast property confiscation. Both princely reformations in Germany, England, Denmark, and Sweden and city-based reformations led by town councils stood to profit by a windfall of land, buildings, and endowments from the takeover of church property. Secular governments thus also gained more comprehensive sovereignty as a large sphere of autonomous institutions was brought under their sway.

Yet another institution defied both the marital ideals of the householders and the celibate ideals of the monks and priests: the town brothel. Augsburg, like many towns in Germany and Italy, founded a city-run brothel in the fifteenth century in order to regulate what was seen as a "necessary evil."[23] The health and working conditions of the city prostitutes were supervised; they could not be forced to work when they were ill or pregnant, and had a certain accepted place in public city functions such as processions.

With significant numbers of the young male citizenry unable to marry while they served their apprentice and journeymen years, and an increasing proportion left with no prospect of being able to marry at all, the town brothel was designed to keep men from committing worse offenses such as raping or seducing "respectable" women. The male sexual drive was assumed to be insistent; if not given an acceptable outlet, it would inevitably find an unacceptable one.[24] Although the brothel was supposedly off-limits to vowed celibates as well as to married men, both were known to visit it on occasion.

The period from the 1520s to the 1560s saw the closing of town brothels both in cities that went with the Reformation and in ones that remained or returned to being Catholic. The sixteenth century was an age of revived puritan asceticism throughout Europe, both in Spain and Portugal, which became bastions of anti-Protestant Catholic renewal,[25] and in the regions that embraced the Protestant Reformation. Both sides clamored for strict control of morals through the enforcement of ideals of celibate and/or marital chastity.

The polemics of the reformers continue to echo in history books, painting the monasteries as places of constant sexual vice. Such descriptions cannot be taken literally but should instead be recognized as expressing a clash of conflicting ideals of moral purity, each founded on deep sexual anxieties. The fifteenth century had already seen a wave of monastic revival, separating many orders into houses that had renewed the strict rules of their founders (Observants) and houses that had not (Conventuals).[26] This earlier reform of monasteries was foundational for the Catholic renewal of the sixteenth century, which sought to counter the Reformation through a renewal of its vision of a strict celibacy for priests combined with a faithful, abstemious monogamy for the married.

This does not mean that there were not sufficient instances of monks' visiting brothels or seducing wives or daughters in confession, and of bishops' gathering fines for the children of priests living in concubinage, to raise temperatures across the contested regions of Europe.[27] But it is probably more accurate to think of the laxity of monasteries and convents as a sort of leisured affluence or class arrogance than as rampant sexual vice. When the reforming mobs broke into the Dominican monastery in Augsburg, they were outraged to find the monks playing at bowls.[28] Likewise, Catholic reformers pressed nuns to take up hairshirts and fasting and give up parties with good food and plays.[29] In short, much of the vitriolic exchange of accusations of "whoremongering" that filled the air itself expressed a renewed ascetic temper, combined with a new confidence that such rules of personal life could be enforced by more powerful states and their new morals police. Both Protestants and Catholics sought to create their godly realm.

The sexual anxiety that fueled this new rigor was surely founded not merely on outrage at the sins of others, but also on the moral crusaders' awareness of their own struggles and lapses. Protestant reformers had themselves recently departed from vowed celibacy after long struggling with a way of life that told them they could obliterate the sexual drive if they had enough ascetic discipline. In rejecting this view of human potential in favor of one that held that the sexual drive must be satisfied, and that God's ordained means of satisfaction was marriage, they adapted rather than abandoned the ascetic anthropology of Saint Augustine.

The righteous guildmasters, who forbade journeymen to marry

and now led the reformed morals police that sought to punish fornicators, had themselves arisen from years of apprenticeship during
which they had had to delay marriage and had frequented the brothel
as their accepted sexual outlet. When they finished vilifying the
monks as enemies of their godly city, they turned to correcting one
another.

The reform in Augsburg, as in many German cities, began with
pamphlets written by Luther that articulated the challenge to the celibate church. Evangelical preachers, themselves monks or priests, rose
up and began to preach the new word in town churches. This led very
quickly in the mid-1520s to the challenge of more radical reformers,
who sought to break altogether from the established order of church
and state.[30] Those who came to be identified as Anabaptists sought
covenanted church communities set radically against society. They
believed in strict moral discipline for their members, but a discipline
that came from the congregation itself, not from civic authorities.

Some played with new visions of the family, including a restored
Old Testament patriarchal polygamy and an endogamous union of
converted church members that renounced outside control.[31] Such a
reform stood in stark contrast to the aspiration of reforming princes
and city councils to take over church property and create integrated
state-churches under their control. The Anabaptists were shortly
driven out of reforming cities and territories, their women and men
hunted down and forced to conform or be executed. The great in-
gathering of Anabaptists to create the godly city at Münster was repressed by a combined army of Catholics and Protestants, who left the
movement's leaders to die in iron cages hung from the cathedral.[32]

The challenge of Anabaptism and the Peasants' War of 1525
turned Luther and other reformers to a reliance on princes and town
magistrates as their arm of enforcement, and prompted them to shelve
the more radical visions of dissent and social equality suggested by
their motto "a priesthood of all believers."[33] The few women who
had found a voice as preachers and pamphleteers in the first years of
the Reformation were now firmly told that they were to keep silent
in public and obey their husbands, even if those husbands were Catholics who beat them for their new beliefs.[34]

After excluding the more radical reformers, the first task of the reforming town councils was systematically to take over churches and

monastic property and to integrate the income from these properties
into the town treasury. The buildings abandoned by the monks might
be turned to new charitable purposes, perhaps becoming a hospital
under the control of a town-appointed administrator. But in this process of abolishing monastic institutions and either expelling or pen-
sioning off their residents, the reformers at Augsburg, as in several
other cities and territories, encountered unexpected resistance from
nuns, who often more adamantly than monks resisted the abolition of
their way of life.[35]

While the monk or town priest who accepted the Reformation
might take up a new ministerial role as a Protestant married clergyman, the nun lost a vocation to a higher spirituality that also constituted an independent sphere of learning and administration. She was
offered as a substitute only the option of being a pensioner or, if she
was young enough, the wife of a clergyman, something that many
nuns saw as both unappealing and a definite demotion from their previous status. Nuns, more than monks and priests, came from elite
classes and disdained to marry below their class.[36]

The nuns' refusal to leave their convents was met with various
strategies by reforming authorities. In some cases nuns were harassed
by mobs, forced to hear reforming sermons (to which some responded by singing and praying their rosaries), denied clergy for mass
and confession, or even dragged from their convents by their families.
In other cases they were allowed to stay on but forbidden to take new
novices into their orders, which would thus eventually die out.[37] Reformers faced a particularly difficult puzzle when nuns adopted the
Lutheran theology but insisted on maintaining their convent life.

The abbesses of great houses were drawn from the nobility and
ruled over extensive properties. Imperial abbeys such as Gandersteim
had histories of learning and rule that stretched back to the tenth century.[38] A Reformation-leaning abbess who was also an independent
territorial ruler could not easily be crossed by reformers, since she had
the power to appoint reforming preachers to her churches. Thus in
several places an anomalous situation arose in which nuns continued
their convent life even as they patronized the reformers, and Catholic
and Protestant nuns lived side by side in the same convent.[39]

Some of these Protestant convents survived through the eighteenth century, to be closed only by the Napoleonic occupation, not

by the Reformation. In the case of Augsburg, four out of the eight convents outlasted the Protestant period into the 1550s, when the city was taken over by Jesuits and Catholic reformers; none of the pre-Reformation male monasteries survived this period. Yet the overall effect of the closing of monastic communities, male and female, was a decrease in the charitable help available for the poor.

Even when the buildings and benefices taken over were turned into new charitable institutions such as city-run hospitals, the sheer variety of help previously available to the needy was diminished. For example, in Zwickau, when the Beguine house where the sisters had lived humbly and nursed shut-in elderly and sick was closed, no replacement was provided for those services.[40] Charity was no longer seen as a "good work" by which one could commend one's soul to God and gain forgiveness of sins, and so benefices for good works fell off in reformed cities.

The poor were now likely to be seen as criminally vagrant rather than as deserving of charity. Funds previously used for the poor were taken into city councils, sometimes serving as sources of loans for councilors. Where new charities were opened, the status of such work was demoted, now to be done by low-paid menial laborers rather than by those exemplifying a holy way of life. The pattern of increased centralization of control under city councils greatly decreased the variety of social, church, and charitable institutions that mediated between the state and the household and its individual members, making forced conformity to a uniform way of life ever more difficult to evade.

The existence of female religious communities challenged Reformation anthropology on two levels. Not only did it represent a rejected view that celibacy was a higher vocation to holiness than marriage, but it also defied the beliefs that marriage and motherhood were the only legitimate calling for all women under God's ordinances of Creation, and that a woman must always be under the control of a male head of family. Thus the very fact of women's living together and managing property and resources independently *as* women was an offense against the Protestant understanding of proper gender relations. This view was expressed in a 1534 memorial in the Augsburg town council, which declared that God had made woman subject to man because of her weaker nature: "How should it come to any good when women join themselves in a separate life, contrary to the ordinance of God, yes, against nature, they give themselves to obedience to a woman, who has neither reason nor the understanding to govern whether in spiritual or in temporal matters, who ought not to govern but to be governed."[41]

The abolition or at least the limiting of convents in Reformation cities was followed by an earnest campaign to reform the morals of the citizenry as a whole or drive out those who resisted such reform. In Augsburg in the 1530s a series of reform ordinances were passed that transferred control of marriage and morals from confessors and church courts to the city council. Sexual sin was now defined as a crime as well as a sin, to be met with punishments such as fines and imprisonment on bread and water.[42] Some reformers called for a revival of the Old Testament code of capital punishment for adultery, and their calls were successful for a time in Geneva and Scotland.[43]

City populations were put under close surveillance by new morals police that searched for hidden sexual vices of fornication and adultery, sins that had previously been disciplined by guildmen only when they became public and notorious. Blasphemy, drunkenness, gambling, fighting, and rowdy behavior—vices to which young men were regarded as being prone—were now to be strictly punished.[44] Such policing of morals ended by violating the very institution of the patriarchal household that the reformers lifted up as their ideal, as homes were invaded to gain evidence of moral infractions.

The closing of the public brothels did not put an end to prostitution, but only drove it underground, where it was unregulated and clandestine. Many cities experienced increases in rape, adultery, and fornication—or at least there was greater documentation of such crimes—after the brothels were closed. But the distinction between "respectable" and "unrespectable" women was abolished, which meant that anyone who had sex outside marriage might be called a "whore" or a "whorer." The respectable wife found to be unfaithful was as much a "whore" as the woman who made her living by prostitution. A wife who dallied with a journeyman whom she might, on her husband's death, make her husband differed from a woman who took in regular customers only in the frequency of fornication; they did not enjoy a different social status.[45]

Town councils and courts now assumed the role of inquisitors, ferreting out the details of the sexual sin, how it had come about, how often and under what circumstances it had taken place, in order to mete out appropriate punishment. Their efforts to enforce moral standards encountered particular difficulty when the perpetrator was the male head of a household. To accede to the complaints of a wife that her husband had committed adultery and to imprison him subverted the very patriarchal order the council sought to uphold. Complaints of wife-beating were further complicated by the belief that husbands had the right to punish their wives with "moderate" physical correction, but unruly violence threatened the social order.[46]

Reformers did not recognize domestic violence as either a sin or a crime, and no Protestant marriage court allowed divorce on the basis of wife-beating. Yet they found themselves dealing with many cases of marital quarreling and violence as the surveillance of morals extended into relations between husband and wife in the household itself. The reformers' usual response was to counsel increased forbearance on the part of the husband and increased submission and docility on that of the wife, rather than to impose any punishment on the husband that might suggest that wives had a right to be protected from violent husbands.

MARRIAGE AND SACRAMENTALITY IN REFORMATION THEOLOGY

Did the reformers' rejection of the superiority of celibacy over marriage, and their acclaim of marriage as the normal vocation of most men and all women, lead to a more companionate view of the marital relation and a more positive view of sex, as Reformation defenders such as Steven Ozment have argued?[47] In order even to approach an answer to this question we must turn to the reformers' theology of sexuality, marriage, and gender relations, and particularly the theology of Luther, the founder of the attack on the traditional teachings of the Latin church on marriage and celibacy.

The Catholic view had been drawn from an Augustinian theology of the debasement of sex through the Fall and the impossibility of engaging in the sexual act without sin. Luther renewed the Augustinian emphasis on human sinful depravity and the loss of free will in the fallen state. For Luther marriage was an ordinance of creation given in Paradise for the purpose of procreation. Yet even in Paradise woman would have been man's inferior and under his headship, though this subordination would have been mild and voluntary, and sex itself would have been lust-free and delightful, producing many children without pain.[48]

The Fall, for Luther as for Augustine, had brought the debasement of sex into lust, and a more coercive subjugation of woman to punish her for her priority in sin. Luther thought of Paradise as a sort of autonomous family farm run by a benevolent patriarch and his docile, hardworking, fertile wife—a rural-peasant version of the householder idea we have been examining. Adam and Eve would thus have been a patriarchal but companionate couple sharing the work of the farm.

Luther believed that the Fall had caused an expansion of new institutions of army and state beyond the householder family, institutions necessary to control and punish an insurgent sinfulness that had not been present in Paradise. Woman was strictly excluded from participating in these new institutions of coercive control and thus became more marginal in her roles than before the Fall, when the sphere of government had not existed. In Luther's words, "The rule remains with the husband and the wife is compelled to obey him by God's command. He rules the home and the state, wages war, defends his possessions, tills the soil, plants, etc. The wife, on the other hand, is like a nail driven into the wall. She sits at home."[49]

Luther's view may be seen as an idealized version of a self-subsistent rural household independent of the organized institutions of urban society—commerce, the army and the state—which he rightly recognized had reduced women's sphere of activity.

For Luther, marriage had been given to men and women by God in Paradise as the basic unit of society for companionship and procreation. Since the Fall, all—that is, all *men*—had been afflicted with sinful lust. Thus the celibate ideal was both wrong and impossible, as it went against both created and fallen nature. All *should* marry because God's intention from the beginning had been to unite men and women in marital union and bid them to procreate. Almost all *must* marry because the lustful urges that had arisen from the Fall could be contained without sin only in marriage. Without marriage, lust would quickly lead to fornication for all but an exceptional few (again, men) who could be celibate without falling into sexual sin.[50]

Luther saw the celibate ideal as an insult to God, who had handed down the ordinance of marriage for companionship and procreation. It necessarily led to worse rather than better morals, since without marriage most men would fornicate; this was proved by the "whorish" monks who endlessly fell below rather than rose above "nature," as they pretended. In this, Luther's view adapted Augustine's three "goods" of marriage: procreation, remedy of concupiscence due to the Fall, and companionship.

Luther departed from Augustine, however, in refuting the assumption that one could control the sexual urge, and hence rise above the need for marriage as a remedy of concupiscence, through conversion to ascetic life. However, for Luther, the third "good," of companionship that mirrored the relation between Christ and the church, could not be described as a sacrament because marriage was an ordinance of nature, not of Christ. Based on his study of the New Testament, Luther accepted only baptism and the Eucharist as sacraments that imparted redeeming grace. He rejected as sacraments marriage, ordination, penance, confirmation, and extreme unction.[51]

This does not mean that these expressions of Christian life became unimportant for Lutherans; indeed, Lutheranism revived the rite of confirmation and linked it with the educational preparation of youth for church membership, after it had virtually disappeared as a significant rite in the medieval church.[52] The desacramentalizing of marriage has been puzzling to those who have argued that Luther and the reformers raised the status of marriage from its inferior position in medieval Christianity. Lutherans also opposed the medieval canonical acceptance of clandestine or unblessed marriages, insisting on parental approval of the marriage of youth and also on public blessing in church.[53] Why, then, the insistence on marriage's nonsacramental nature?

The desacramentalizing of marriage needs to be seen in the context of a heightened separation of creation and redemption in Lutheran and reformed theology. Christian theology in the first centuries had assumed a dialectical relation between creation and redemption: Christ renewed the union of God with creation, being himself the divine ground of creation. Sacraments were signs of the renewed grace in nature, and ultimately that the whole of creation was itself a sacrament. Looked at through the eyes of faith, sacraments were everywhere; for the thirteenth-century theologian Bonaventure, for example, contemplation of nature was the first stage of the "mind's road to God."[54]

The reformers combined nominalism with a neo-Augustinian theology of fallen nature to radically separate humans from any "natural" connection with God, thereby also denying the sacramental potential of nature. Nothing natural could be a bearer of God's grace. Not only the sacramentality of marriage but the medieval church's proliferation of sacramentals must be rejected. All holy candles, water, relics, and other physical objects seen as possessing qualities of the divine presence that could bring protection and healing in everyday life must be cleared away.[55]

The rejection of the idea that holiness could be expressed through sexual continence reflected the desacramentalizing of the body. The counterpart of the patristic and medieval view of sex as polluting and sinful was the belief that the body could become holy, a bearer of the presence of the divine, through abstinence from sex. The virginal female body in particular, "intact" and unpenetrated by the male, was an icon of embodied holiness, prefiguring the resurrected spiritual body.

Reformation theology rejected root and branch this theology of embodied holiness. All bodies were natural, finite, prone to sin, distant from God. Christ's redeeming act had transcended nature and its proclivity to sin, bringing a redeeming grace that was beyond nature and unavailable through it. The sacraments of baptism and the Eucharist, for Luther, had been instituted by Christ to transfer to elect, repentent Christians the grace won by Christ's cross. But marriage was not such an instituted bearer of grace. To marry was to obey God's creational ordinance to form families for the sake of procreation and to contain and channel sinful lust. It belonged to the realm of nature and control of sin, not to redemption. Thus it could not be called a sacrament.

Zwingli and Calvin took this desacramentalizing of nature beyond Luther and applied it to baptism and the Lord's Supper as well. Baptism did not convey redeeming grace by its material properties, but was rather a sign of a preordained election by God. The Eucharist did not physically embody Christ but was instead an intellectual "reminder" of Christ's redeeming act.[56] Luther's spirituality was sufficiently steeped in medieval sacramentalism to resist these further moves.[57]

Desacramentalizing rationalism is also expressed in the privileged status in Reformation worship of sound over anything that can be seen, touched, or smelled. The "Word" preached and sung become the primary sacramental occasion for God's presence, for in the spoken word God could be experienced (evidently) without material embodiment. Reformation churches stripped away any visual decoration and turned the altar into a small table, with the pulpit in its center. Rows of pews put the congregation in a disciplined position to listen to and hear God's word, without coming and going or pressing forward to see the act of consecration, or looking at images, touching relics, or smelling incense, as in Catholic churches.

Susan Karant-Nunn has studied the impact of this effort to strip Protestantism of sacramental objects of holiness that could be carried off into daily life. The rite of baptism lost the sacramental elements of salt, unction, holy candles, clay, and spittle that were part of the Catholic ritual, and retained only the bare act of pouring water on the baptized with the words of baptism. Even then, the minister was instructed to pour out the water immediately to prevent people from taking it home as holy water with which to bless themselves.[58]

The medieval church had developed a rite of marriage that began at the southern door of the church (where Adam and Eve were traditionally depicted); the blessing of the couple might be followed by an optional nuptial mass. Wealthy parishioners might have the priest come to their home to give the blessing and join in the festivities.[59] In either case, medieval canon law tied the validity of the marriage not to the priest's blessing but to the words of consent spoken by the couple, followed by consummation.[60]

Most of the actual rituals of marriage belonged to folk traditions carried out by the family. These could be quite elaborate, taking place over a year or more, with the groom's family's making inquiries about the bride's suitability, negotiating the dowry, trousseau, and gifts, formally conveying the bride to the groom's house with her gifts (the bridal bed and bedding were brought by the bride), and bedding the couple down together, each stage accompanied by toasts, dances, and feasts.[61]

Protestant reformers sought to curb much of this family ritual, which they saw as a source of sinful waste, gluttony, drunkenness, and lascivious dancing. They rejected the canonical view that consent of the couple alone was essential for a marriage's validity, insisting instead on parental consent for the young and a formal joining of the couple in church before the minister and congregation. The nuptial mass was replaced by a sermon in which the minister emphasized the scriptural doctrines of marriage in the Creation and Fall.

The couple was reminded that woman was punished by subordination to her husband and pain in childbirth, and man by hard labor for the sin of having listened to his wife. The wife was to pay strict obedience to her husband, and the man to love his wife as Christ loved the church. Marriage was seen as an oppportunity to instruct not just the couple but the whole congregation on the proper roles of men and women in marriage.[62] This sober rite clearly was not particularly enjoyable for the congregation, and ministers continually complained that members skipped the church service and attended only the dance and feast.[63]

Marriage manuals to be read by ministers and lay people offered another opportunity for instruction on the doctrine of marriage. Both German reformers and English Puritan divines composed an extensive literature on the Christian household.[64] The manuals sought to balance the themes of companionship and male headship. Husband and wife were to love each other and be companions in all things, with the household representing a sort of corporate enterprise in which husband and wife were coadministrators of a realm that was both home and livelihood.

The household was typically thought of as including not only children but servants of various kinds. The wife was a "subregent" under her husband in the task of disciplining these subordinates. The New Testament household codes were regularly invoked in these texts to delineate the threefold hierarchy of the family under the paterfamilias: wives were to obey husbands, servants masters, and children parents. Thus the companionship of husband and wife was never that of equals, and was assumed to work harmoniously only when the wife understood herself as an obedient subordinate and the husband as a beneficent but authoritative patriarch.[65]

The underside of this doctrine was always the suspicion that the wife might resist proper subordination. It was this female impulse to insubordination that had caused all sin and evil to come into the world. Reformers darkly hinted that it also explained why women were prone to witchcraft.[66] Female weakness and rebelliousness must be constantly curbed lest they lead to disorder and even greater evils, such as diabolic opposition to the rule of God, husbands, ministers, and magistrates.

Popular literature and woodcuts carried this negative underside of the patriarchal view of marriage relations even further, often depicting a wife out of control, riding on her husband and making him her servant, in a reversal of divinely ordained order that could be righted only by the husband taking a firm hand to discipline his wife with a "good beating."[67] Thus praise of marital companionship and harmony was itself based on the acceptance of a relation of super- and subordination, and unfolded against a background that constantly suspected and must curb its reversal.

DIVORCE IN PROTESTANT THOUGHT AND PRACTICE

The Protestant desacramentalizing of marriage also led to another consequence—namely, the possibility of divorce, an option that had been rejected by the medieval church on the ground that a valid sacrament was indissoluble. As the control of marriage shifted from Catholic church courts to Protestant marriage courts led by ministers and magistrates, petitions for divorce began to be heard. But these Protestant marriage courts established narrow grounds for divorce, seeing it not as a remedy for marital disharmony but as a punishment for marital fault, to be granted rarely and only when all efforts to correct the fault had failed.

Luther entertained various justifications for divorce, having to do with both an inability to carry out the marital duties and a rupture of the primary marital bond. Thus, for him, a husband's impotence (a ground for annulment in the Catholic system), a wife's refusal to have sex, adultery, and desertion were all possible reasons for divorce.[68] But he was not enthusiastic about any of it. In the famous case of William of Hesse, for example, whose wife did not give him sexual satisfaction, Luther recommended bigamy rather than divorce.[69] He and other reformers saw themselves as being guided by Scripture in this matter. Matthew's version of Jesus' words, which allowed divorce for adultery, was decisive for them. The bigamy of the patriarchs suggested that this practice could sometimes be permitted in accordance with God's word.[70]

In practice, Protestant marriage courts accepted only adultery and desertion as grounds for divorce. In the case of adultery, reconciliation and forgiveness were to be sought; only when such efforts failed was a divorce granted, with remarriage allowed solely for the innocent party. If both parties were guilty of adultery, neither could remarry, making Protestant practice effectively the same as the Catholic grant of separation without remarriage. In the case of desertion (usually on the part of the husband), the wife often had to wait years, until it was clear that the husband's whereabouts were unknown and/or that he was not likely to return, before she was granted a divorce with the right to remarry.[71]

Only Martin Bucer insisted that companionship was the primary purpose of marriage, and that marital disharmony could be a ground for divorce.[72] In the seventeenth century, Milton would translate Bucer's treatise on marriage into English to bolster his own argument that disharmony was a ground for divorce.[73] But neither Bucer nor Milton thought of companionship or the lack thereof in egalitarian terms; both believed that it was wifely docility to the husband's commands that assured harmony, and that when this was lacking, divorce was appropriate. Thus, while Protestant teaching on marriage spoke of companionship as a purpose of marriage (as did Catholic teaching), a hierarchical understanding of that quality was assumed that disallowed equal partnership between husband and wife in marriage.

CELIBACY AND MARRIAGE IN THE CATHOLIC REFORMATION

The Catholic response to these Protestant challenges was one of sharp rejection of key divergences from traditional teaching on celibacy and marriage, yet in a context of shared patterns and assumptions. The process of secular takeover of charities and princely control of church offices occurred in Catholic areas also. In Spain, the center of the Catholic Reformation, the king had already won control over the appointment of bishops and abbots, a power that extended to Spanish America.[74] In France, pope and king struggled over the extent of royal control over church offices, but in practice royal control and Catholic renewal went hand in hand.[75] City councils in Catholic cities also took over charities, but without expelling religious orders.

The general trend toward narrowing economic opportunities for women extended to both Catholic and Protestant regions. Catholic humanists and reformers no less than Protestants insisted on female subordination in the family and in society. The revived use of Roman law to deny women's legal self-representation and to appoint guardians for single women or widows found favor across western and southern Europe.[76] Catholics and Protestants did not differ on patriarchalism, only on some details of its implementation.

The Council of Trent, convened for eighteen years from 1545 to 1563 to formulate a doctrinal and pastoral response to the Reformation, resoundingly negated the Protestant rejection of the superiority of celibacy over marriage as well as the nonsacramental and dissoluble character of marriage. This latter it saw as denigrating marriage. The mandatory celibacy of all priests was reaffirmed, even though some Catholic humanists pushed for change in this rule. The council sought to shore up priestly discipline through the institution of seminaries where those preparing for the priesthood could be separated from rowdy university culture and strictly "formed" for a celibate life.[77] Celibacy was to be enforced by close supervision and punishment of infractions.

Celibacy for vowed women, meanwhile, was to be enforced by strict cloister. This insistence on cloister as the means of ensuring discipline for nuns rendered the papacy and Catholic reformers hostile toward any efforts on the part of Catholic women to found active women's orders for service and evangelism. Nonetheless, a number of efforts were made to create such active orders in the sixteenth and seventeenth centuries, and some of these partially succeeded by defining themselves as institutes rather than religious orders.[78]

Trentine legislation reaffirmed that marriage was a sacrament and as such was indissoluble. It also reduced further the impediments to marriage due to consanguinity and affinity. Although a valid marriage could not be dissolved, annulment could allow remarriage, and conflicts might be resolved through separation without remarriage. Trent also rejected clandestine marriage and ruled that the validity of a marriage depended on the public announcement of banns and vows of consent before a priest and two witnesses.[79]

Like Protestants, Catholics sought to wrest fuller control over marriage from laypeople. The medieval tradition had made consent, regardless of priestly witness, the ultimate basis for validity, using marriage courts to enforce vows taken privately. Now any marriage entered into outside the Catholic church became invalid and hence dissoluble, leaving an option for those who converted to Catholicism to replace marriages previously blessed by Protestants.

In conclusion, both Protestants and Catholics reaffirmed a patriarchal ordering of church, family, and society in the sixteenth century, in a context of increasing marginalization of women by an expanding political, economic, and cultural life that excluded them. Yet the cultural styles of the two movements were markedly different. Protestantism, particularly in its reformed version, expressed its authoritarianism through a whitewashed ambiance stripped of visual and tactile stimulation. To hear God's word and obey it comprised the dynamic of spirituality.

Catholicism, by contrast, endorsed and extended the use of visual and tactile symbols. Exorcism became popular in the struggle of Jesuits to take over Protestant areas, turning the duel between Catholic "orthodoxy" and Protestant "heresy" into a public and corporeal display of the conflict between God and the devil.[80] Processions, sacramentals of all kinds, and a style of church art and architecture that emphasized theatrical, emotional stimulation were typical of the public life and worship of renewed Catholicism during this period.[81]

The first of these two cultures might be seen as owing much to the pleasure-deferring bourgeois, and the second to the royal court, where subjects were awed into submission and loyalty by the display of divine glory. Whereas Protestant spirituality might be characterized as one of sensual deprivation to emphasize verbal command and obedience, Catholic spirituality was one of sensual overload, but likewise in the service of authoritarianism. For both, the marriage bond was essentially hierarchical, a matter of male headship and female submission, an ordering that was the foundation and basis for all the other hierarchies of church and society.[82]

CHAPTER 4

The Making of the Victorian Family: 1780–1890

The period from the French Revolution to the end of the nineteenth century saw a gradual transmutation of the social and economic roles of the family. Over these years the family would lose more and more of its productive functions, a trend that would continue into the twentieth century as even finishing processes such as dressmaking and cooking from primary ingredients disappeared from the home. Educational, religious, and health roles also eroded. The home would cease to be a place for teaching children the skills of future work, for family prayer, for nursing the sick, for birth and death. The pharmaceutical skills of housewives who made medicines from their herbal gardens would be lost to new generations of daughters. Institutions such as schools, hospitals, pharmacies, and asylums would take over functions formerly performed within the family.

But as many productive, educational, health, and religious activities shifted to institutions outside the family, the ideology *about* the family and its crucial importance for social wellbeing intensified. Language borrowed from monastic communities and evangelical crusades would invest the family with new salvific significance as a place of refuge from the fallen world. Ideal woman, segregated in the idealized home, would assume a halo of angelic purity and suffering love borrowed from Mariological femininity. Children, too, would be idealized in a new way, thought of no longer as offspring of sinful depravity but rather as innocents to be carefully nurtured and protected from evil by their all-loving mother.

In the pages that follow I will trace, in all too summary a fashion, key aspects of the reorganization of economic and social roles that laid the basis for these dramatic shifts in the ideological identity of the family, women, and children in relation to adult men and to the expanding world of economic, political, and social organizations from which the family was differentiated. The pioneers in shaping this narrowed and intensified form of family were the upper bourgeois, the merchant entrepreneurial and professional classes.

From these strata, emerging victorious over the old aristocracy in the nineteenth century, the trend spread to the petite bourgeoisie and became the ideal that the working classes sought to emulate as the proof of their success and respectability. In the public mind this middle-class model of the family installed itself as the "normative" standard against which all other forms of family were judged as deviant. Yet this ideology of the middle-class Victorian family concealed much about the actual realities of its daily life, including the extensive domestic work roles necessary to sustain it, most of which fell to the housewife as worker and manager. The enormity of her workload was masked by the demand that she appear to be a fragile and leisured "lady".

The middle-class family norm also mystified the realities of working-class families as well as those of black ex-slaves in the United States. It made their adaptations of traditional family work patterns to new economic circumstances appear morally reprehensible, calling for intervention by middle-class social reformers. Needless to say, debate over state policy in relation to the supposedly "deviant" families of the "lower classes" continues to be shaped by the same perceptions today.

PATTERNS OF CHANGE IN ENGLAND, FRANCE, AND THE UNITED STATES

The great houses of the English and French aristocracies had traditionally been seats of political power as well as loci for the management of territories farmed by dependent peasants. In the sixteenth century such households claimed dozens or even hundreds of residents besides the lord, the lady, and their legitimate children. Kin, mistresses, illegitimate children, servants of various gradations, clients, and friends would all assemble in the great hall for feasts. There was little privacy. Even intimate activities such as birthing and rising from bed were attended by a retinue of clients seeking the lord's patronage. Servants slept in corners in the same room as the lord and lady, or in halls or work areas.[1]

The seventeenth century in England saw a deep division between the "family values" of the aristocracy and those of the Puritan middle class. The luxury and sexual freedom of the upper class conflicted with the ascetic rigor of the Puritan ethic, which demanded strict chastity of both husband and wife, as well as patriarchal submission by servants, children, and wife to husband, all within a context of husband-and-wife conjugal partnership. According to Lawrence Stone, a historian of the English family in this period, by the eighteenth century a fusion had taken place between the Puritan values of asceticism and conjugal partnership and the sensual freedom of the aristocracy, even as that aristocracy itself continually drew into itself new families from the wealthy merchant class.[2]

This new family pattern stressed the separation of the core family from the network of kin, domestic servants, clients, and farm workers. The great houses were redesigned to support this redefinition, with workers being expelled to discrete cottages and servants banished to their own quarters in the upper stories or at the back of the house, accessed by different staircases so that the two classes would not meet by accident. Corridors were laid out with separate doors leading into each room, replacing the older layouts in which one room had opened onto another, and certain rooms could be reached only by going through other rooms.[3]

Members of the male elite shaped their own private quarters, with a study, library, billiard room, and smoking room that women were not to enter. The lady of the house reigned in the parlor. Nurseries kept children away from their parents and with their nannies. The adult members of the family now dined alone, waited on by discreet servants, no longer feasting in a large company. Decorum, cleanliness, precise pronunciation, elaborate table etiquette with an array of utensils and plates, and the privatization of personal functions, such as excretion and sex, that once had been performed openly—all these became the rule that set the elite apart from the lower orders.[4]

These great houses of landed and commercial wealth constituted, however, but a tiny minority of the population—in England about 3 to 5 percent.[5] In the eighteenth century the Enclosure Movement gathered a vast amount of common land into the hands of the landed class for the purpose of sheep raising, and in so doing greatly reduced the numbers of small independent farmers. Much of the rural populace was proletarianized as landless agricultural workers and domestic servants, and many migrated to the cities to labor in workshops and factories.[6] Still others found new opportunities in the colonies.

In France, meanwhile, independent peasant farmers continued to form the backbone of agriculture and would gradually adapt themselves to market conditions in the nineteenth century.[7] From medieval times, peasant families had functioned as collective units that united production for use and for market with reproduction and socialization of children. The wife in such a family economy had a heavy work role. Aided by her daughters, she spun thread, wove cloth, and made clothes; cultivated vegetable and herb gardens for food and medicine; cared for chickens, pigs, and cows, collected eggs and milk, and made cheese and sausages; produced a number of articles for family use, such as candles; and helped the men and older boys with the planting, weeding, and harvests when needed. She sold her surplus in local markets to buy food, clothes, and other items not produced at home.[8] Over time, other factors would come to influence this situation. From the sixteenth century into the nineteenth, the urban-based guilds, with their strict control of artisan production for the market (discussed in the previous chapter), were undercut by merchant entrepreneurs. These merchants bypassed the guilds by drawing on rural labor, either hiring those who had lost their land or had insufficient acreage or taking advantage of seasonal unemployment. The merchant entrepreneurs sought to integrate several stages of production of a product and its marketing, using low-paid labor, particularly by young women.

For example, silk merchants in the Loire area of France in the early nineteenth century controlled all stages of production. The work was done in a series of workshops, with peasant girls spinning the cocoons into skeins, which were then taken to millers, then to dyers, then to spinners, warpers, and weavers, and finally to those who folded and packed the cloth for sale.[9] Several different stages might be carried out in or near cottages and could thus draw on group family labor. The guilds had once prospered by monopolizing several stages of such production and its marketing, but they were now replaced by either sex-segregated labor in workshops or group labor by family members, who were given materials by a merchant or his agent and returned the completed goods in exchange for low wages.

This kind of "putting-out" system in the hands of merchant entrepreneurs preceded industrialization.[10] The factory would mechanize this work with new machinery and integrate it into one large center where workers assigned to all stages of production could be assembled together to labor under a rigorous work schedule—thereby separating productive work from the household. However, the "putting-out" system of production should not be seen simply as a proto-industrial scheme that disappeared with the advent of factories. Indeed, forms of it continued side by side with factories, employing women who took in piecework for assembly in their homes and then returned the finished product to the entrepreneur. These female pieceworkers typically worked long hours for even lower pay than women in factories, who were themselves paid less than men. Married women with young children accepted such work because it allowed them to stay at home, rather than having to find child care.[11]

As the artisan guilds were undercut by the "putting-out" system of home-based assembly, and as some farmers lost their land, a family wage economy began to replace a family productive economy.[12] Former peasant farmers might work together as a group in their cottages, receiving raw materials and assembling them for return to the merchant, using all members of the household and receiving a wage based on the quantity produced. Such cottage industry was often combined with remnants of home production and agriculture for use—gardens, chickens, or the like.

As early factories were developed, the family wage economy continued. Sometimes an entire family would migrate to a factory town and find employment in various sectors of the factory, surviving by pooling the wages of husband, wife, and children. Some early factory owners, such as Benjamin Walcott, who remodeled New York Mills in 1825, even organized the whole complex for family labor. Walcott built a series of cottages in two rows on either side of his factory, where employee families could live and also work together in the factory. Each cottage had some land on which vegetables and fruit could be grown and livestock kept, thus allowing the survival of certain aspects of the farming life. The husband and children worked in the mills, as did any servants, slaves, or kin residing in the household, each receiving a wage according to his age and time spent at work. The wife usually did not do wage labor but was involved in home production. The wages themselves were often paid in kind—cloth, food, and the cost of shelter—rather than in money.[13]

Other factories, such as the textile works of Lowell, Massachusetts, in the 1820s, intentionally drew their work forces from the young women of farming families, offering them strictly supervised dormitories in which to live. The factory owner served in loco parentis, seeing that his young female workers were in by ten in the evening, said their prayers, and went to church regularly.[14] The female workers often sent part or all of their wages back to their parents to supplement the family economy, rather than controlling it entirely themselves. The assumption was that such work represented an intermediate step between childhood and marriage, during which period the single girl in her teens and early twenties was expected to contribute to the family wage and save money to found her own family.[15]

The paternal factory based on employing families did not entirely disappear in the later nineteenth century. The Amoskeag Manufacturing Company, for example, which created Manchester, New Hampshire, as a planned factory town in 1837, continued into the 1930s to employ multiple members of families who lived in nearby boardinghouses or family residences in an environment almost completely controlled by the factory, down to the endowment of churches. At its peak in the early twentieth century, it was the largest textile factory in the world, employing seventeen thousand workers. It drew increasingly on new immigrants, particularly French Canadians, who came as families and depended on a family wage from many members' working in the factory.[16]

Both the family productive economy and the family wage economy assumed that the work of all family members, other than the very young and the elderly infirm, was necessary for survival. Although the adult male was paid more than women or children, his wage was in itself insufficient to support the family. The wife combined reproduction and production for use and market across a life cycle, while children were incorporated into home-based work as soon as they could help out.[17] Sending out children of seven or eight to work in the factory followed a traditional pattern of child labor.

Families that depended on a household wage earned in workshops or factories outside went through a work life cycle. Single young women went out to work long days, the typical workday in early factories being twelve to fourteen hours. Married women might continue to work until they had their first child, but that generally happened shortly after marriage. Families with small children were usually impoverished; the wife might supplement the husband's wage with various home-based work such as taking in piecework, boarders, or laundry, or selling home-cooked food. As the children grew and could be sent to work, the family might prosper, but its income would fall again as the children moved on to found their own households. Again the wife might return to work to add to the family income.[18] The situation could become especially desperate if the male provider became infirm or died and the wife was left to make a living alone. Adult children, particularly daughters, were sometimes kept from marrying in order to continue to contribute to their natal household.

The timing of marriage, childbearing, and child-raising was calculated with an eye to the family work force. The European working classes typically married late, women in their midtwenties and men in their late twenties to thirties, thus reducing the number of children born.[19] French peasants with land practiced a stem-family strategy in which the eldest son remained in the paternal household and married only after his father died and he inherited the farm, caring for his widowed mother if she survived his father. Primogeniture prevented the family land from being divided. Younger sons were given cash to find land or work elsewhere, and daughters a lesser amount for dowries. If the family farm did not have sufficient means to provide these endowments, the siblings might remain unmarried, working as servants on the paternal land.[20] For Catholics, religious orders offered alternatives for unmarried family members.

It was virtually impossible for an unmarried woman to earn a living wage by herself. Most single women depended on living with kin in return for contributing to a household wage.[21] A widowed mother with young children would be in perilous straits, forced to eke out a living by needlework, doing housework and laundry for others, and taking in boarders if she had room.[22] Some such women had no choice but to turn over their children to town orphan asylums.[23] Prostitution was the way of last resort to earn money.[24] The elderly widow with no adult child to live with also would have to turn to an asylum.[25] Such institutions, as we shall see later in this chapter, were increasingly founded in European and American towns to serve this destitute population.

In contrast to the late-marrying practice of most working-class men and women, members of landless families that survived through cottage industry seem to have married younger, in their early twenties, often combining the tools and skills of a man and a woman in the same industry. Such couples would have several children right away in order quickly to create a family work force.[26] In France, birth control became widespread not only among the middle class but among the working class in the nineteenth century, as a way to prevent unwanted children in the later stages of a woman's reproductive cycle.[27]

The number of children was also limited by high child mortality rates. Fifty percent or more of children died before the age of twenty, particularly in their first year, and many pregnancies ended in still births or miscarriages. Ill health and malnutrition caused by poverty and polluted work environments contributed to reproductive failure and maternal and child mortality.[28] The average life expectancy was in the early thirties in France and England in 1800,[29] but more women died in their childbearing years due to overwork, poor health, and multiple pregnancies.

Few children could expect to reach adulthood with both parents still alive. The average marriage lasted about twenty years, broken by death rather than by divorce, with many men, but fewer women, re-marrying.[30] Many children thus grew up in mixed households with stepparents and half-siblings, or were sent to other households to work by stepparents who were hostile to raising them.[31]

Artisan families that demanded the work of the wife often sent infants to rural wet nurses for their first two years, increasing the likelihood of mortality.[32] By six a child would be employed in the home economy, and at eight to twelve sent out to work as a servant in another household or in a factory. If a family lacked enough children to work, it might take in youths of other families.[33] Thus children were regarded primarily as a work asset, with only a short period of unproductive life, rather than as the objects of intensive nurture and dependency that they would become in the Victorian middle-class family.

The United States in the late eighteenth and early nineteenth centuries diverged significantly from the model seen in England and

France, as pioneer societies cleared and settled land wrested from native peoples who lived in very different social organizations and cultures. The first generation of westward colonization, in pushing into western New York from New England, reproduced something of the self-subsistent, home-based economy and the religious and ethnic cohesion of seventeenth-century New England, the "little commonwealth."[34]

As Mary Ryan has shown in her study of social development in Oneida country, New York, when pioneer settler Hugh White moved to the area in 1790 from Middletown, Connecticut, where his ancestors had lived since 1638, he brought with him these earlier New England traditions. He bought and settled a fifteen-hundred-acre tract of wilderness, building a homestead for himself and his wife that would one day be inherited by his eldest son, and laying out adjoining farms for his five sons and two daughters. Other pioneers from New England followed similar patterns of settlement. Whitetown, named for Hugh White, was a tightly meshed network of patriarchal families living on largely self-sufficient farms, whose male heads made up the town council and the elders of the First Presbyterian Society, founded in 1794.[35]

These three interconnected institutions—families, town council, and church—comprised the society of Whitetown, a society that closely monitored the behavior of its members. Church trials called to account those who strayed from the straight and narrow of moral behavior, either sexually or in church attendance. Family houses' few rooms were crowded, affording little privacy. Such a familial society in which family members scrutinized each other and reported bad behavior for church rebuke left little place to hide even personal thoughts, much less deviant behavior.[36] Education, prayer, and town meetings all took place in households.

In this society the money economy was secondary, with households obtaining most needed goods through barter with each other's home-based production. The household housed a work force consisting of the male head of the family and his wife and children, as well as other kin and non-kin workers, apprentices, white indentured servants, and black slaves. There was no separation of public from private, for the household was virtually coterminous with society, economically, politically, and culturally.

In less than a generation, however, this tight-knit society began to change, as open land stopped being available for the next generation, and artisans' shops, textile factories, stores, and banks appeared in the diversifying town center. A more ethnically and religiously hetero-geneous population also moved in, with Catholics, Baptists, and Methodists all founding churches. Many single men lived in board-inghouses while they sought jobs in workshops or white-collar posi-tions as clerks.[37] Enlightenment thought introduced a new skepticism about Christian truth, and some male heads of households no longer led family prayer or were even church members. The building of the Erie Canal in 1822 brought an influx of unchurched people, along with a spate of brothels and taverns.[38]

REVIVALISTS, UTOPIANS, AND THE ASYLUM MOVEMENT

The unraveling of the godly commonwealth alarmed the older set-tlers of western New York as it had their Puritan forebears a century before. The 1820s–40s would see waves of revivalism in this region, in what is commonly referred to as the "burned-over" district of the Second Great Awakening.[39] The primary organizers as well as the subjects of these new surges of revival and conversion to the godly life were, though, not male heads of family, but women and their young adult children.[40] The revival itself was both promoted and expressed by a proliferation of missionary, charitable, and reform associations, founded not only by the wives of the affluent merchant class, descen-dants of the first settlers, but also by women of newer, upwardly mo-bile families of artisans, such as printers and watchmakers.

The aim of these missionary, charity, and reform societies was to re-create the godly society by incorporating the unchurched resi-dents. Missionary societies distributed Bibles and tracts to this new "underclass." Charity societies surveyed the town for people living in poverty and sickness, especially abandoned wives with children, and brought them food, blankets, and clothes even as they tried to help improve their morals and religious observance. Reform societies ze-roed in on the two issues of sexual laxity and intemperance, seeking to close down brothels and taverns or at least convert those in them who had gone astray—not only the female deviants, prostitutes, and barmaids but also their male clientele.

These societies, spearheaded by women of the upper and up-wardly mobile middle classes, adopted the evangelical method of house-to-house visitation. In Rochester, New York, the Female Charitable Society, founded in 1822, divided the town into neighborhoods, with delegations of women regularly visiting each home in their region and reporting back to the society.[41] In this way the moral and economic condition of the town was kept under regular surveillance. If the means was no longer male-led church trials to denounce the deviants, but female aid aimed at persuasion, the hoped-for end was nevertheless to re-create a society made up of families of disciplined, temperate churchgoers.

The revivals that took place in the town churches, led by charismatic preachers such as Charles Grandison Finney, were imbued with a millennialist perfectionism. The ideal was a strenuous transformation of self, kin, friends, and others in expanding circles that would purge out all sin and lead not just to calm and social order, but to the full realization of Christ's reign on Earth. In a revival sermon delivered from the pulpit of Rochester's Third Presbyterian Church in November 1830, Finney declared that if Christians were truly united and dedicated to their task, they could convert the world and bring on the millennium within three months.[42]

Such revivals virtually brought town business to a halt for days as a continual round of sermons, prayer circles, and protracted meetings commenced. The result was waves of new converts gathered into the churches, but also waves of new organizations geared to different age and gender groups and dedicated to distributing tracts on temperance, sexual rectitude, strict observance of the sabbath, or abolition of slavery. The proliferation of such societies created new networks of association beyond the family, bringing women and single young men together in sisterly or brotherly bonds, no longer under the control of the family patriarch.[43]

Not all the town fathers rejoiced in these new societies of moral and social uplift. Efforts to prevent business from being conducted on Sundays and to close taverns interfered with profits.[44] Some moral reform societies veered from saving fallen women and converting wayward youth to informing on established family men who visited brothels on the side.[45] Antislavery campaigns challenged both slave owners and those who profited by the cotton produced by slave labor. And Universalists, devoted to Enlightenment reason, objected to efforts to monitor thought and behavior along evangelical lines.[46]

These tensions opened up fissures between social ameliorators and perfectionists—between those who sought to moralize society for the sake of a social order under middle-class leadership and those who espoused radical perfectionist visions that challenged the social and economic systems responsible for both affluence and poverty.[47] More radical groups, particularly those of Quaker background, began to question the social hierarchy itself: the dominance of rich over poor and white over black, and even the legal and social subjugation of women.[48] The Grimké sisters, speaking on an antislavery tour in the 1830s, brought the disturbing message that both the power of whites over blacks, in racism and slavery, and the power of men over women were contrary to God's original and ideal order for society, in which all were created equal and no one group was given sovereignty over another.[49]

The reaction to such "ultras" was generally to rein in the reform societies and to moderate the perfectionist demand to fit in with a more modest quest for social order, under the leadership of the men of the established classes—the same men whose wives led the work of charity for the "worthy" poor (no Catholics need apply).[50] But not all those inspired by the millennial vision were persuaded to modify their ideals. Some radicals experimented with utopian societies that were seen as model expressions of the redeemed society.

Utopianism was not new to America in the 1830s: Christian utopians from the left wing of the Reformation, such as Jean Labadie, Jacob Zimmerman, and Conrad Biessel, had imported their monastic colonies of Bohemia Manor, Woman in the Wilderness, and Ephrata to Maryland and Pennsylvania in the colonial period.[51] The Shakers, with their claim to be the Millennial Society of Christ's Second Appearing, had come to America in 1774 and subsequently spread their colonies across New England and west to Kentucky.[52]

The first decades of the nineteenth century brought more German pietist communitarians, including George Rapp with his Harmony Society, the Zoarites, and the Amana Perfectionists,[53] as well as some socialist utopians who, inspired by the thought of the Scots factory owner Robert Owen and the French social theorist Charles Fourier, who sought to live out these theories on American soil.[54] The utopian socialists responded to the chaotic conditions of poverty and exploitation in early factory owners by founding egalitarian communities that reintegrated work and family, production and reproduction, as one. Some paternalist factory owners who sought to provide housing and moral oversight for their workers drew inspiration from these utopian projects, though leaving out their socialism.

Some utopians built villagelike communities, with individual or group houses arranged in neat rows, communal kitchens and dining halls, workshops, barns, and farmland all owned in common. An assembly hall brought everyone together for governance and culture; nurseries and schools raised the community's children. Other thinkers such as Fourier favored a single multistoried and winged apartment building with a central courtyard and surrounding farmland, where the members of the community could live and work together.[55]

Utopians imagined that the hierarchies of rulers and ruled, workers and owners, and men and women would be overcome in such communal societies. All would own the land and means of production and make decisions about its governance together. Communal dining and children raised in common would relieve women of their domestic isolation and allow them to participate as equals in work, culture, and political governance.

Utopians also experimented with new forms of the family. The Shakers, for example, created celibate communities of men and women living side by side as equals. The Mormons, for their part, revived patriarchal polygamy.[56] The Oneida Perfectionists, under the paternal leadership of John Humphrey Noyes, lived in a condition of "complex marriage" whereby all men and women might have sexual access to one another. Birth control was practiced both for eugenics and to permit sexual pleasure to be enjoyed without fear of unwanted pregnancies.[57] Josiah Warren's colony, Modern Times, championed "free love," not as a form of promiscuity but as the right of women as well as men to divorce and remarry in order to form love relations based on free choice, not on economic and social coercion.[58] Frances Wright conceived of her Nashoba Colony as a place not only where women could experience equality and free love, but also where racial segregation would be overcome and blacks and whites brought together.[59]

Such experiments in sex, family, gender, and race relations were deeply unacceptable to most white Americans, who reacted to them with horror. Indeed, few utopian colonies were long-lived, though celibate communities under cohesive religious rule far outlasted the secular socialist experiments. Nevertheless, the literature of utopianism and visits to such communities fed a vision of radical reform that would continue to inspire those seeking an egalitarian family and society.

Despite the short-lived history of many utopian communities, the utopian impulse of the Jacksonian era had a significant impact in widespread enthusiasm for the building of large asylums to house what were increasingly seen as dangerous alien populations: the insane, the criminal, and the destitute. Colonial America had seen these groups not as social problems but rather as the expected effects of the condition of a fallen humanity prone to sin, and of the divinely ordained hierarchical ordering of society into rich and poor. That period's solution was town-sponsored charity for unfortunate neighbors (mostly given to people in their own homes), vigorous public punishment for the criminal, and expulsion of the foreign vagrant.[60]

With the open migration of diverse ethnic groups, nineteenth-century towns no longer had the option of expulsion. The use of stocks, public whippings, and executions came to be seen as cruel and more likely to inflame the passions of the mob than to serve as a sobering deterrent. Deviants were now viewed as social problems to be solved, and the preferred explanation for such problems was some variant of the failure of the family to inculcate orderly habits.

Thus the criminal had been introduced to crime by a vicious family, or abandoned by his family to fend for himself or herself in a dissolute environment.[61] Insanity was caused by chaotic family and social conditions.[62] The poor, especially orphans, lacked families to give them disciplined habits and were on their way, through drink and vice, to crime.[63] Outdoor aid, or charity given to the needy in their homes, was widely criticized as merely leading to dependency and idleness, rather than teaching needed discipline.[64]

The chosen solution to these various social disorders was to build a large asylum, typically an imposing institution, multistoried and winged, set apart from the city in a rural environment. Each type of institution specialized in a different disorder—the penitentiary for criminals, the insane asylum for the mentally ill, the orphanage for abandoned children, the workhouse and the almshouse for the poor—but the method was similar. Inmates were incarcerated in a total institution and subjugated to a strict routine organized by the clock.

Rising together at the bell at five-thirty in the morning, all ate together in silence, then moved on to a fixed schedule of work. Visits or letters from family and friends were discouraged, since these relations were seen as the cause of the problem. It was assumed that separating problem populations from their bad environments and giving them a strict schedule of discipline, carried out in enforced silence, would enable them to be resocialized and eventually released to become hardworking citizens.[65]

Whereas earlier charity work for the poor and orphans had been performed by an alliance between the church and female benevolent societies (an alliance that largely continued into the postbellum era), the new institutional solutions were secular, state-funded, and administered by a new state bureaucracy. Despite the reformers' great promises of the quick eradication of crime, insanity, and poverty, the institutions themselves rapidly degenerated into overcrowding and punitive, custodial care, rather than the humane reform of habits.

Still, the penitentiary, the insane asylum, and the orphanage remained the solution of choice for nineteenth-century Americans in response to crime, insanity, and childhood poverty, even as their ameliorative claims disappeared. Prisons remain the chief solution to crime for today's Americans, who incarcerate more of their population, predominantly persons of color, than any other nation.[66] Much of this popularity lies in the perception of such "criminals" as belonging to alien classes and ethnic groups, not the familiar class of kin and neighbors, and the desire to "get them off the streets"—that is, remove them from threatening visibility.

ABOLITION, SUFFRAGE, AND LIFE IN THE SOUTH

The Civil War represented a significant break with the economic patterns of the antebellum period, particularly for the South but also for the North. Antislavery northern women, confident that a Union victory would bring the abolition of slavery, threw themselves into war work, rolling bandages and knitting socks for the soldiers.[67] Through the Sanitary Commission, northern women were organized into seven thousand local societies that supported services for the Union army, providing clothes for soldiers and nurses and medical supplies for the wounded.[68]

Suffragist women hoped that their war work would issue in their own enfranchisement along with that of the Negro. But in this they were to be deeply disappointed. The Fourteenth Amendment cited the adjective *male* as a qualification for voting for the first time in constitutional history, thus explicitly excluding all women of either race. The Fifteenth Amendment, for its part, outlawed racial discrimination as a bar to voting. Suffrage leaders Elizabeth Cady Stanton and Susan B. Anthony opposed the passage of the amendment until it included gender as well, aided by Sojourner Truth, who spoke for the rights of black women.[69] But Republican senators and former male allies in the antislavery movement opposed their efforts, insisting that this was "the Negro's hour."

The result was a splitting of the suffrage movement into two groups, the National Woman Suffrage Association, led by Stanton and Anthony, and the American Woman Suffrage Association, led by Lucy Stone. The division would not be healed until the end of the century.[70] In the antebellum women's-rights movement, leaders such as the Grimké sisters and Lucretia Mott had decried racism as well as slavery and discrimination against women, but that alliance of issues was lost after the split over the amendments.

The classist and racist views of white women such as Stanton came out as they expressed their outrage at the notion of inferior black (and immigrant) men voting while superior women of the white leadership classes were denied the same right. As a result, the woman suffrage movement increasingly allowed itself to argue for the vote along class and race lines, as a way to double the political voice of white elites, while tolerating the disenfranchisement of black men under the Jim Crow laws that sprang up in the South after the Civil War.[71]

White elite women of the South lived in a very different world from that of women such as Stanton and Anthony. A few southern women of the planter class, such as South Carolinians Angelina and Sarah Grimké, had responded to their experiences of slavery by becoming abolitionists, but they could hardly be outspoken in such views without leaving the South.[72] Most such women had acquiesed to slavery as a necessary evil, while seeing themselves as victimized by the burden of domestic management of slaves.[73]

The plantation system created a totally different economy and family than did the industrializing North. Southern plantation-class white women were isolated on widely separated estates and had little chance of forming women's associations of the kind that underlay northern women's benevolent and reform societies. The southern economy was agricultural, based on raising and selling staple crops such as tobacco and cotton for the national and international markets. But far from living in leisure off the profits, the white mistress of the plantation was the primary manager of a domestic economy that depended on raising pigs, chickens, and dairy cows for milk, cheese, and butter, growing vegetables and fruits, weaving cloth, and making clothes, rugs, quilts, candles, soap, and medicines for domestic consumption by the whole household.

The plantation mistress did part of this work herself and supervised the slaves who did the rest. She was the keeper of the keys to the storehouse and of the account books for the domestic economy, as well as the chief doctor for the sick, white and black. All the while, she had to maintain an appearance of fragility and affluent leisure that belied the actual difficulty of her extensive work.[74] During the Civil War this work would only be intensified, since the plantation served as the primary economic base for the war, sending its agricultural surplus to feed the army and providing clothes and other supplies for the soldiers.[75]

The sexual dynamics of slavery set the biracial household of Big House and slave cabins into a repressed and volatile relationship. The white mistress was to comport herself as and raise her daughters to be the epitome of sexual virtue, while her husband and sons were allowed a wide latitude to sexually use black female slaves. White women often projected the blame for such sexual relations on the black women themselves, who were imaged as sexually promiscuous animals in contrast to the asexual and "pure" white women. The black male was meanwhile denied the right to protect his own wife and daughters from sexual and physical abuse.[76] Around the edges of this system lay the fear of slave uprising and revenge, fantasized as the rape of white women and the massacre of the white family.

The slave woman bore the brunt of this system of physical and sexual exploitation. She shared an equal burden of field labor with the black male, even when pregnant or recently delivered of a child, and was the reproducer of slave labor for the master, bearing both the children of her own marriage and those forced upon her by white men (the latter children also became slaves, since southern law decreed that the condition of the child should follow that of the mother).[77] In addition, she did domestic work for her own family, attempting to create a small space of comfort apart from white exploitation.[78]

If slavery severely curtailed any independence for the black family, characterizing blacks as an extension of the white household with no right to a life of their own, that does not mean that strong family ties were not formed by blacks under slavery. Indeed, blacks clung to family relations precisely as the sphere where they most sought to define their own lives against slavery. On their emancipation, the first thought of many ex-slaves was to search for relatives who had been sold or fled and to seek to reassemble the family, registering their marriages officially, a right previously denied them.[79]

Emancipated blacks wished to distance themselves from all of the patterns of life they had had to endure under slavery, desiring above all to have their own land that they could cultivate for their own family. That their wives would never again have to work in the kitchens or fields of white farms, but could instead devote themselves to caring for their own families, was a prized objective. While some white women grew restive in the roles of full-time housekeeper and mother, for black woman they spelled a cherished hope.

Southern whites, however, were determined to disenfranchise blacks and prevent their economic independence by forcing them to serve as low-paid wage labor. Out of this struggle emerged, in the decades after the Civil War, the sharecropping system, which called for black families to plant and reap and then share crops with whites who financed their work and kept them in permanent debt. As much as black men took pride in trying to exempt their wives and daughters from such fieldwork, often they had no recourse but to use all family members in planting and reaping.[80]

Black women and men were actually *de*skilled in the postbellum era—that is, denied the possibility of doing whatever skilled work they had done under slavery, such as cloth weaving (women) or carpentry, tanning, blacksmithing, and shoemaking (men).[81] After the war, the main paid jobs allowed to blacks were in agriculture or domestic service. The first real professions within the black community were the ministry (for men) and teaching (mostly for women). Black mothers valued education for their children and often worked long hours to keep them in school in the hope that they would thereby escape from poverty.

For black women, domestic service was always an option. By refusing to work as live-in maids, such women distanced themselves from slave roles and could return to their own families at night.[82] Thus blacks in the South, contrary to white perceptions, sought to create intact nuclear families with a husband and father as head of the household. But the low wages paid black men left no alternative but a wife and children who also worked just to bring together the bare means of survival. The large percentage of female-headed black families that began to appear toward the end of the century was not a continuation of family patterns of blacks after slavery, but an expression of a new situation encountered in urban migration. In cities there was little work available for black males, but plenty for black females in domestic service.[83]

EMERGING IDEALS OF DOMESTICITY

If the Civil War broke the plantation economy of the South, the industrial development of the North was greatly accelerated by the conflict. The decades from 1870 through 1900 would see continuous capital growth, new waves of immigration from Europe, and westward expansion to settle the continent. Immigrant Irish, Polish, Italian, and Jewish women would be incorporated into domestic service and low-paid textile labor, especially the "sweating system" of the garment trades. The invention of the sewing machine would provide a new tool for such work for women, both in their own homes and in garment-assembly workplaces.

Technical advances such as gas lighting, domestic plumbing, furnaces, and stoves added comforts to middle-class family life while at the same time extending the demands of housekeeping through more elaborate furnishings, higher standards of cleanliness, and more intensive ideals of maternal nurture. Wealthy merchant families had begun the pattern of separating home from workplace in the 1830s and 1840s, and this was extended to successful artisans and shopkeepers in the decades after the Civil War.[84]

No longer did husbands run their businesses from offices attached to their homes; instead, they went out to work in separate office buildings. Families no longer lived above or behind the workshop, with the wife's keeping the books and helping to sell goods in an attached store. However, such patterns of family business where wife, husband, and older children worked together, with combined living and work space, would not disappear entirely: they can still be found today in small groceries or restaurants founded by new immigrants.

But the middle-class pattern in the United States, as in England and France during the same period, was to separate the family home from the workplace. In part this was achieved by building houses in new suburbs surrounded by flower gardens (no longer the homely vegetable gardens that provided food for the table). Paid work then became identified with men who left the home for an extended workday, while women focused primarily on unpaid labor or "house-work"—cleaning, cooking, and caring for children. No longer a place of production, the home was now reshaped as a refuge from the "world" of work and business.

What emerged was a Victorian ideal of the family—the "modern family"—that continues to function today in the nostalgic imagination as a normative model. In this middle-class vision of the family, home and work, female and male "spheres," were strictly separated. The ability of the male "breadwinner" to support a full-time house-wife was the mark of middle-class success, a standard that most working-class Americans could not emulate due to the low wages paid to their men. The woman who worked—that is, left the home for a paying job—was seen as nonnormative. Such work was allow-able for young women or "spinsters," but it was regarded as selfish and destructive to family life for married women with children.

Once again, the ideal belied the reality for many middle-class women. Like the myth of the leisured plantation wife, it masked the actual work for use done by the nineteenth-century housewife, which was still crucial for economic maintenance: growing vegeta-bles and fruit in the garden, canning and preserving food, and making soap, medicines, and clothes. Since only the richest sector of the mid-dle class could afford servants, this work was done primarily by the wife. When money was needed, housewives still resorted to the strat-egies of taking in boarders and doing piecework in their homes. Daughters, too, were pressed into service in both domestic work for use and outside jobs that contributed to the family wage. Sometimes funds were found to send a brother on to higher education, while the sister sacrificed her own education.[85]

The images of both woman and child were reshaped. The child was no longer the born sinner whose perverse will must be broken by stern discipline, but a malleable being to be gently nurtured in piety and self-discipline.[86] Women, even wives and mothers, were asexual innocents, permanent servants of the domestic sphere of purity and goodness against the evil outside world. A new religious ideology imagined the home as a magic circle of pure womanhood and innocent childhood, an unfallen garden of Eden set against a sinful male realm of business and politics. As women were stripped of the productive functions of the family economy, they took on intensified roles as nurturers of prolonged childhoods and healers of the bruised egos of men who journeyed daily between the world and the home.

A polarized dualism of masculinity and femininity evolved in Victorian thought, shaped by the separated spheres of home and work, of woman as nurturer and man as worker. The woman was to be sexually pure, physically delicate, emotional, dependent, and loving, in contrast to the man, who was sexually virile, physically strong, aggressive, dominant, and rational. Men and women were socialized to model themselves after these opposite, interdependent ideals as their true "natures."

This ideology of Victorian womanhood played a compensatory role over against the new male world of secular industrial society. Although the doctrine of chaste, altruistic femininity had been built on Mariology and on aristocratic traditions of the lady and was already widespread in women's magazines in the 1830 revival era,[87] it was reshaped in the Victorian era to cast the home as a benevolent realm of uplifting nurture providing refuge from the competitive business world. In effect, middle-class America gave up trying to create a godly society and retreated to making a godly home.

Home and womanhood were to be everything that the outer world of business was not. At home the natural aristocracy of birth still held sway in male-female relations, even though this concept was discredited in the public, political world. In the home, a religious world of fixed certainties was to be maintained, in contrast to the secular world of rationalism and skepticism. In the home, emotion and intimacy reigned, against an outside world dominated by unfeeling technological rationality. In the home, sublimated spirituality compensated for an outward capitulation to the fierce materialism of the commercial quest for profits. Home was an Eden of beauty and peace located in a quiet suburb far removed from the ugly world of the factory. It was women's job to create this dreamworld of a home where men could come to rest and recuperate from their daily immersion in harsh conflict.

This ideology of true womanhood not only domesticated women but feminized religion. As the precepts of the American separation of church and state increasingly segregated religion from the world of politics and business, the family and private life became the sphere of religion. Morality was to apply to private relations in the family, not to public political and business associations. The church and its ministry, no longer critics or buttresses of the public world of magistrates and judges, instead became an auxiliary to the home and its privatized piety and morality.[88]

Christian virtue was now identified with female virtue. Like woman, feminized Christianity was seen as essentially nurturing, altruistic, loving, affective, and passive. Anger, conflict, and even too much rationality and critical thinking were deemed both un-Christian and unfeminine. In Victorian images, Jesus had limpid eyes, delicate features, and silky hair and was surrounded by children, no more the glaring medieval pantocrator as world ruler, warrior, judge, and king.

Victorian culture typically declared that women were more naturally religious than men, and indeed it was a woman's role to nurture piety in her children and to moralize her husband and sons, if possible. Far from suggesting that this spiritual superiority might qualify women for public leadership in church or state, however, Christian leaders used it to argue for their segregation in the home. Only by staying sequestered could a woman maintain her purity and be a source of purity for her children and restoration for her husband when he returned to rest in her bosom.

In 1869 Horace Bushnell attacked the struggle for women's political rights in a treatise entitled "Women's Suffrage: The Reform against Nature."[89] Bushnell, a leading Congregational minister, proposed that the duality of the Old and New Testaments, law and grace, corresponded to that of masculinity and femininity. The male represented law, and the female represented grace or the Gospel. The Gospel revealed forgiveness and altruistic love that transcended the law, but these values were not suitable to the real world of sin and conflict, in the public order. Here the male, as the representative of law, must rule in both state and church. Womanliness, like Christlikeness, was "not of this world," so woman, though the spiritual superior of the male, was therefore unfit for public office, whether political or ecclesiastical. (On these grounds Jesus also would have been unsuited for ordained ministry, but Bushnell did not pursue the implications of his argument.)

Victorian womanhood was seen not only as more spiritual but also as less sexual than maleness. Though she be the mother of children, the chaste wife should be innocent of her own biology and incapable of desiring sexual pleasure. Sex was to be endured for the sake of maternity, not enjoyed for its own sake. One effect of this repression was the socialization of middle-class women into a culture of illness. Women were assumed to be too delicate to bear the rigors of physical labor, and any mention of bodily functions was presumed to be shocking to their psyches. The decline in the number of children borne by white middle-class women in the later nineteenth century may suggest that some of this ideology of asexuality was used to limit both sexual access and pregnancy.[90]

The notion of women's delicate and sickness-prone nature was also exploited by eminent doctors and educators to argue against women's education. Medical specialists insisted that women had limited physical energy and that what little they had must be devoted to the tasks of maternity. Any effort to divert this minimal store of energy to outside tasks such as "brainwork" would lead quickly to invalidism. Moreover, women who lived too much in their brains would become sterile and lose their capacity to bear children.[91] The large number of educated professional women who remained single was cited as proof of this latter prediction, raising a dire specter of the white middle classes' losing the "race war" against sturdy blacks and immigrants who were having large families.[92]

But the very existence of such arguments in late-nineteenth-century America pointed to the fact that more and more middle-class women were breaking the barriers of domestic segregation. The suffrage campaign carried on its struggle for "eighty years and more" to win the vote and full legal standing for women as citizens.[93] The teaching profession, already opened to women in the earlier part of the century in primary education, now expanded to secondary and higher education, with more and more colleges opening their doors to women. A few women even won places in the professions of doctor, lawyer, and ordained minister.[94]

A new wave of organizing by Christian women arose in the 1880s under the banner of the Women's Christian Temperance Union. Under the leadership of Frances Willard of Evanston, Illinois, the WCTU expanded beyond the traditional evangelical crusade for temperance and claimed the new causes of winning woman suffrage, ending child labor, and putting an end to war. Rather than accepting segregation in the home by the ideology of true womanhood, Willard used it as a launching pad for her mission to uplift and perfect the world by ridding it of vice and violence. Her slogan of "making the world homelike" coopted the ideal of the home but turned it into a way not to retreat from but rather to transform the outside world.[95]

Working-class women were also organizing, seeking to start their own unions or join male ones in order to raise their wages and ameliorate the harsh conditions under which they worked.[96] Yet this effort found little support from male union leaders or the white Protestant ministers of the Social Gospel movement, who embraced a democratic socialist vision that they identified with the "politics of Jesus." White unions saw even low-paid women's jobs as a threat to working men; their preferred solution was a male "family wage" that would allow the husband and father to support his family, emulating the middle-class pattern of a dependent wife and children.[97]

Thus the reform era of the late nineteenth century presented contradictory faces. Middle-class white women endeavored to break out of their segregation in the home to claim equal political rights, education, and professions in the world. White working-class men, meanwhile, sought a family wage to disemploy their wives and send them home to be full-time wives and mothers. For their part, working-class women saw their pleas for an equal wage go largely ignored. During the same period, black men were being lynched in the South for any appearance of "uppitiness," and the outcries of black women against the mistreatment of their people were scarcely heard by white reformers, male or female.[98] Such contradictions would continue to characterize Reformers of the early twentieth century.

CHAPTER 5

From the Progressive Era through the Great Depression: 1890–1940

American women's work in 1890 still reflected the conditions that had been established after the Civil War. According to the census of that year, 16 percent of women sixteen and older worked for wages, accounting for 16.5 percent of the work force. Women workers were predominantly young and single and either newcomers to urban areas from farms or immigrants from Europe. Wage work for women was seen as comprising a stage of life between school and marriage, during which young women worked to contribute to the family income and to save for their own homes at marriage.

But these statistics are misleading and do not reflect the actual extent of women's productive labor. A majority of black women, for example, typically undercounted in such statistics, worked and continued to work after marriage, most in agriculture or as domestics and laundresses. Fully 44 percent of foreign-born or second-generation immigrant women also worked, and many of these continued to work after marriage as well. They labored in factories and in the garment trades and as cleaners. Only 10 percent of white women from older American families worked for wages, but this figure does not count the work of mothers and daughters on farms or of the many who took in laundry or sewing in their homes.

Most waged women did menial or low-skilled labor for low pay. Forty percent did domestic, laundry, or institutional cleaning. Another 20.3 percent worked in mills and factories, mainly in textiles or food processing.[1] A new area of female work was beginning to open up in sales and clerical work in offices. Women had long done selling, but in association with family-run businesses. Now mass production and distribution through department stores were creating a separate market and venue for products bought and used specifically by women (e.g., women's clothes), and with them came a new need for saleswomen (men typically sold products bought and used by men).

Clerical duties—both secretarial work and accounting—had been the province of men a generation earlier, seen as aspects of an apprenticeship undertaken prior to owning one's own business. The advent of the typewriter, however, reshaped clerical work as a separate female job without upward mobility. Expanding high school education and business colleges were giving women the literacy and skills needed for these new secretarial roles.[2]

A small sector of women worked as primary-school teachers, librarians, and nurses. These jobs, mostly or entirely filled by women, were only beginning to demand upgraded educational standards in 1890. Normal schools were being established to train teachers, but many did not require a high school credential. Nursing schools attached to hospitals provided little medical training; nursing in fact still overlapped with cleaning work. Women librarians were also expected to dust and repair books and had scant professional training. Only a handful of women had become doctors, lawyers, or ministers and worked on the low-paid margins of those professions. Together, all of these white-collar female workers accounted for less than 15 percent of waged women in 1890.[3]

WOMEN IN SOCIAL REFORM: SETTLEMENT HOUSE TO GOVERNMENT BUREAUCRACIES

A remarkable generation of American women associated with the settlement-house movement would transform social work from volunteer charity into a female profession by the turn of the century. These women came mostly from middle-class white Protestant backgrounds and were the first generation of graduates from female colleges. Unlike their working-class sisters, these women were not expected to work between education and marriage but instead supposed to remain at home to aid their families. Many experienced a frustrating disorientation after the intense, idealistic experience of learning in a female-bonded environment. For women such as Jane Addams and Ellen Gates Starr, college friends at Rockford Female Seminary, the founding of a settlement house became a way to channel the experiences of female bonding, education, and idealism into social service.[4]

Hull House, founded by Addams and Starr in 1889 in a poor immigrant section of Chicago, would evolve into one of the defining institutions of social reform in American life over the next two decades. The inhabitants of the Italian and Jewish neighborhoods surrounding Hull House mostly worked in tenement sweatshops with no indoor plumbing. Saloons abounded, while public schools were nonexistent. Hull House's residents, who grew to number twenty-five by 1896, along with eighty or more nonresident volunteers, sought to mediate between middle-class Americans like themselves and the exploited immigrants through educational and social services.

A gymnasium and youth clubs provided alternative places for recreation and social life for neighborhood youngsters, while a kindergarten and day nursery served working mothers. Classes in sewing, nutrition, and household management aided these mothers in their housekeeping, while art classes, choral groups, concerts, lectures, a debate club, and a library raised their cultural level and promoted their assimilation into middle-class American life. The Jane House provided cooperative living for working women, and a public kitchen served hot meals. An employment agency and a meeting place available to unions reached out to the adult working population, male and female.[5]

The work of Hull House soon touched on neighborhood and city reform issues. Campaigns to create safe playgrounds for children, to improve city services such as garbage collection, inspection of factory work conditions, and food contamination, to set up a visiting-nurse program, and to appoint advocates for young criminal offenders brought Hull House alternately into conflict or collaboration with ward bosses and city and state governments. Settlement workers were paid by being linked with wealthy donors, each of whom would provide a particular woman with a fellowship.[6] The ethos of their work was still that of self-sacrificing service to the poor, in the Christian female charity tradition, but the modest funding by women philanthropists made it a half-step between voluntary and waged work. Hull House was thus a kind of secular Protestant service order, and an alternative family for its members.

But soon Hull House began to seek to institutionalize its reforms through local and state governments, which would then pay for the services of the workers. The founding of a separate juvenile court, for example, required female probation officers to work with the youth, and the inclusion of art and music in school curricula called for cities to pay teachers in those areas. Inspection of factory conditions and contaminated food was accompanied by agitation for legislation and paid inspectors. Florence Kelley's efforts in the inspection of sweat-shop conditions in factories brought not only state regulation but a job for her as Chief Factory Inspector for the State of Illinois, charged with enforcing the new laws.[7] Julia Lathrop's investigation of city-funded asylums won her an appointment as head of the Illinois Board of Charities, which aimed to reform the government of such institutions.[8] Both women were Hull House residents.

No longer merely a form of charity in which a caseworker dis-tributed aid donated by the rich to impoverished clients, social work was now being transmuted into a professional social science allied with the state. At the Chicago School of Civics and Philanthrophy, founded at the University of Chicago by Hull House associates Sophronisba Beckinridge and Edith Abbott, the focus was on re-search into social conditions as a means to establish the data needed for government reforms. The social welfare agencies created by those re-forms would be staffed by the school's graduates.[9]

A major milestone in this move of settlement-house women into government reform came with the founding, in 1912, of the Chil-dren's Bureau in the federal Department of Commerce and Labor. The bureau had been the brainchild of Florence Kelley and another settlement-house worker, Lillian Wald, both then associated with New York's Henry Street Settlement. The two women began their campaign in 1903, enlisting the aid of a network of social welfare or-ganizations with which they were connected. In 1909 they were able to put the idea before President Theodore Roosevelt at the first White House Conference on the Care of Dependent Children. Al-though the conference itself focused on the needs of children with-out parents, Wald and Kelley saw their proposed Children's Bureau as a locus for broad-based welfare reform on behalf of children and their mothers.[10]

Congress authorized the proposal during a period of progressive fervor in 1912, when Progressive Party candidate Theodore Roosevelt was challenging Woodrow Wilson for the presidency. Although Roosevelt would ultimately lose the elections, Wilson would accept much of his party's reform agenda. Julia Lathrop was appointed to head the Children's Bureau and quickly staffed it from the ranks of the progressive women's network, hiring mostly female candidates. To begin the bureau's work in the area of child welfare, Lathrop chose to concentrate on birth registration and infant health rather than on more controversial goals such as child labor laws or mothers' pensions.

At Lathrop's direction, the bureau published a series of pamphlets on prenatal and infant care that became best-selling government publications. Drawing on a nationwide network of women's voluntary organizations, including the General Federation of Women's Clubs, the Association of Collegiate Alumnae, the Women's Christian Temperance Union, the Parent and Teacher Associations, and the Congress for Mothers, the bureau was able to put an army of women into the field to canvass each region for unregistered births and to talk to mothers about prenatal and infant care.[11]

The Children's Bureau was soon flooded with letters from mothers who poured out their troubles; each was answered with care. Following then-popular behaviorist principles of strict time schedules for raising infants, the pamphlets and interventions of the bureau advocated a particular, middle-class philosophy of child-raising that went against the grain of many ethnic traditions and also greatly extended the burden of time and care expected of "good" mothers.[12] A new class of female government professionals was thus in effect indoctrinating the nation's mothers in their duty to be "full-time," stay-at-home mothers, an ideal out of the reach of many ethnic and black women.

The Children's Bureau in its first years was a federal department of government that nonetheless defied bureaucratic methods of operation and conventional notions of government's role. It drew on the methods of voluntary charity work and on a culture of female altruism toward and care for others, especially women, children, and the poor. Many of the employees at the bureau were single and lodged together, continuing the pattern of settlement-house life in the federal capital. Lacking a large staff or funds, the bureau used the female reform networks both to do its work in the field and to lobby on its behalf with the federal government, thus interconnecting public and private agencies. For instance, Lathrop called on this network to bombard the House Appropriations Committee with protests when it turned down her request to expand her funding and staff; the House subsequently approved the request 276–47.[13]

The 1890s had seen an expansion and consolidation of women's uplift and reform organizations. In 1890 the National and American Woman Suffrage associations had overcome their bitter split after the Civil War and united, signaling a new unanimity on suffrage across the spectrum of women's groups from moderate to radical.[14] The Women's Christian Temperance Union, founded in 1874, had itself adopted a broad platform of suffrage, pacifism, and social reform in the 1880s under the leadership of Frances Willard.[15] For its part, the Women's Educational and Industrial Union, established in 1877, brought middle- and working-class women together on a reform agenda that championed the regulation of factory conditions, better wages and working conditions for domestics, minimum wages for factory work, maternity leave, and old-age pensions.[16] The new emphasis on "scientific housekeeping" in collegiate home-economics courses was directed beyond the private home and into "municipal housekeeping." Reform of working and social conditions and public sanitation was thereby defined as an extension of a woman's housekeeping role in the family.

Also in 1890, older literary clubs such as Sorosis, founded in New York City in 1868, had united with reform clubs to create the General Federation of Women's Clubs, attaching a moderate reform agenda to the women's club movement generally.[17] At the end of the decade, the National Consumers' League, a women's group founded in 1899, would engage in factory inspections to ascertain conditions, publishing lists of "white stores" that carried goods produced and sold under good working conditions, and thereby using women's power as consumers to promote reform in factories and stores.[18] The Women's Trade Union League, which would emerge in 1903 out of the struggles of women in the garment industry, would persuade middle-class women to support working women's efforts to unionize.[19]

This network of national women's organizations, together with hundreds of local variations, coalesed into a united front to win suffrage in the 1910s. In 1914 the General Federation of Women's

Clubs would formally declare its support for suffrage after holding back for decades out of fear that the more conservative and apolitical clubs would defect.[20] Suffrage had now become mainstream, no longer associated with a challenge to women's domestic role. During World War I, mainline suffrage movement leaders such as Carrie Chapman Catt demonstrated their patriotism by their loyal endorsement of the war effort, despite earlier links with pacifism.[21] Suffrage was passed by the House of Representatives in 1918 and by the Senate in 1919, to be ratified by the thirty-sixth state in 1920. A prohibition amendment was approved during the same period, indicating a union between women's vote, social reform, and temperance.[22]

RACISM, SOCIALISM, AND DIVISION AMONG WOMEN

The mainstreaming of suffrage was paid for by a capitulation to racism and WASP nativism. The implicit antiblack attitudes of many club women had come out into the open in 1900, when black club leader Josephine Ruffin had applied for membership in the General Federation through her representation of both the black New Era Club and the integrated New England Women's Club. The New Era Club was accepted and then rejected when its black constituency was discovered. A compromise vote in 1902 allowed state federations and the national federation to adopt different policies, effectively eliminating black clubs from the latter organization.[23]

Catholic and Jewish women also felt unwelcome in state and general federations of WASP women's clubs. In response, many blacks, Catholics, and Jews founded their own women's organizations, focusing more on group interests than on women's issues alone.[24] Catholic women were typically directed by their bishops to oppose suffrage in the 1910s,[25] but despite rebuffs by the white suffrage movement, black women's groups such as the National Federation of Afro-American Women and the Federation of Colored Women's Clubs, as well as the black female sororities, strongly supported the cause.

Black women hoped that their enfranchisement would help break down the de facto *dis*enfranchisement of black men under the Jim Crow laws. (This, of course, was precisely why many Southern white women—and men—opposed women's suffrage.) Instead, the laws that denied black men the vote through poll taxes and tests were now applied to black women as well. Appeals were made to white feminists of the National Women's Party, asking them to protest on black women's behalf, but they refused to take up the issue, claiming that it was a matter of race, not gender![26]

As the suffrage movement accommodated itself to mainstream racist, capitalist, and white female domestic culture, a new radical wing of women emerged in the 1910s, associated with socialism, sexual liberation, and economic critique of women's family roles. Women such as Crystal Eastman, Emma Goldman, and Margaret Sanger frequented radical socialist circles in New York. They rejected Christianity as oppressive to women and were members of the New York feminist group Heterodoxy.[27] They identified with "feminism," a new term in that period. Feminists saw themselves as seeking a more thoroughgoing transformation of gender relations for both women and men than was promised by the "bourgeois" suffrage movement.[28]

These women of the Left were not all of one mind on the connections between socialism and feminism, but they shared a new celebration of women's right to sexual freedom. Ridiculing the asexual, female-bonded maternal culture of the Progressive-era women's movement, they claimed the right to free sexual unions with men based on affection, not bondage in legal marriage. They read Freud's writings on the Id and the Superego and Havelock Ellis's exaltation of sexuality as the liberator of women from Victorian repression.[29] They championed birth control as a way of freeing women to enjoy sexual pleasure and equal partnership with male companions, no longer constrained by the fear of unchosen maternity. Birth control had been illegal in America since the 1870s under the Comstock laws, but radicals such as Emma Goldman flouted those laws to distribute contraceptive information and devices.[30] Margaret Sanger would turn this aspect of the leftist feminist movement into a personal crusade in the 1910s and 1920s, while gradually distancing herself from socialism.[31]

Perhaps the most distinctive thinker in socialist feminist circles of this period was Charlotte Perkins Gilman. Her major book, *Women and Economics*, published in 1898, attacked the idealization of woman's superior morality, supposedly achieved through her identification with the home and motherhood. In fact, Gilman argued, her confinement to child-raising and drudgework in the privatized family, and the denial of any larger role for her in society, had turned woman into a pathological personality. The narrowness of her sphere prevented woman from greater human development and truncated her capacity for companionship with her husband and enlightened parenting of her children.

What woman needed was to be freed from housework and exclusive child care so that she could combine stimulating work with a family life. Improved parenting of children and companionship between husband and wife as equals would then be possible. Cooking, housework, and child care should, Gilman believed, be socialized and professionalized; she envisioned apartment buildings for working women and their families with collective kitchens, professional cleaning services, and shared child care.[32] This vision drew on a long American tradition of utopian communal societies going back to the 1830s, as well as the collective living of settlement houses—but Gilman's ideal imagined not extended communities but private apartments where families could each have their own space, with access to food service, cleaning, and child care all located within the building.

Like many middle-class women who thought of waged work as liberating women, Gilman had in mind interesting professional work such as teaching or writing, not long hours of low-paid labor in factories, laundries, or canneries or even in the typing pools that were most working women's lot. Other socialist women enthusiastically took up Gilman's theme and tried to design apartment houses for professional women with socialized child care and housekeeping services. Such schemes floundered, however, on the inability to conceive how such work could be done if not by other women whose low pay would not allow them similar amenities![33]

More successful in this period were a number of efforts made by women to alleviate their housework by banding together in dining clubs where they and their families could take their meals together.[34] But the socialization of women's child care and housework was not to be the favored direction of American family development; rather, in the 1920s, such ideas would be equated by conservative alarmists with Russian Communist experiments in collective kitchens and crèches and condemned as subversive.[35] Instead, government and corporate America sought to emphasize the goal of individual homeownership in suburbs set apart from cities and outfitted with ever-expanding household technology.

The women's movement emerged in 1920 from the long struggle to win suffrage committed to apply women's newly won political power to significant social reforms. One aspiration widely shared by suffrage women was world peace. They truly hoped that World War I would be the war to end all wars. The Women's Peace Party, founded in 1915 by Jane Addams, came out of the war with a new name: the Women's International League for Peace and Freedom. WILPF members looked to the League of Nations for a model of how arbitration might replace war as a way to settle international disputes. They expected and promoted disarmament, the dismantling of the United States' wartime military forces, in order to invest in peacemaking alternatives.[36]

But the Navy and the War Department had different ideas: they wished to maintain a large postwar military force as the means to win American global power. War Department head John Wingate Weeks saw this plan threatened by the broad consensus for disarmament within the women's movement, now armed with the vote. At first the women were merely dismissed as "fluffheads" who were unacquainted with reality, but soon the tactics against the women's peace movement turned nastier. Reviving the un-Americanism campaign that had marginalized socialists and jailed their leaders during the World War I "Red scare," groups in favor of a strong military defined the women's movement as a Communist front, doing the bidding of the new Bolshevik government in Russia.

The infamous "spider chart," created by and leaked from the War Department and widely reprinted by patriotic groups including the Daughters of the American Revolution, linked in a subversive network not only the WILPF but such other women's groups as the National Consumers' League, the Women's Trade Union League, the Women's Christian Temperance Union, and even the National Council of Parents and Teachers, the Girls' Friendly Society, and the American Home Economics Association. Most of the prominent women leaders were named on the chart, among them Carrie Chapman Catt and the leadership of the child welfare establishment of the federal Children's Bureau.[37]

While mainstream women leaders vigorously protested this blanket smearing of women's organizations, they also purged their movement of its more radical ideas and elements, including the socialists within the WILPF. The result was a sharp repression of any more far-reaching vision of social transformation that had been imagined as emerging from women's new political power. The fear of being labeled subversive or un-American also exacerbated differences among women's groups.

In the final decade of the suffrage struggle, the movement had split between the mainline leadership under Carrie Chapman Catt and a radical wing led by Alice Paul, who applied the direct-action tactics of British suffragists, courting arrests and force-feeding in prison.[38] Paul organized the National Women's Party in 1915, rejecting the nonpartisan stance of Catt. After the war and the winning of suffrage, the National American Woman Suffrage Association transformed itself into the respectable League of Women Voters, whose goal was to educate the electorate of all parties. Paul and others, by contrast, refounded the National Women's Party in 1921 and by 1923 had narrowed their focus to one central cause: the passage of an Equal Rights Amendment to the Constitution, which would eliminate sex as a legal classification and repeal all laws that discriminated against women (or men) as a gender group in any area, from property rights to divorce to employment opportunities.[39]

The Equal Rights Amendment (ERA) was bitterly opposed by mainstream women reformers in the League of Women Voters and the federal Children's Bureau. These "social feminists," as they have been called, maintained the view that women were by nature different from men—both more altruistic and more nurturing (a major basis for linking women with social reform and peacemaking) but also weaker and more vulnerable due to their maternal function. Since settlement-house days these social feminists had worked to pass protective laws that would limit the hours and conditions of women's work. Heavy lifting, long hours, and night work were all seen as jeopardizing women's capacity to bear healthy children.

In supporting protective legislation specifically for women, the social feminists buttressed the arguments of male union leaders, who also favored protective laws, but for different reasons. Women's low pay was seen as threatening male jobs; shortening their hours and curtailing the types of work they could do would keep women out of better-paying jobs and confine them to sex-segregated labor.[40] Working women's own preferences were seldom consulted by either middle-class social feminists or male trade unionists. Many working women resented being shut out of better-paying jobs that they were able to do. Some welcomed shorter hours even if that meant less pay, but others saw night work as enabling married women with children to care for their families during the day while leaving child care to a husband at night.

The disagreement between the social feminists and the Women's Party over the ERA became a bitter ideological dispute in the 1920s, dividing egalitarians from those who argued for separate spheres and female difference as a presupposition of women's work for women. The division shattered the illusion of a united front of women reformers, held over from the last decade of the suffrage era. No longer devoted to a common cause, women were now set against each other, with the Daughters of the American Revolution attacking women peace leaders as subversives while those same social and peace feminists vilified ERA supporters as elitists who lacked an understanding of the needs of working women.[41] This debate would be revisited in the revived struggle to pass the ERA in the 1970s.

THE "NEW WOMAN" OF THE 1920S

The 1920s saw the popularization of a new "new woman" very different from her predecessor in the Progressive era, who had imbibed social ideals at a women's college and devoted herself to social reform, remaining unmarried and bonding with other women. The "new woman" of the twenties, by contrast, was the flapper—young and both sexually and economically liberated, but using her liberation for personal pleasure and adventure, not for altruistic service to others. The flapper did not bond with her sisters in social service, but rather competed with other, similarly liberated women to attract and "hold" a man. She assumed that women's subordination to men was now a thing of the past, but neither did she aspire any longer to be morally superior to them; rather, she sought to be an engaging social and sexual partner, to show herself to be a lively, sporty "pal" to men.[42]

Unlike the socially and intellectually serious graduates of women's colleges in 1900, the flapper was a coed who spent her college years partying, hopefully emerging with a Mrs. Or else she was a young secretary whose work in the business world allowed her to flirt around the water cooler. But this image of the liberated woman, claiming her own sexuality and wages, was stripped of the radical visions of transformation of gender relations held by the socialist feminists of the 1910s. The movies and magazines that popularized this image of the "new woman" harnessed female sexual liberation to socially conservative goals. At heart, the flapper longed to surrender her freedom for marriage and a family. The "right man" who came along at the end of the story would take her away from the glittering world of independent life and put her where she really wanted to be—in the home, with him firmly in charge.

Distributing information about birth control was still illegal in the 1920s, with the repeal of the Comstock laws a decade away, in 1936. Sexual liberation was presumed to mean "petting," stopping short of intercourse, until after marriage. But popular stories no longer featured romantic tales of the "good" woman seduced and impregnated by a heartless Romeo. The "new woman" was expected to know how to prevent an unwanted pregnancy, even if the means were still not widely discussed. As a wife, the new woman was supposed to "keep her man" by remaining sexually attractive, capable of giving and receiving sexual pleasure.

Sexual pleasure for its own sake, no longer primarily for procreation, was widely promoted in new marriage-advice literature. Achieving mutual orgasms was now a kind of "duty" for married couples. Rather than liberating women for "free love" relations, sex was tied to keeping the monogamous marriage intact. The popular movie, *Why Change Your Wife,* with Gloria Swanson, showed a dowdy, bookish wife, about to lose her husband to another woman but winning him back by transforming herself into a lively, sexually attractive vamp.[43]

Older social feminists who remained in charge of women's organizations from the League of Women Voters to the Children's Bureau to the Women's Party were uncomfortable with and suspicious of the new woman of the 1920s, seeing her as undermining their ideals and a reform culture that was linked to a view of female moral purity. For these women, shaped as they had been by the Progressive era, birth control and sexual liberation both demeaned and threatened women's power based on moral superiority. The male sexual drive was viewed with distaste as animalistic; women triumphed over it and also limited pregnancies by forcing men to accede to female purity. To "descend" to men's level of sexual lust was, for women, to cede both this higher ground and also to make themselves vulnerable to sexual exploitation by men, a contest they could only lose.[44]

Such fears for the likely fate of the flirtatious coed or secretary were not unfounded, though in the twenties they appeared "old-fashioned." Feminists of the 1960s would try to reclaim the social feminism of the Progressive era as a legacy of lesbian love, but the claim would be anachronistic.[45] Female bonding, even the lifelong companionship between female couples (called Boston marriages) common among reform women, such as Jane Addams and Frances Willard,[46] was connected to a higher female morality precisely because it was culturally unthinkable as sexual.

The split between affective female friendship and (hetero-) sexuality allowed such women to bond with other women while distancing themselves from sexual relations. By contrast, the sexualization of women in the twenties was normatively heterosexual; when it redefined female bonding as sexual, it labeled it as a deviant, perverse sexuality.[47] The celebration of lesbianism in a post-sixties feminism belongs to a new cultural turn that reclaims female bonding while assuming that all women are sexually active.

It is important that we not be misled by the dramatic shift in popular imagery of women, from the white-clad suffragist on parade of 1915 to the flapper coed of 1925. Female cultures were diverse in the twenties, but the general trend was toward shoring up conservative values of family and gender relations under the guise of the "modern," sexualized woman. Changes in sexual culture, female employment, education, and the vote were surely significant, but to a large extent they were used to refocus rather than to transform patterns of female subordination to men in public and family life.

The 1920s witnessed a complex realignment of religion and secularity, of the privatized self, of family and public culture, of sexuality and social morality, of femaleness and maleness. Americanism vis à vis "foreignness" was also being redefined as American culture became more ethnically and religiously diverse. Public culture in business, entertainment, politics, and academic life was shorn of Christian religious references and allied with values of scientific rationality and efficiency. Women reformers who sought to be "modern" allied themselves with such secularity. While they retained notions of altruistic morality from nineteenth-century Christian society, they distanced themselves from a specific Christianity, thus leaving themselves with a hypothesis of female altruism rooted only in biology—a thesis vulnerable to changing views of female biology and "nature."

Women social workers and peace activists no longer spoke of bringing about the Reign of God as the goal of their efforts, as they would have in the nineteenth century. Jane Addams, though herself a member of a Congregational church near Hull House, intentionally resisted defining her work in terms of Christianization, sensitive to the culturally diverse (largely Catholic and Jewish) constituencies with which she worked. Assimilation into white Anglo-Saxon Protestant middle-class culture was still implicitly the norm of Americanization, but the avant-garde of social reform eschewed explicitly religious language.[48] Likewise, female educational professionals claimed a language of secular rationality, not of religiously based ideals.[49]

But the severing of Protestant Christianity from liberal social reform meant that the language of the Christian crusade became identified with conservative, even racist social ideologies that were hostile not only to the sexually liberated woman but also to reforms promoted by the Children's Bureau, such as child labor laws. The Catholic hierarchy, which had opposed woman suffrage, dropped its opposition once the vote was won, and turned instead to organizing Catholic women to use their votes to support socially conservative causes. In 1920 the Catholic bishops set up the National Council of Catholic Women under the bishops own social agency, the National Catholic Welfare Council.[50]

Official Catholic women's groups championed a view of woman as different from but complementary to man. Women were now described not as morally inferior but rather as more moral and altruistic than men, a status that was quickly harnessed to conservative causes. Women were mandated as having a special role in the fight against liberalism, secularism, socialism, and feminism, with all their pernicious fruits in society: liberal divorce laws, legalized birth control, federally funded maternal and infant health care (seen as interfering with the rights of the family), child labor laws, and the Equal Rights Amendment. Catholics equated this conservative crusade with an aggressive Americanism, seeing themselves as saving both true Christianity and

American society. Mrs. Francis Slattery, president of the Boston League of Catholic Women, made the connection explicit in her 1929 Christmas radio address when she urged, "Let us fashion ourselves on the model of the Holy Family. Let us bow our heads in deepest reverence to the cross of Christ and raise our arm in salute to the flag of flags—the Stars and Stripes of America."[51]

Protestantism during this period was deeply divided between modernism and fundamentalism, between those who accepted liberal biblical criticism and those who insisted on a plenary verbal inspiration of the Bible. This split also reflected a division along lines of social policy. Fundamentalists insisted that the biblical view of the family precluded women's public ministry or political leadership, while liberal Protestants championed justice for the (white male) working class but were largely silent on racial issues and traditionalist on women's place in the home.[52]

Paradoxically, the Pentecostal and Holiness wings of conservative Protestantism subverted the subordination of women by allowing them to preach and lead prayer services under the inspiration of the Spirit. Women preachers, prayer leaders, and faith healers were common in Pentecostal churches, and at least two such figures became national celebrities: Aimee Semple McPherson, founder of the International Church of the Four Square Gospel, and Kathryn Kuhlman, whose revival ministry would blossom into a radio empire in the 1940s.[53] These women charismatic preachers supported conservative values of women's subordination to men within the family while themselves wielding great public influence and amassing significant wealth. Another woman preacher, Alma Bridwell White, founder and bishop of the Pillar of Fire Church, united the promotion of women's equality in church and society with nativist anti-Catholic and anti-Semitic views, sentiments that eventually led her to collaborate with the Ku Klux Klan.[54]

Right-wing Christian America found its most explicitly nativist and racist expression in this latter organization. Founded shortly after the Civil War, the Ku Klux Klan was revived 1915 and went on to feed on the antiforeign paranoia of the Red Scare during World War I. In 1923 the Klan sought to make use of women's new power in society by organizing a special women's branch. To justify its ends, the Klan adopted some of the language of social reform, claiming to be protecting the American family and civilization by crusading against liquor, sexual vice, and sexually suggestive movies—all empires presumed to be controlled by Catholics and Jews.

The Klan portrayed liberal America as having gone soft, and as being ripe for the picking by subversive foreign agents who spread moral degeneracy. The Klan itself, in contrast, was depicted as a morally rearmed masculine Protestantism, militant in its defense of white womanhood and the family against un-American forces. This image of fierce WASP masculinity prepared to protect the American family was in some tension with the promotion of women's Klan groups, which were to use women's votes to win political office and thereby consolidate white Protestant power against blacks, Jews, and Catholics. Conflicts soon arose between male and female Klan leaders over the autonomy of the female branch.

Taking their cue from progressive groups such as the Consumers' League, Klan women mobilized to boycott Catholic, black, and Jewish enterprises and to drive their owners' families out of town. In the twenties, in some states such as Indiana, the power of the male and female Klans was so widespread as to make them indistinguishable from the local white Protestant establishment. Even the women's club movement, which never purged itself of racist and nativist views, could be seen as not that different from the Klan. Both sought to use white "native-born" women's new power to shore up white power in general, while excluding blacks of both sexes from political and economic access to mainstream society and marginalizing Catholics, Jews, and recent immigrants.[55]

Given these deeply conflicting social forces, it is not surprising that the social feminist reform establishment of the Children's Bureau and its volunteer army sought to slant their own reform agenda in a more conservative way. During World War I they presented their goals of child labor laws, maternity and infancy health clinics, safe milk, and pensions for single mothers as measures necessary to safeguard youth's ability to defend America. This linking of children's health with national defense allowed the Children's Bureau, in the early 1920s, to consolidate its power within the federal government and to cement its alliances through state agencies and women's volunteer organizations.[56]

Lobbying on behalf of the women's reform agenda was professionalized in 1920 with the founding of the Women's Joint Congressional Committee (WJCC), which created a unified conduit for most of the major women's organizations. These included the General Federation of Women's Clubs, the National Consumers' League, the League of Women Voters, the National Trade Union League, the Mothers' Congress and the Parent-Teacher Association, the American Association of University Women, the Women's Christian Temperance Union, the Federation of Business and Professional Women, the Home Economics Association, and the National Council of Jewish Women.[57]

The inaugural triumph for this women's lobbying establishment was the passage of the Sheppard-Towner Maternity and Infancy Act in 1921. This first federally funded health-care act provided states with matching grants to set up prenatal and child health-care centers for pregnant women and infants. A Women's Bureau was also created within the Labor Department, parallel to the Children's Bureau, to oversee the welfare of women workers. The effect of these acts was to open up an expanded network of employment for women as public-health nurses and welfare managers.[58]

Not everyone was pleased with this emphasis on healthy maternity. The Women's Party saw it as setting women apart as a gender devoted primarily to motherhood,[59] while Margaret Sanger objected to the fact that birth control was not among the health services to be provided.[60] Doctors also complained that it intruded into their professional sphere. The Sheppard-Towner Act would be terminated in 1929, in part through the lobbying of the American Medical Association,[61] but by then the preventive health care promoted by it would be incorporated into regular medical practice. The female reform establishment, too, would suffer setbacks in the second half of the twenties as antiwelfare forces asserted themselves in Congress and throughout the nation, but it would blossom again in its final heyday in the early thirties, when much of its legislative agenda would be passed during the New Deal.

The profile of women's work and the family economy in the United States changed significantly between 1900 and 1930. By 1930, the percentage of women in the work force had increased to one in four, but even more important was the difference in the *types* of work women did. Fewer now worked at the lowest job levels, as domestics or laundresses; 75 percent of these jobs were filled by black women, as white immigrant women moved up but blacks were barred from better jobs.[62] A vast new field of female labor opened up as women found jobs doing clerical work, in sales, and as bank tellers and telephone and telegraph operators, as well as in new specialty positions, as hairdressers and cosmeticians.[63]

The number of women in the "female" professions of teaching, nursing, librarianship, and professionalized social work also increased, as did the percentage of women college teachers, which rose to 32.5 in 1930.[64] But at the same time, some prestigious male professions closed ranks against women, most notably medicine, which greatly upgraded its requirements and economic status while making it ever more difficult for women to obtain entrance to medical schools and appointments as interns. Six percent of doctors were women in 1910, a figure that declined to 4.4 percent by 1930.[65]

More white women now continued to work after marriage and regarded their work as a "career," not just a sojourn between school and marriage. Twenty-nine percent of women workers were married in 1930.[66] The 1920s had seen the opening salvos in the debate over whether women could combine family and careers. Black and poor ethnic women, of course, had long worked after marriage and motherhood at low-paid, arduous jobs, but that had occasioned no debate; the issue arose in the 1920s because of the new visibility of white women professionals who kept working after marriage. This was a change from the earlier pattern at the turn of the century, when "career women"—what few of them there were—had typically remained single.

An important impetus driving more women to work after marriage was the new domestic consumer economy. Having an automobile, electricity, a telephone, a refrigerator, a gas stove, a vacuum cleaner, an electric iron, and other appliances came to be seen as the norm for the "American way of life." Those who did not yet possess these amenities felt inadequate until they obtained them. Mass-media advertising and installment buying urged Americans to aspire to a standard of high consumption and to spend beyond their means. As economic wants increased, so, too, did the need for added income. With fewer working children, the wife became the primary second breadwinner in an expanded consumer economy focused on the family as the site of consumption.[67]

While domestic appliances lightened women's domestic workload, higher expectations for the household's life-style forced wives to put in as many hours on housework as their mothers, though the labor was not as arduous as before, when women had had to boil clothes and wash them by hand, cook on wood stoves, and can food for the winter. But less help from servants, daughters, or other family members meant that the wife usually did this work by herself.[68]

The small number of women professionals who juggled work and family brought an impassioned response from male experts, who arose to condemn the working mother in terms that recalled other experts' warnings, in 1900, against women's going to college, which they claimed would result in neurosis, physical breakdown, and sterility. Then, as we have noted, women were said to have less energy by nature, and to need what little they had for maternal functions. Higher education would cause this energy to go to their brains, depriving their wombs.[69]

By 1920, the focus of the argument had shifted to the child. Motherhood was said to be a "full-time job"; working mothers meant neglected children prone to delinquency, and homes broken by divorce.[70] Married women professionals replied by characterizing the stay-at-home wife as an underdeveloped neurotic. A child could thrive better, they insisted, with a mother who was more vigorous due to having outside interests, and routine housework and child care could as well be done by qualified hired help. Others, staking out the middle ground, spoke of the need to provide part-time work for women and infant and day-care centers run by professionals.[71]

A new generation of women social historians pointed out that women had always both worked and cared for children, but that when work, once centered in the home, had been severed from it, it had created a conflict between the two that had not existed before. Housework needed to change, as paid work had changed, in order to adjust the relations between home and work.[72] Feminists argued that women should not have to choose between marriage and work, any more than men had to. Both work and family were part of being a whole human being, and women had a right to such fullness of life, just as men did.[73]

THE DEPRESSION AND WOMEN'S WORK
This debate about the possibility and appropriateness of women's combining work with family for their own fulfillment had hardly be-

gun before it was derailed by the economic breakdown of the Great Depression. In the Depression's first years, U.S. industrial production fell by 50 percent, and unemployed men stood in long lines waiting for handouts. The working wife became the scapegoat of this economic collapse, as government, business, unions, and media all decried her as "selfishly" laboring for luxuries while depriving men of needed jobs.[74]

Banks, businesses, and school districts announced policies of not hiring married women or firing women who got married (this trend had already existed in the twenties, but it was elaborated and made public policy in the context of the Depression).[75] The federal government, in section 213 of the Economic Recovery Act of 1932, decreed that a married person could not hold a federal job if a spouse was also employed by the federal government. Although the language was neutral, it was understood to refer to wives, not husbands.[76]

In response to this concerted attack on the working wife, the women's network of organizations, including the National Women's Party, came together with something of its old unity in suffrage days. Appealing for a reversal of section 213, (which would, despite this effort, remain in force until the end of the decade),[77] the women's organizations and women leaders in the federal government, such as Grace Abbott, who now headed the Chidren's Bureau, argued that in fact women took few places away from men, since they worked mainly in sex-segregated jobs that men would not want. Moreover, women worked out of economic necessity to support their families, not for extra luxuries.

These arguments on behalf of the working wife were partly true: most working women did hold low-paid domestic or clerical jobs or jobs in the female professions, such as nursing, that men would not take. But the defensive logic of the women's establishment had the effect of confirming as normative, rather than questioning, the assumption that women should work only in low-paid, sex-segregated fields, and during economic crises when they lacked a male breadwinner.[78] To complicate the situation further, because of the nature of their work, women were less likely to be laid off than men; most of the job loss during the Depression was suffered by male workers in heavy industry and business.[79]

Although most men would not accept female-identified jobs such as nursing or typing, much less domestic work, other female professions were targeted for male employment, notably the upper levels of teaching, librarianship, and social work. These jobs had improved their professional qualifications and become better paid in the 1920s, making them more attractive to men (despite pay cuts during the Depression). Women had made up 85 percent of public school teachers in 1920, but the figure fell to 78 percent by 1940. Men also increased their presence as librarians (from 8.7 percent to 15.1 percent) and social workers (20 percent to 33 percent). Although still a minority in these professions, men generally took over the upper-level administrative jobs.[80] Male professions in which women were a minority meanwhile closed their ranks: in college teaching, for example, the proportion of women declined from 32.5 percent to 26.5 percent between 1930 and 1940.[81]

While women were being forced down in but not out of the general work force during the Depression, the New Deal administration under Franklin Roosevelt, particularly through the influence of his wife, Eleanor, contributed to the empowerment of the female network in federal and state bureaucracies. This network, shaped in the Progressive era and the settlement-house movement, became what Robyn Muncy has called "a female dominion in American reform".[82] In 1933, after intense lobbying by the women's organizations, Frances Perkins was appointed secretary of Labor, the first woman ever to run a government department.

Perkins had come from settlement-house work to head the New York Consumer League, and had been New York's Industrial Commissioner when Franklin Roosevelt was governor of the state.[83] The Labor Department under Perkins oversaw both the Women's Bureau, headed by Women's Trade Union veteran Mary Anderson, and the Children's Bureau, under Hull House graduate Grace Abbott. Other leaders of the women's reform network were elevated by Roosevelt to fill federal agencies concerned with the needs of women and children. Mississippi social worker Ellen Woodward and Bryn Mawr sociology professor Hilda Smith supervised women's projects administered by the Federal Emergency Relief Federation and the WPA (Works Progress Administration), respectively,[84] and Rose Schneiderman, a longtime women's union leader, was appointed to the National Relief Administration's labor advisory board.[85] These and other high-level women appointees shared a common background in women's organizations and social reform; many were graduates of elite women's colleges.[86]

Despite the visibility of a few individuals in the New Deal, and the prominence of Eleanor Roosevelt as their supporter and conduit of communication with the president,[87] women in general did not fare well in the administration's policies of relief and public works. The operating assumption of New Deal relief policies was that it was male, not female, unemployment that was the problem to be solved. Women were able to qualify for relief only if they could establish that they were the sole breadwinner of their family and had been so prior to their unemployment.[88]

Public works projects such as construction and forestry were aimed at employing men; women were included in only 16 percent of such projects, and then mostly to do sewing or cooking for male workers or families. A few thousand out-of-work female teachers and librarians got jobs in adult education, book repair, and cataloging.[89] Eleanor Roosevelt's efforts to duplicate the Civilian Conservation Corps for women eventually created eighty-six camps that employed sixty-four hundred women in forest conservation,[90] but that was an insignificant figure compared to the number of men employed by the Conservation Corps. Moreover, women received unpaid summer training or at best were paid fifty cents a week (compared to a dollar for men).

Wage differentials for men and women not only continued but were legalized under New Deal legislation. The National Industrial Recovery Act of 1933 enshrined minimum wages ranging from 14 percent to 30 percent lower for women than for men doing the same jobs.[91] Some work was excluded from minimum wage requirements, such as that described as "light and repetitive," a euphemism for female labor.[92] Agricultural and domestic work, an area in which poor black and Hispanic men and women predominated, was also exempt.

Many affected employers responded to minimum-wage legislation with speed-ups or a proliferation of piecework that women took home, thus bypassing minimum wage.[93] Again the female social reform network protested these injustices, but to little avail. Much of the same pattern of sex discrimination remained imbedded in the provisions for minimum wages and maximum hours contained in the Fair Labor Standards Act of 1938.[94] This time the women's protest was muted by the realization that some women benefited even from a lower minimum wage, since it still raised their pay above its previous level.

The passage of the Social Security Act of 1935 inscribed in law much of the social reform agenda that the women's network had been working on for thirty years. The act founded the American welfare state, making provisions for unemployment insurance, old-age pensions, and stipends for the handicapped and disabled. The Social Security Act also awarded stipends to dependent children, a provision that would be expanded into Aid for Dependent Children, given to mothers, in the act's 1939 revision.[95] Meanwhile, the Fair Labor Relations Act banned the employment of children under the age of sixteen, long a demand of women reformers.

These reforms nonetheless fell short of the women reformers' hopes. Many categories of female jobs were not covered by Social Security, particularly low-paid positions filled by black and Hispanic women. Employers of black and Mexican agricultural workers still paid men a pittance for a day's work that included the labor of their wives and children. Minimum-wage, maximum-hour, and child labor and schooling laws were ignored when it came to these types of female and child workers.[96] The working wife, for her part, was discriminated against in old-age pensions, receiving less for her own earned Social Security pension than she would as a widow of an insured husband.[97] Women reformers had also hoped in vain for the provision of universal health coverage.[98] Finally, the supervision of aid to dependent children was assigned to the Social Security Administration, not the Children's Bureau, thus dismantling this base of women's work in the federal government even as much of its reform agenda was achieved.[99]

In evaluating the pattern of women's work in relation to the family during the Depression, we can see that long-term trends discernable in the twenties continued. More married women worked in 1940 than in 1930—35 percent compared to 29 percent—and more of them were middle-class whites.[100] Women were forced down in, but not out of, the work force. Unemployed teachers and other whites took clerical or domestic jobs, in turn compelling black women to stand on street corners seeking occasional domestic work.[101] By the end of the Depression, more women were working than in 1930, but in more menial and sex-segregated areas, while the percentage of women professionals had declined.

Yet in spite of the argument that women worked only out of desperate need, the family consumer economy established in the 1920s continued to be the American norm. Middle-class wives took jobs not simply to put bread on the table but to ensure that their families could continue to drive cars and buy electrical appliances,[102] even as these same women reverted to mending clothes, canning food, and taking in boarders to "make ends meet." Both marriage and fertility rates (especially for whites) dipped,[103] but children stayed in school longer rather than going to work.[104] Birth control was at last legalized, making family planning more accessible.[105]

One major result of the Depression was that the feminist insistence of the twenties that women should both work and have families in order to be complete persons was silenced. Wives who hung on to jobs, and the women who defended them, now had to argue family necessity, not self-fulfillment. In this regard the legacy of the women reformers of the Progressive era in the New Deal was an ambivalent one. They were unsympathetic to the call for birth control and the combining of marriage with family for women, despite the trends in this direction. While they claimed a major role for women in government for the first time, that was the exception that largely reinforced the rule that defined motherhood as a "full-time" job precluding a career for most women. Thus the whole discussion of how family and work might be adjusted to one another, allowing real companionship between men and women in both work and family, was suppressed, not to be broached again until the 1960s.

CHAPTER 6

Changing Ideologies and Realities: 1940–1975

The thirty-five years between 1940 and 1975 saw dramatic shifts in competing ideologies about women's roles in American society. As the needs of war production in World War II took over the economy, women were urged to enter nontraditional professions—to drive tractors, make ships and airplanes, and replace absent men in almost every sphere of civilian life. Young women wearing overalls and carrying welding torches were exalted as new heroines. But by 1944 the welcome mat for women in heavy manufacturing was already being rolled up. American women were now told that it was their patriotic duty to leave their jobs to make room for the returning vets, and to devote themselves to home and family.

In the 1950s working women were seen as pathological deviants from a "proper" sexual destiny, and working mothers as the cause of divorce and juvenile delinquency. Then the mid-1960s brought a major revolt against the "feminine mystique" as a new feminist movement was born. Women challenged the prescriptions of psychologists and churchmen about their separate roles and natures, characterizing them as sexist ideologies designed to deny women their full humanity. Yet despite these conflicting social messages, American women continued steadily to increase their share of the work force, even in the 1950s. More married women worked, and women with younger children, driven less by changing ideological arguments than by the need for an income to support themselves and their families.

WOMEN'S WORK IN WORLD WAR II
The conversion to war production in the early 1940s did not initially favor women's employment; indeed, many women were laid off from

manufacturing jobs as factories retooled for military production by male workers. Women were not at first accepted into training programs for the new jobs.[1] But as the need for workers exceeded the supply of available men, government war propaganda urged women to enter defense work as a patriotic duty. Rosie the Riveter was glamorized as the "new woman." Making guns and planes was compared to sewing to argue that women were capable of such work.[2] Manufacturers broke down jobs into smaller components to make them easier for women.[3]

The needs of the war economy would bring six and a half million more women into the work force, drawing on older and married women as well as teens. Protective legislation prohibiting women from night work and overtime, as well as child labor laws, were now relaxed to expand the work force.[4] Some two million of these women went into war production, while a million more filled clerical roles in a burgeoning federal bureaucracy. Women also took all sorts of other jobs in the civilian economy as men vacated their posts for the military—doing everything from driving buses and taxicabs to playing in symphony orchestras that had not employed women musicians before.[5]

Women continued to fill traditional female jobs as well, doing clerical work, sales, and service. But the opening of new opportunities in fields formerly closed to them allowed many women to greatly improve their income. Despite the official image of the war worker as a previously unemployed wife or girlfriend who entered the work force temporarily to do her bit to win the war and bring her man home, more than half of such women had worked before the war. They now left female jobs for jobs in war production, often migrating to new regions of the country, because the pay was much higher, though most were no doubt also inspired by the thought of contributing to the war effort.[6]

Many women who entered new work areas experienced hostility and harassment from male workers, though some found mentors willing to help and encourage them.[7] Labor leaders were at best ambivalent defenders of the new women workers, reluctant to promote equal pay for women unless pay levels for men were directly involved. Where jobs were reclassified as separate, "female" work, lesser pay was still the rule. Women were seldom promoted to leadership roles in the unions themselves, even though they flocked to become union members.[8]

Although hours were long and conditions often difficult, many women war workers gained new self-confidence through their experiences. They proved to others and to themselves that they could do work once thought to be beyond women's capacity. They also coped with crowded housing, a lack of transportation, and new environments in which family networks were absent. They found a new sense of competence and autonomy that would transform their lives. Even when forced out of their new jobs at the end of the war to return to more traditional female employment and family life, many eventually translated their expanded self-confidence into further education and innovative careers beyond what they might otherwise have pursued. A former shipbuilder could imagine becoming an architect, or a waitress aspire to own a restaurant.[9]

More than half of the wartime female work force was married, and a third were over thirty-five. Almost three million of them had children under fourteen.[10] Working mothers had to reconcile long work hours with the deprivations of war conditions: rationing, shortages of consumer goods, long shopping lines, double school shifts, the lack of gasoline for cars.[11] Although the government would eventually recognize the need to help working mothers by subsidizing day-care centers, these were still few, inconvenient, and sometimes woefully inadequate. Less than 10 percent of working women found child care through such centers;[12] most mothers either relied on relatives or paid neighbors to care for their children while they worked.

Those women who did not take paid jobs were called into volunteer war work. They sold war bonds, saved valuable scrap material, cultivated victory gardens, and served in the Red Cross or as air-raid wardens, all the while coping with shortages and other war difficulties and worrying about their absent male relatives. Although only one in eight American men actually saw combat, half of those who did would be killed or injured. Three hundred fifty thousand women also served in the armed forces or as military nurses, and some were injured or killed in combat zones, though none was permitted to participate in combat.[13]

Black women continued to experience racial discrimination in employment. Only a handful were allowed into segregated female military units, and few found well-paid war work. Most were hired by defense factories to do janitorial work, seldom to weld planes or ships.[14] Black men made more gains in employment in the civilian economy and in segregated military units, and their improved income actually allowed some black wives to stay home and care for their children rather than working.[15] A few black women made inroads into white-collar female work, as telephone operators or in clerical or sales jobs, again usually under segregated conditions. Yet even these modest improvements enabled many black women to leave the lowest-paid work. The proportion of black women working in agriculture dropped to 8 percent and in domestic service to less than 48 percent at the end of World War II, down from 70 percent in 1940.[16]

The war years also saw major mobilizations of black Americans against racial discrimination. A. Philip Randolph's threat to march on Washington in January 1941 persuaded President Roosevelt to sign Executive Order 8802, banning racial discrimination in the defense industry. Black leaders did not miss the opportunity to point out that the United States needed to win a victory for democracy at home as well as abroad by making black Americans equal citizens.[17] Although this argument had little effect during the war (the military would be desegregated only in 1948), the new consciousness and organizing of the forties would bear fruit in the civil-rights movement of the next decade.

Not all American minorities made gains during the war. Japanese Americans suffered a devastating loss of their homes and property when Roosevelt signed Executive Order 9066, authorizing the confinement of Japanese Americans in internment camps. A hundred and ten thousand of them, including entire families, were forced to leave their homes and businesses to live in cold, crowded barracks in camps surrounded by barbed wire and patrolled armed guards.[18]

Even though American women were proving their capacity to meet new demands, government, corporate, and union leaders had no intention of permitting a lasting change in gender relations in American society. War propaganda made it clear that women were doing men's jobs strictly "for the duration." As soon as the war was won and the veterans returned, it would be women's duty to vacate their new jobs and return to homemaking, preferably adopting a redoubled attitude of feminine submissiveness to nurture the male battered by the war experience and ease him back into homelife.[19]

Already by V-E Day, government contracts for war production had been canceled and female workers assembled and dismissed. Few women would be rehired when the factories retooled or got new contracts, even though some would seek to protest through their unions.[20] Contrary to the official propaganda that women were eager to quit working and start families, some 75 percent declared that they wanted to continue to work, and in their present jobs.[21] About two million women were laid off, and many others were surely happy to greet a returning husband and stay home; but 80 percent of women kept on working, most of them forced to revert to lower-paying female jobs. Some who left work to start families went back when their children were older. The percentage of the work force that was female dropped briefly, but by the end of the fifties it would rise again, to 35 percent, almost equaling the wartime high. The ratio of female to male wages, however, would steadily decrease. By the midsixties, women's wages would average only 58 percent of men's, and in fields with a high concentration of women, such as sales, women would make only 40 percent as much as men.[22]

THE FAMILY IDEOLOGY OF THE 1950S

The population of working women was no longer celebrated in the 1950s as it had been during the war. The reigning social propaganda pictured the suburban housewife and full-time mother as the normative American woman. Those women who departed from this norm through paid employment were decried as the "lost sex"—unhappy, maladjusted, and in need of therapy to reconcile them to their biological destiny of motherhood and submission to their husbands.[23] Freudian psychologists labeled women who sought independence as suffering from "penis envy."[24] Male child-raising experts such as Dr. Spock rejected the strict Watsonian time schedules of the 1930s in favor of a new permissiveness that tied mothers all the more closely to a twenty-four-hour regimen of response to their children's needs.[25] This intensified demand for attention to children was coupled with messages of fear and guilt. Either underattentiveness or overprotectiveness could result in weak, neurotic offspring, especially boys, responsibility for which defects lay squarely and exclusively on the mothers' shoulders. Psychiatrists such as Edward Strecker blamed maternal overprotectiveness for the huge number of American males (1.6 million of them) rejected as unfit by the military during World War II.[26]

The fifties brought a wave of intensive propaganda promoting women's exclusive devotion to domesticity. The American popular media, as well as social scientists, told women that their "natures" disposed them to feminine submission, the cultivation of housewifery, and auxiliary existence through their husbands and (male) children. Nonconformity to these roles threatened their own wellbeing and that of their families and society. This campaign was reinforced by the domestic repercussions of the Cold War, when paranoid fear of "communist infiltration" cast suspicion on anyone who favored social reforms in American society.[27] The spectacle of labor and political leaders being dragged before the House Un-American Activities Committee to answer for their possible Communist leanings sent out ripples of fear that touched even the most modest levels of society.*

The network of women's organizations from the suffrage days, including the Women's Bureau of the Department of Labor, the American Association of University Women, the Business and Professional Women's Clubs, the Women's Trade Union League, and various associations of Negro, Jewish, and Catholic women, survived into the fifties, but their members were now mostly elderly. The National Women's Party continued to lobby Congressmen year after year for passage of the Equal Rights Amendment, making some progress in the forties and fifties toward its endorsement by the two major political parties. Newly founded equal-rights groups, including a number of state committees as well as the Catholic Saint Joan's Society, rallied to the cause.

This work for women's rights would bear fruit in the revived feminist movement of the sixties, but in the fifties it was viewed as the ramblings of a bunch of eccentric old ladies from a bygone era.[29] Furthermore, most such groups remained encapsulated in a narrow sector of the white upper middle class and made only token efforts to reach out to women in the labor movement or to blacks.[30] Their existence was unknown to Betty Friedan, for example, when she began to question the suburban dream of domesticity in the late 1950s.

College campuses in the decade after the war would see a flood of male veterans pursuing higher education under the GI Bill, often

---

* Just how far things went may be illustrated by a personal anecdote: in 1953, when I was seventeen and the editor of my high school newspaper in La Jolla, California, a local retired Navy officer accused me and my staff of being "Communists" because of the occasionally critical tone of our columns and editorials (I had written an opinion piece criticizing the commercialization of Christmas!).[28]

with a young wife and baby lodged in nearby married-student housing. Women's share of college diplomas fell to 25 percent, as men greatly increased their presence on campuses.[31] From 1940 to 1960, women's numbers declined in medical schools (from 12 percent to 5 percent), in science and engineering (from 21 percent to 10 percent), and in college teaching (27.7 percent to 24.5 percent).[32] Prominent educators such as Lynn White, president of Mills College, advocated separate education for women to prepare them for housewifery and motherhood.[33] Although few colleges followed this prescription formally, in effect women were steered by high school and college counselors into cultural enrichment and secretarial skills rather than the rigorous academic work, particularly in the sciences, that would lead to more prestigious careers.[34]

In the war years and into the fifties the median marriage age fell to twenty for women (twenty-two for men),[35] the lowest in American history, while the birth rate rose through the popularity of the three- and four-child family. Early marriage and high fertility compensated not only for the war years but also for the Depression, when many Americans had put off marriage and childbearing due to poor economic prospects.[36] For their part, educated women were now much more likely to marry and have children than at the turn of the century, when the smaller cohort of college graduates had often remained single and pursued careers in social work and teaching. Indeed, being single and women's living together were seen as pathological states in the fifties, in contrast to the Victorian era, when they had enjoyed an accepted niche in society.[37]

The divorce level also continued to rise in American society, particularly after the war, when many hasty wartime marriages unraveled as vets returned to find the women they had married grown accustomed to autonomy. One fourth of marriages ended in divorce in 1945, and that ratio persisted through the 1950s. By 1960 there were 2.2 divorces for every 8.5 marriages.[38] The enthusiasm for marriage was unabated, however, and most young divorcés quickly remarried, though women with children had less chance of remarrying than men. Fifteen percent of all American women with children were single heads of households, with the figure more than double for black women what it was for white (17.6 percent of black women compared to 8.5 percent of white women).[39]

The boom economy brought far more American families into the middle class, and the GI Bill assured millions of the dream of home-ownership. Although in the mid-1950s a third of Americans remained at or below the poverty line, that represented a major improvement over the thirties, when about half had been poor.[40] Televisions and other household appliances seemed within every family's reach, though for many families what made such middle-class amenities affordable was the employment of the wife. Women who bore three children in their early and middle twenties were looking for jobs by their midthirties, but their truncated education and interrupted work experience ensured that the jobs they found were primarily in low-paid, female-identified areas. Women as college professors sank to 19 percent by 1960, down from 32 percent in 1930. In 1960 62 percent of working women were in sales or clerical and service work, while only 12.4 percent worked in professional or technical fields.[41]

The dominant culture of enforced domesticity for women and repression of social criticism, combined with relatively high prosperity for more Americans, make the fifties look like an era of exemplary wellbeing and social consensus to those who now regard the decade with nostalgia. But the appearance was deceptive. In the 1960s social scientist Michael Harrington would uncover the "other America," the lower third that remained shut out of consumer affluence.[42] Meanwhile, the continuation of pervasive racism and segregation of black Americans was beginning to be challenged by an awakened civil-rights movement. White women, too, encapsulated in their suburban families or unnoticed as they toiled in low-paying jobs, were about to discover their discontent.

THE CIVIL RIGHTS MOVEMENT
Despite the repressive atmosphere created by McCarthyism, the civil-rights movement slowly grew in the fifties to expand into a national crusade by the early sixties. A diversity of other liberation movements would explode later in the decade: a new feminist movement, anti-poverty and welfare campaigns, the push for gay and lesbian rights, and an awakening critique of racism by other ethnic groups, such as Native Americans and Hispanics, modeling their quest on the ideology and gains of the Negro-led civil-rights movement. This criticism would eventually evolve from calls for reform into revolutionary demands for the radical transformation of American society and, in the

case of the antiwar movement, withdrawal from military intervention and imperialism in U.S. foreign policy.

A new stage in the struggle against racism was triggered by the
May 17, 1954, decision of the U.S. Supreme Court in *Brown vs. Board
of Education*, outlawing school segregation as inherently unequal.
While many school boards made gestures of compliance, white leaders in the deep South dug in their heels and prepared for organized resistance. By July of the same year, the first White Citizens' Council
had been formed in Mississippi, and others soon followed. White
groups, seeing themselves as protecting southern culture against a second northern invasion, resorted to terrorist tactics, lynching and
shooting blacks who dared to lift their heads. In August of 1955 the
lynching of fourteen-year-old Emmett Till outraged blacks across
the nation.[43]

That December, Rosa Parks refused to go to the back of the bus in
Montgomery, Alabama, sparking a yearlong bus boycott that would
end bus segregation in that city.[44] The fight to integrate schools finally
forced President Eisenhower to protect blacks from violent white
mobs by sending federal troops to Little Rock, Arkansas, in September of 1957.[45] That the black civil-rights leadership was strongly
rooted in the black church was signaled by the establishment that year
of the Southern Christian Leadership Conference (SCLC).[46]

White southern students were likewise drawn into the struggle
through progressive segments of their own churches, such as the
Methodist Student Movement.[47] In 1960 the student wing grew
more militant with the organization of lunch-counter sit-ins that began in Greensboro, North Carolina, and spread across the South.[48] In
April of that year young activists founded the Student Nonviolent
Coordinating Committee (SNCC) to set a standard of militant confrontation vis à vis the older clergy leaders in the National Association
for the Advancement of Colored People (NAACP) and SCLC.[49]

Although the new president, John F. Kennedy, was supportive of
an active role for the federal government in civil rights, white southern violence only escalated, with the burning of the buses of freedom
riders, beatings, shootings, and jailings of civil-rights workers who
sought to integrate schools and register voters. In August 1963 Martin
Luther King Jr. drew hundreds of thousands to a march on Washington, where his "I have a dream" speech galvanized the nation.[50] Presi-

dent Kennedy had made a major speech of his own endorsing civil rights in June of the same year, and called on Congress to pass a comprehensive civil-rights act.[51] This would occur in 1964, after Kennedy's assassination.

Despite the participation of black women and an increasing number of white women, both southerners and northerners who went south, in movements such as SNCC in the early sixties, issues of sexism were never addressed. An implicit masculinism pervaded the civil-rights movement and its antiwar counterpart, Students for a Democratic Society (SDS, founded in 1959). Biased by popular views of black society as "matriarchal" due to poverty and the repression of the black male, the civil-rights movement was seen as restoring the masculine dignity of the black man castrated (both literally and psychosocially) by white racism.

These views made black women feel it was their first job to support black males and empower the black community as a whole, not to be concerned with "women's" issues. White women, traditionally the symbols of sexual untouchability in whose name black men had been lynched, were doubly problematic at the intersection of race and gender, though northern white women came into this situation with scant comprehension of its history. White women involved in the movement admired the strong black women as role models of empowerment, and felt nurtured by the older blacks who were the intrepid "mothers" of the movement.

But white women, especially those from the North, had little understanding of how their own white-femaleness functioned as a symbol of feminine beauty and conquest for black men, or how this infuriated black women, especially younger ones. This in turn made it difficult for black women to trust white women enough to try to articulate these conflicts for them. The sexual component of race relations was both explosive and silenced; both the inferiorization and the sexual use of women in the movement were raw nerves that neither black nor white women dared discuss in the early sixties.[52]

THE RISE OF LIBERAL FEMINISM

A clearer articulation of injustice to all women was meanwhile beginning to be developed in a very difference locus: the federal government. The leaders of the network of women's organizations in and around the federal government expected certain token female appointments from the president, but Kennedy, himself a "macho" Irishman, failed to make any such appointments. Instead, as a way to "pay his dues" to his female supporters, he established, in 1961, a Commission on the Status of Women, to be led by Esther Peterson, a labor activist whose position as head of the Women's Bureau was thus elevated to a higher level of decision making (Eleanor Roosevelt was named the committee's honorary chair).[53]

The Equal Pay Act of 1963 promoted equal pay for women working in the same jobs as men, though to little immediate effect for most women due to the sex segregation of the labor force.[54] Meanwhile, the president's commission was gathering data on the status of women in federal and private employment as well as on protective labor laws, women's education and financial security, and child care. Its report, submitted in October 1963, was moderate, calling for greater equity in the workplace for women, along with benefits that would help them balance work and family roles, such as maternity leaves, tax deductions for child care, and financial support for education and job training.[55] The ERA was nowhere mentioned. Peterson, in the tradition of the labor movement and the Women's Bureau, was opposed to the amendment and hoped to circumvent it through piecemeal reform.[56]

After Kennedy's death, the commission ensured that its work would continue by persuading President Johnson to appoint both a Citizens' Advisory Council and an Interdepartmental Committee on the Status of Women, which were to oversee the implementation of the commission's recommendations. Meanwhile, encouraged by the work of the presidential commission, the states began to form their own such commissions on the status of women, and soon all fifty states had them, all gathering information on women's status and recommending reforms. This meant that there was a growing recognition of the inequity of women's actual economic, legal, and social situations in American society and a network of activists in and around government to pursue legal reforms on these issues.[57]

Then, in 1964, a legislative "accident" suddenly put the question of women's equality at the center of federal reform. During the debate on the Civil Rights Act, intended to put the power of the federal government behind the demands of blacks for economic and political equality, Howard Smith, a conservative Virginian who chaired the

House Rules Committee and was personally opposed to the act, proposed the addition of the word *sex* to Title VII, which would ban racial discrimination in employment. Although this was widely viewed as a "joke" designed to scuttle the whole act, Smith was himself a longtime supporter of the ERA and had been influenced by the National Women's Party's continual lobbying for the addition of the word *sex* to any bill advocating equality between males, on the theory that (white) women should also be included.[58]

Whatever Smith's real motivation, some congresswomen and other advocates, such as Pauli Murray, a black lawyer on the president's commission, lobbied vigorously for the amendment to Title VII.[59] The Civil Rights Act was passed with its inclusion. However, the Equal Employment Opportunity Commission (EEOC), appointed to oversee the enforcement of Title VII, had no intention of following up on cases of sex discrimination, which it regarded as an inappropriate extension of its charter—even though such cases comprised the majority of the complaints pouring into the EEOC's offices.[60]

The conflict came to a head in June of 1966 at the third annual meeting of the state commissions on the status of women in Washington. Convinced that energetic enforcement of new legislation on behalf of women would not take place without an outside women's movement (comparable to the NAACP) pressing for it, women in government circles met with Betty Friedan, whose 1963 book, *The Feminine Mystique,* had given her a national platform as a spokesperson for women. The result was a decision to form a National Organization for Women (NOW) to serve as the needed outside advocate. It was Friedan who insisted on the word *for* in the name (instead of *of*), since she saw it as a movement of women *and men* working for women's equality.[61]

The inaugural meeting of NOW took place in October 1966, with Betty Friedan as first president and Richard Graham, an activist for women's rights on the EEOC, as one of the vice presidents. The leadership reflected elite white professional circles in higher education, labor, government, and business; church women were also supporters of NOW from the beginning, and the first board included two nuns.[62] Yet the organization's advocacy of redress of sex discrimination in employment reached beyond the elite to all classes.

NOW's first test case was on behalf of airline stewardesses forced to give up their jobs upon marrying or when they turned thirty-five. Pressure was also brought to bear on the EEOC to reverse its decision allowing employers to publish sex-segregated newspaper advertisements for employment. NOW's leaders joined their voices with those of other women's advocates to insist that President Johnson amend Executive Order 11246 (of September 1965) to add the word *sex* to the phrase "race, creed, color and national origin" in calling for affirmative action. This Johnson did in October 1967, in effect confirming the inclusion of sex discrimination on the same basis as race discrimination in government policy.[63]

From the beginning, Friedan had a more radical vision than that of the Women's Commission. She wanted to do more than merely ameliorate the stresses of women between home and job while maintaining the basic sex segregation of those spheres; it was her goal to transform such relationships to reflect full equality. Men and women needed to be equal partners in child raising as well as in the paid labor force, without any sexual discrimination between male and female jobs. To achieve this, the relations of home and work must be adjusted to allow equal participation of both genders in both areas. This meant that NOW must concern itself with other issues such as women's reproductive rights, including the legalization of abortion, and endorsement of the ERA.

The NOW Bill of Rights for Women, announced by Friedan in her first presidential address in 1967, spelled out the organization's agenda: 1) passage of the equal-rights amendment to the Constitution; 2) enforcement of all laws banning sex discrimination in employment; 3) maternity-leave rights in employment and Social Security benefits; 4) tax deductions for home and child-care expenses for working parents; 5) child-care facilities funded by law on the same basis as public schools; 6) equal and unsegregated education, including loans and fellowships; 7) job training opportunities, housing, and family allowances for women in poverty, without prejudicing the decision of either parent to stay home to care for his or her children; 8) the right of women to control their reproductive lives by removing from the penal code laws restricting contraception and abortion.[64]

Some more conservative women reacted against the broadening of NOW's agenda by leaving to form their own organizations. One of these was the Women's Equity Action League (WEAL), which focused on the enforcement of existing laws and the passage of new ones to ensure equity in education and employment of women. Among its major actions was a suit against three hundred colleges and universities for sex discrimination in such areas as sex quotas and equal scholarships for women students, as well as equal hiring and pay for women employees, both clerical staff and faculty. WEAL would later undertake similar suits against banks and city governments.[65]

Another early group that spun off NOW was the National Women's Political Caucus (NWPC), led by Representatives Bella Abzug and Shirley Chisholm and activists Betty Friedan and Gloria Steinem, who sought to put women's issues on the agendas of state and national political parties and to elect women candidates from both major parties.[66] Women's caucuses on academic life, federal employment, athletics, and professions were founded between 1967 and 1971, spreading feminist advocacy to mainline institutions. Women's studies as an academic discipline was born in the early seventies, giving rise to national associations for women's studies and journals such as *Feminist Studies* (1972), *Quest* (1973), and *Signs* (1975).[67]

THE NEW LEFT, WOMEN'S LIBERATION, AND GAYS

The proliferation of feminist concerns in established institutions was soon to be matched and challenged by more radical women's liberation movements arising from a younger generation of women activists from the SNCC and SDS and the campus and urban New Left movements. Just as NOW had been created in response to the alternate promotion and betrayal of women's issues by the federal government, so radical feminism had its beginnings in the heady advocacy of social liberation and the consequent betrayal of women by the New Left. This experience of betrayal was rooted in a combination of the masculine bravado typical of male leaders of the SNCC and SDS and their appropriation of the ideology of sexual revolution as an integral part of social liberation.

Sexual revolution had not been on the agenda of either the older civil-rights movement in the South, under its clergy leaders, or the old Left, which to some extent mentored the socialism of the New Left. Both of those movements, rooted in the black church in the one case and in immigrant working-class labor movements in the other, had conservative attitudes about personal life-style. Demonstrators were to present their grievances in racial and economic arenas while adopting respectability in their dress and personal decorum, in order not to distract from the serious issues at hand. When northern students flocked to the South to work in the civil-rights movement wearing the "scruffy" clothes of the counterculture, they were sternly admonished by southern black leaders, who ordered them to clean up and wear neat clothes, particularly in public actions.[68] What for whites was a personal style of disaffiliation with class privilege was for blacks simply an expression of disrespect for hard-won respectability.

Sexual revolution in American culture had had its first fling in the "Roaring Twenties," only to go underground during the Depression and World War II. By the late fifties, the affluence of suburban America was eroding the work ethic and suggesting new forms of sexual experimentation such as "wife swapping." The "beatniks" flaunted their revolt against middle-class conformity, and writers such as Herbert Marcuse merged Freud with Marx to claim that instinctual and social liberation went hand in hand. These ideas were in turn appropriated by the new youth culture of the sixties, itself made up of the children of white middle-class affluence.[69]

Young women who joined the SNCC and SDS were, by the mid-sixties, confronted by a complex message of social and sexual revolt. They should be ready to live in poverty, working night and day as volunteers doing the typing and cooking for a movement that urged them to "put their bodies on the line" against racists and militarists, while also being willing to be sexually accessible to males of the movement, thus proving that they were not "uptight." Women sought to show their dedication to the "revolution" by giving in to the demands of male leaders for both their manual and their sexual services. Only slowly and tentatively did a few women begin to question these demands as exploitative; when they did so, they were met by ridicule and verbal violence on the part of leftist men.

In November 1964 several white female SNCC workers wrote a modest "position paper on women in the movement," protesting their lack of leadership positions, only to be dismissed by Stokely Carmichael's joking retort that "the only position for women in the movement is prone."[70] More such wounding experiences followed. Efforts to present papers on women's issues at gatherings were greeted with hoots and obscene catcalls such as "Take her off the stage and fuck her." Women felt further excluded as draft resistance became the key expression of revolutionary dissent: only men could resist the draft, while women's duty was to sexually reward such male heroes by "saying yes to men who say no."[71]

Athough women of the Left were attracted by the notion of claimng their own sexual feelings, they were hurt by a style of impersonal male sexuality that lacked not only commitment but emotional involvement and care. The men of the Left themselves purported to reject the impersonality of the "organization man" in favor of the sensitivity and poetic feeling associated with the "feminine," but this pose was belied by their crude treatment of sexual relations with women. By 1968 these pent-up feelings finally broke through as women withdrew from male-led movements into their own "rap groups" where they could "speak bitterness" about their experiences of sexism.[72]

The consciousness-raising group became a key tool for these new women's groups. The slogan "The personal is political" expressed the belief that the very uncovering and sharing of personal experiences of sexism could be radicalizing, birthing a joint "analysis" of the system of sexual domination that oppressed women, and bonding such women together as a community.[73] Consciousness-raising sessions absorbed much of the energy of such groups, though some also engaged in street theater, dressing as witches to hex the stock exchange or crowning a sheep "Miss America" to protest the sexual objectification of women in beauty pageants (an event that the news media exploited to dub feminists as "bra burners," though no bras were actually burned).[74]

Soon the women's liberation groups, as they came to be called, were seeking larger outlets. They wrote newletters to communicate their ideas to others and founded bookstores, publishing houses, health clinics, alternative schools, and day-care centers. Women's music expressing women's liberation was written and promoted through music stores, new record companies, and women's music festivals.[75] Following the ideology of the New Left, these women's liberation groups rejected hierarchy and attempted radically egalitarian forms of organization, an effort that sometimes led to the backstabbing of any woman seen as becoming too much of a "star."[76]

Many of these projects replicated the traditional women's work of volunteer services, yet women's liberation groups imagined them to be new and radical through rhetoric and organizing style and a belief that they were founding an alternative political and economic sphere liberated from dominant male institutions. This ideology of disaffiliation also caused them to spurn the sort of political and legal reforms that were the focus of the liberal feminists of NOW and WEAL. Trying to elect women to Congress was seen as the epitome of "cooptation." Such leftist rejection of participation in the political process would eventually have the effect of promoting the election of conservatives, particularly as antifeminists of the Right began to recognize the possibility of organizing their constituencies for block voting.

By 1970, discussion of lesbian sexual preference was growing in leftist feminist circles. Many women's liberation groups were disposed to affirm lesbians who "came out" to their consciousness-raising comrades, due to both their socialization in and their feelings of abuse by the culture of male leftist sexual revolution. Female-female love held the promise of allowing women to embrace their sexuality apart from male sexual exploitation.

Following the tendency of New Left culture to take every critical insight to its logical extreme as its highest and best meaning, some lesbian feminists were soon claiming that only lesbians were *real* feminists. The ultimate way to separate oneself from all expressions of male domination was to reject "sleeping with the enemy." Every woman was said to be a potential lesbian and should explore sex with women in order to be fully "women-identified." Feminist projects and centers now became more likely to be lesbian-identified, with some questioning the right of heterosexual women even to participate, and excluding their male children. In Jill Johnson's landmark book *Lesbian Nation* (1973), feminist separatist nationalism, modeled after black nationalism, imagined women's organizing a separate world for themselves alone.[77]

If these developments alienated many liberal women who considered themselves feminists, they also displeased some lesbians. Lesbians had their own movement history distinct from that of NOW and the New Left, neither of which groups had welcomed them. Both gay men and lesbian women had organized their own support groups in the 1950s, Mattachine and the Daughters of Bilitis. Gay males now grew more openly militant, in late June and early July 1969 engaging in five days of rioting to protest police raids on Stonewall, a gay bar in New York. The Stonewall Rebellion became a landmark event for this new militancy. Lesbian women, for their part, mostly did not have a parallel bar scene and felt alienated by the male elitism and impersonal sexuality of the gay movement. Yet while many lesbians had strong ties to men in the gay community, they were also close to heterosexual men and women in their own families and in their workplaces, and did not feel they needed to withdraw from the rest of humanity to affirm their identities, like the feminist separatists.[78]

Some lesbians looked to the feminist movement for a welcoming community, but in 1969 Betty Friedan was hostile to what she called the "lavender menace," fearful of the tarring of feminism as lesbianism.[79] This reservation was soon swept away, however, by the acceptance of lesbianism among younger and more radical feminists. By 1971 NOW had made a turnabout and voted to add support for lesbian rights to its agenda of women's rights.

The NOW resolution saw antilesbian bias as linked to hostility to women's autonomy: "Because she defines herself independently of men, the lesbian is considered unnatural, incomplete, not quite a woman—as though the essence of womanhood was to be identified with men." While not acceding to lesbian separatism as normative for feminism, the resolution affirmed that "a woman's right to her own person includes the right to define and express her own sexuality and choose her own lifestyle."[80]

MAINSTREAMING FEMINISM: GOVERNMENT AND THE CHURCHES

By 1972 some of the stresses of factionalism and radical political correctness that had split segments of feminism began to ease. Radical feminists began to realize that despite their ultimate commitment to "overthrow patriarchy," running women's centers on an impoverished volunteer basis was burning them out while not really changing the "system," and that incremental reforms might have their place. The success of legal actions brought by groups such as WEAL to expand opportunities for women in universities and other institutions won their respect. A new recognition of the strength in diversity grew: different styles of feminism in different subcultures could reach far more women than a uniform ideology and program. Black feminists, too, were beginning to articulate their own distinct context for and perspective on feminism.[81]

This growing sense of solidarity in diversity was facilitated by the expansion, across the country, of local NOW chapters that were largely independent of the national organization. These chapters adopted much of the style of egalitarian leadership and consciousness raising of the women's liberation groups, while still working for legal reforms. National NOW's acceptance of more shared leadership and of the usefulness of consciousness raising as a means of socializing new recruits to feminism, as well as its moderate endorsement of lesbian rights, helped heal some of the old conflicts.[82]

The period from 1971 to 1973 would see major victories for feminism. The Ninety-second Congress, of 1971–72, prodded by congressional feminists such as Bella Abzug, passed an array of women's rights laws, including the Equal Employment Opportunity Act of 1972 and the Comprehensive Health Manpower Training and Nursing Training Acts of 1971, prohibiting sex discrimination in all training aspects of health-profession programs. The Revenue Act of 1971 allowed parents with a combined annual income of up to eighteen thousand dollars to deduct child-care costs of up to four hundred dollars a month from their federal taxes. Title IX of the Educational Amendment Act barred sex discrimination in all educational institutions that received federal funding.

Congress also passed the Child Development Act, which would have provided free day care for families of four with an income of less than $4,300 and aid on a sliding scale for families with higher incomes, but the bill was vetoed by President Nixon, who claimed it would "weaken" the family. The most stunning victory of all was the passage of the Equal Rights Amendment by the House and then the Senate. Several other laws passed by this Congress also contained sections prohibiting sex discrimination.[83]

The next year, 1973, brought the Supreme Court ruling that abortion was legal in the first two trimesters. The landmark *Roe vs. Wade* suit had been filed not by NOW but by women lawyers working independently, not wishing to harden the resistance to their cause by identifying the issue with feminism.[84] Nonetheless, the decision was greeted by NOW and feminists groups generally as a major victory.

In the late sixties the main news media had treated feminism with derision, but that all changed in the first months of 1970 when national publications such as *Time* and *Newsweek*, as well as NBC and CBS, ran respectful major stories on it.[85] Feminism was now on the map as a significant phenomenon in American society. Mainstream politicians and opinion makers were surprised by its successes and its broad influence. Conservatives, meanwhile, were caught off guard by the passage of the ERA after a fruitless fifty-year struggle, and by the legalization of abortion in the *Roe vs. Wade* decision.

These feminist victories, however, soon mobilized political and religious conservatives. By 1973 American society's brief honeymoon with feminism was waning, as reactionary leaders such as Phyllis Schlafly fought to stop the ERA from being ratified by the states. Schlafly's campaign was backed by far-Right groups such as the John Birch Society, Pro-America Incorporated, the Christian Crusade, and Young Americans for Freedom.[86] The linking of feminism with abortion and lesbianism would, as moderate feminist leaders had feared, fuel a right-wing antifeminist backlash that would only grow in subsequent years.

The backlash against feminism would not just pit Christian conservatives against "secular humanists" or "atheistic Communists," but would set Right against Left within the churches themselves. Just as the first wave of feminism in the nineteenth century had risen out of the abolition movement, which was based in large part in the churches, so the second wave of feminism was partly rooted in the church-supported civil-rights and peace movements. Many women who went through civil rights and the New Left to women's liberation and "came out" as lesbians had begun their journeys in church youth groups and campus chaplaincies, and had never entirely cut their ties to their Christian identity.

Also, like their nineteenth-century predecessors the Grimké sisters and Lucretia Mott, many feminists with roots in the church understood their embrace of women's liberation as a fuller expression of a liberationist Christianity. Translating their commitment to women into a movement devoted to achieving equality in the church as well as in society, they helped to develop a new, feminist theology. They were inspired in this by the great preachers of the civil-rights movement, such as Martin Luther King Jr., who had identified the American "dream" of equality with the call to justice of Jesus and the prophets.

Christian seminaries in the sixties were filled with young men of the Left, many of whom had entered to avoid the draft but ended by channeling their seminary training into a ministry of social justice.

Some seminary professors were also transformed by their involvement in civil-rights, peace, and urban ministry work, and wrote theologies for a church committed to these causes. Black theologians such as James Cone meanwhile began shaping a black theology in response to urban riots and the cry of "black power."[87] Liberation theologies were also being written in Latin America in the late sixties, and their texts and authors were making their way to North American audiences in churches and seminaries.

Yet even these male mentors in a Christianity of the Left ignored gender and were not initially supportive when, inspired by their work, women asked about "women's position in the movement." Remnants of Christian socialism from the Social Gospel movement of the twenties and thirties lingered in the traditions of many ministers and theologians, who thereby assumed that justice for the "workers" would mean women's retirement from work for "full-time" housewifery. The neo-orthodoxy that reigned in theological training in the sixties silenced this Social Gospel tradition, but that did not preclude it from also being hostile to feminism.[88]

The women of the sixties who began to synthesize feminism and a liberationist Christianity thus did so largely on their own. They were unaware of the existence of foremothers who had created feminist theological thinking in earlier centuries, such as Margaret Fell, cofounder of the Society of Friends, in the seventeenth-century, or the Grimké sisters, Lucretia Mott, and Elizabeth Cady Stanton in the nineteenth. The recovery of such heritages of feminist theology would come about through a new wave of women's studies in historical theology, birthed through the women's movement in the churches in the 1970s.[89]

Yet these questions of feminism in the church were being raised at precisely the moment when the churches themselves were relaxing their historical ban against the ordination of women, and more and more women were entering theological schools to train for the ministry. A few liberal denominations had begun to ordain women in the nineteenth century as part of the earlier wave of feminism, among them the Congregationalists, Unitarians, Universalists, and Methodist Protestants. Mainline Protestants, in contrast, had rejected women's ordination in the 1880s and instead invented a deaconess order to satisfy the urge of women for official ministry.

This situation started to change in the 1950s. In Europe, theologically educated women had been granted pastoral ministries during World War II, when most of the male pastors were in the trenches. After the war, some of these women had declined to "go home" and agitated for full ordination. In the midfifties, the Lutheran and Reformed churches in Scandinavia and Germany began to grant women ordination. A few American mainline churches, such as the Presbyterians U.S.A. and the Methodist Episcopal Church, were aware of these developments and decided in 1956 to follow suit.

For the Methodist Episcopal Church, this decision was also spurred by a 1939 merger with the Methodist Protestants, who had been ordaining women since the nineteenth century. As a small denomination, the Methodist Protestants had lost the vote for women's ordination at the time of the merger, but they continued to argue their case within the new united church. Deaconesses who had earned respect over many decades of service abroad or in inner-city ministries also helped press for this change.

The changes in these churches occurred at a time when there was no organized feminist movement. Many women in these denominations did not even realize in the early sixties that they *could* be ordained.[90] But with rising feminist consciousness in the larger American culture, women began to flock into seminaries in the late sixties and seventies. Their numbers have continued to grow steadily, so that in 1999 they comprised a third of theological students overall (counting seminaries of churches that do not ordain women, such as the Roman Catholic Church) and accounted for 50 percent or more in seminaries of liberal denominations.

Other denominations opened their doors to ordained ministry for women in the 1960s and '70s. The American Lutherans and the Lutheran Church in America took this step in 1965, and in 1976, after a decade-long struggle that included a decision by a group of retired Episcopal bishops to ordain eleven women "irregularly," the American Episcopal Church likewise voted to ordain women.[91]

As their numbers increased in seminaries in the 1970s, women began to press for the hiring of women professors and the development of women's studies in theological education. Such curricula, which often started with a single marginal omnibus course on women in Christianity, have now grown into a signifiant part of all theological disciplines, with specialized offerings devoted to women and feminist critique in the Old and New Testaments, theology, church history, ethics, pastoral psychology, and liturgy. Continuous research and writing over the last three decades has established a major "canon" of scholarship in these areas for theological students.[92]

The churches themselves have also been deeply influenced by the advent of women and feminist studies. Women ministers now constitute 10 to 20 percent of the clergy of most denominations, and many congregations now take for granted having a women as their pastor. Hymnals, Bible translations, lectionaries, and prayer books have been revised to make their language inclusive of both genders, at least for references to humans (references to God are much slower to change). Adult lay groups select books on feminist theology as study topics, and concern for issues such as battered women and sexual violence in the family have become part of the ministries of most churches. For some, the presence of women in the ministry has challenged, to some extent, the hierarchical ordering of the clergy over the laity and suggested a more democratic and participatory way of shaping the pastoral and missionary work of the churches.[93]

Issues of gay rights also began to touch the churches and seminaries in the 1970s. Some theological students "came out" as gays or lesbians and asked that seminary housing be opened to gay couples. They formed support groups to discuss issues such as church recognition of their marriages and ordination. This has become one of the most divisive issues faced by the churches, often becoming a flash point for near schism between liberals and conservatives. Gay people have also formed denominational advocacy groups for social support, pastoral counseling, and liturgy, including Dignity (Catholic), Integrity (Episcopal), and the Affirmation (United Methodist).

A new denomination, the Metropolitan Community Church, under the leadership of homosexual evangelical minister Troy Perry, was founded in 1968. Metropolitan Community churches typically minister in gay urban neighborhoods and have creatively combined high church liturgy with evangelical preaching and revival singing in a way that can attract gay Christians across the spectrum of Christian traditions.[94] As the gay issue has been debated vigorously and often acrimoniously in the churches, a literature defending the moral integrity of gay relations has grown in such fields as biblical studies and pastoral psychology.[95] Courses in theological schools now assign readings in such works.

The advent of new forms of liberation theology, feminism, and gay rights in theological schools and churches has deeply polarized the Christian church. Right-wing groups such as the "Good News" movement in Methodism, the Presbyterian Laymen, and Catholics United for the Faith have been formed with the intent of reasserting traditional views of doctrine, gender, and sexual relations. They seek to delegitimize the thinking of liberals who have opened the door to such revisionist theology and to drive those who represent such views from theological faculties, church pulpits, and Christian education directorships.

Thus the backlash against feminism and gay liberation does not simply divide Right from Left in the larger society and culture; it also finds some of its sharpest expression in internal conflicts within the church. In the next chapter we will turn to a more in-depth analysis of this backlash in American culture and in the churches.

In conservative circles and established media, the sixties have now become a byword for a time of chaos, breakdown of "values," and disregard for authority, threatening the foundations of American Christian civilization. But this is a misperception on the part of those who saw with horror only some fringe phenomena, and never really understood the heart of the movements. The center of the civil-rights, peace, and feminist movements of the midsixties to seventies was a conviction of boundless hope.

For a brief decade, but with aftershocks that reverberate today, millions of Americans believed that the beloved community, the new humanity, the society of peace and justice could become real. They believed that "we can overcome," and black and white could walk hand in hand together; that war could be no more; that all social relations could become egalitarian, organized by forms of participatory democracy; that every child could be wanted, no longer thrust on an unwilling or unable mother; that sex could express love, not violence and domination, that justice and peace could reign throughout the Earth.

It was all very American. And in the end it was that unleashing of boundless hope—the possibility of actually fulfilling the millennial American dream of "liberty and justice for all"—that was so threatening to those who believed themselves to be the guardians of normative and divinely decreed relations mandating capitalism, patriarchy, and hierarchy in the family and in society.

CHAPTER 7

The Family Agenda of the Christian Right

The victories of the women's movement, particularly the passage of the Equal Rights Amendment in 1972 and the *Roe vs. Wade* decision by the Supreme Court in 1973, soon inspired a backlash that used those issues to mount a multifaceted assault on progressive politics and social change. Much of the New Right that arose after 1973 was not actually new in its components, but rather represented new coalitions of several constituencies of American conservativism, mobilized by new organizations and leaders and using new techniques of organizing, including direct-mail campaigns and the mass media, both television and radio. It also reflected the politicization of conservative subcultures—for example, Protestant Evangelicalism—that had previously been apolitical or antipolitical.

TWO STREAMS OF AMERICAN CONSERVATIVISM

Two distinct branches of American conservatism can be seen as having coalesed in the mid- to late 1970s, and as continuing in changing alliances today. One of these was the Cold War and pro-business conservatism of the McCarthy era, which itself had earlier roots in the assault on union organizing and the Red Scare at the turn of the century and in the 1920s, renewed as opposition to the New Deal in the 1930s. This right wing championed "free enterprise" against government regulation of business, welfare, and redistribution of wealth to the poorer classes, together with anticommunism and support for an American military supremacy against foreign foes.[1]

In the mid-1970s, Cold War liberals such as Irving Kristol and Norman Podhoretz moved to the right, combining endorsements of anti-Communist intervention abroad and a strong military with attacks on state welfare and antipoverty programs.[2] These neoconservatives would later ally themselves with New Right organizers such as Richard Viguerie, and supply-side economic theorists such as Milton Friedman to become a major part of the "brain trust" for the Reagan administration. They benefited from the great expansion of corporate funding for conservative think tanks such as the American Enterprise Institute.[3]

The members of this group were not averse to adopting the traditional morality of Christian evangelicals, though the Zionist Jewish intellectuals among them were bristled at any mention of reestablishing a "Christian America." Together these men helped spearhead the attack on affirmative action and "multiculturalism" in higher education (i.e., the development of women's and ethnic studies) as diluting the traditional "canon" of Western civilization, though they did not object to the inclusion of a limited ethnic and religious pluralism (i.e., white male Catholics and Jews).

Neoconservatives talked, rather, of the inability of government intervention to right social wrongs, and the need to strengthen the "family" in its local ethnic neighborhood and church/synagogue base as the proper way to control social "deviance," while accepting economic inequality and the meritocracy of the talented. Norman Podhoretz made a case for this version of the neoconservatives' threefold agenda for the Reagan "revolution" in a 1981 *Commentary* article, entitled "The New American Majority." He called for

> economic policy that will unleash the productive energies of an artificially hampered people and therefore foster growth; a program of rearmament that will make our defenses invulnerable . . . [and] a legal structure that will encourage the revitalization of the values of "family, work and neighborhood."[4]

The second branch of conservatism was rooted in the evangelical fundamentalist subculture of the Protestant church. The Progressive era of 1890–1920 had seen the emergence of a liberal Protestant ecumenism that took control of the denominational bureaucracy and of the major seminaries of such churches as the Northern Presbyterians, the Episcopalians, the Methodists, the Congregationalists, and the American Baptists, and was expressed as well in the Federal Council of Churches. Liberals had sought to accommodate themselves to the new challenges of science and industrialization by espousing the Social Gospel and accepting historical criticism of the Bible.

Conservatives within these denominations, as well as conservative churches such as the Southern Baptists, reacted against the liberal Protestant coalition by defining a fundamentalist orthodoxy based on biblical inerrancy and literal adherence to key traditional doctrines, including the Virgin Birth of Jesus and the bodily Resurrection. They adopted a premillennialist view of impending apocalyptic doom for modern secular society, in which only the "born-again" would be saved, contrasting this with the Social Gospel belief in the postmillennial progress of secularized society toward increasing justice.[5]

After the defeat of creationism in the 1926 *Scopes* trial, fundamentalists withdrew from participation in the larger American society. Seeking to protect their own worldview and culture against an American society that was becoming more ethnically pluralist and secular, they founded biblical institutes to train their own leaders.[6]

A reemphasis on traditional morality and patriarchal family patterns was common to both evangelicals and neoconservatives, though the former pursued it more rigorously. These patterns were rooted in the traditional teachings of Christianity and Judaism and reinforced by patriarchal readings of psychology and sociology, as well as popular Freudianism, functionalism, and behaviorism. The feminine mystique of the 1950s, itself a renewal of the cult of true womanhood of the Victorian era, was restated in the 1970s in new evangelical tracts that claimed that traditional gender relations reflected the divinely mandated biblical form of the family. Pop psychologists again attacked feminists as the "lost sex" and suggested they were missing their true vocation by choosing careers over "full-time" housewifery and motherhood.[7]

THE STOP-ERA CAMPAIGN

The crusade against the Equal Rights Amendment became a major organizing issue for this emerging right-wing coalition in the 1970s. In 1982 the amendment failed to achieve the required endorsement by two-thirds of the states. Key "pro-family" themes linking "women's lib," homosexuality, and abortion with assault on the family were all shaped during in the anti-ERA campaign; by defining the Equal Rights Amendment as antifamily, conservatives ensured its defeat. This definition was itself the work of a new coalition of conservatisms. In 1972, when the ERA was passed by the House of Representatives and then by the Senate, it had a more mainstream and bipartisan profile.

As we have seen, the ERA was first proposed to the American Congress in 1923 by the National Women's Party but was opposed by Progressive feminists, labor, and the Left until the mid-1960s on the ground that it would undermine protective laws for women. It was endorsed by the Republican Party in 1940, five years before the Democratic Party followed suit. Many pro-business conservatives favored it for precisely the same reason that the Left opposed it: it would do away with protective legislation that limited the freedom of business.[8]

The demise of many such protective laws in the 1960s allowed the social feminist and labor establishment to get behind the ERA. Its championing by the National Organization for Women put it in the new feminist camp. But when Congress passed it in 1972, it was conceived not as a means of making radical changes in gender relations, but simply as a legal tool with which to clear out many obsolete laws, such as those that forbade wives to establish their own domiciles apart from their husbands or to retain control of their property after marriage.[9]

In 1972, the notion that women should enjoy "equal rights" with men was not seen as controversial, and many states rushed to ratify the amendment. Thirty states did so in the first year after its passage by Congress, and only eight more were needed to make it a part of the Constitution. If it had remained noncontroversial for another year, it might well have passed. As Jane Mansbridge has argued in *Why We Lost the ERA*, the American Constitution was designed to be difficult to amend. The requirement that demands two-thirds of the states to ratify an amendment, each by a two-thirds vote of its state legislature, means that an amendment can pass only if it enjoys a broad consensus with no vociferous opposition.[10] This constitutional conservatism also makes it hard to pass amendments that are favored by the Right but opposed by the Left, such as a balanced-budget or a human-life amendment.

The Supreme Court's 1973 ruling in *Roe vs. Wade* changed the atmosphere, even through there was no legal connection between the ERA and abortion. Conservatives in Congress hurried to pass laws ruling out federal funding for abortion, and the Catholic Church began to mobilize to rescind its legalization. Phyllis Schlafly, who would become a key player in the mobilization of the New Right coalition against the ERA, had not up to that time been involved in any of these issues, but she now found a powerful ally in Sam Ervin, a North Carolina Republican and leader of the anti-ERA forces in Congress, who would lend her government franking privileges to mail her Stop-ERA literature.

In the fifties and sixties, Schlafly's political involvements had been along the lines of the McCarthyite old Right. After growing up in a conservative Catholic anti–New Deal family in St. Louis, Schlafly had in 1949 married a wealthy lawyer fifteen years her senior. Fred Schlafly was a devout Catholic with ties to far-Right groups such as Fred Schwarz's Christian Anti-Communist Crusade and the World Anti-Communist League. Fred Schlafly early on supported his wife's political affiliation with the Right.[11]

Phyllis Schlafly ran for Congress on the Republican ticket in 1952, when her first child was eighteen months old. She ran a second time in 1970, by which point she had six children, the youngest of whom was five. Having lost both races, she returned to school in the midseventies to earn a law degree. Given her history, feminists were quick to accuse her of opportunistic hypocrisy in advocating traditional housewifery, and they were furious when she thanked her husband for "allowing" her to speak in public against the ERA. But this perception of Schlafly as insincere simplifies the complexity of the relationship between the embrace of feminism or antifeminism as an ideology, on the one hand, and women's experiences of family and public life in diverse cultural and class contexts, on the other.

Schlafly was "permitted" and financially enabled by her husband to engage in right-wing politics. She herself believed that a woman already had the right to do whatever she wanted; hence, in her view, the ERA was unnecessary to women's freedom to participate in public life. But wives and mothers, Schlafly felt, should do so only when it was compatible with their family commitments, and only with their husbands' permission. She saw her own combination of dedicated motherhood and political crusading on behalf of the traditional family as falling solidly within these parameters.[12]

Phyllis Schlafly's main interests in the 1950s and '60s mirrored those of her husband: anticommunism, support for a strong military defense, and heated opposition to the East Coast establishment, which they believed had treasonably weakened America's military preeminence as a nuclear power. *A Choice, Not an Echo*, her 1964 book extolling the virtues of the Goldwater campaign, earned her a place as a player on the right wing of the Republican Party against its moderates.[13] But her profile as an extremist lost her her bid for the presidency of the National Federation of Republican Women in 1967.

Schlafly responded to this defeat by the party establishment by building her own political and funding base, the Eagle Forum, directed at conservative Republican women. Schlafly had her own newsletter, the *Phyllis Schlafly Report*, which went out to the group's members, and she conducted yearly training sessions on how to be politically effective. Thus, when Congress passed the ERA and the Supreme Court legalized abortion, Schlafly not only recognized the organizing potential of linking anti-ERA and antiabortion sentiments to a defense of traditional womanhood; she also already had a political organization under her own control to throw behind the crusade.

Over the next ten years, Schlafly would hone her arguments against the ERA even as she built her organizational base into a district-by-district grass-roots movement among conservative housewives, particularly in the southern and midwestern states that had not yet ratified the amendment. The success of her crusade depended on the politicization of a disaffected constituency—middle- and lower-middle-class housewives who felt their traditional roles were being denigrated by the rise of professional women—by raising the specter of radical changes in gender roles that would supposedly be brought about by the passage of the ERA.[14]

Schlafly meanwhile appealed to state legislators by playing on their fears of a federal bureaucracy spinning out of control and dictating state passage of laws for social change. She reached out to conservative women by arguing that the ERA would dissolve the old guarantees that a husband had to support his wife, force federal funding of abortion on demand, and abolish the exemption of women from military combat and the draft. She also invoked volatile fantasies of sexual/gender androgyny, asserting that the ERA would create sex-integrated toilets and mandate homosexual marriage. Her rhetoric whipped up antifeminist fear and loathing by portraying pro-ERA feminism as being bent on destroying all respect for marriage and motherhood—antifamily, antichildren, and pro-abortion. Feminism, she asserted, was just a series of

> sharp-tongued, high-pitched, whining complaints by unmarried women. They view the home as a prison and the wife and mother as a slave. . . . Women's lib is a total assault on the role of the American woman as wife and mother and on the family as the basic unit of society. . . . Women's libbers are promoting free sex instead of the "slavery" of marriage. They are promoting Federal "day care centers" for babies instead of homes. They are promoting abortions instead of families.[15]

Pro-ERA women were caught off guard by this assault launched by a highly articulate woman, and they found it difficult to contradict her exaggerated caricature of their rhetoric without backing off from their defense of legal abortion and gender equality in the workplace. One reason for the weakness of their defense in the later 1970s was that many of the laws that the ERA was expected to change had been struck down by the Supreme Court a few years before, using the equal-protection clause of the Fourteenth Amendment. NOW and other pro-ERA organizers could thus no longer cite extant and compelling examples of gender-discriminatory laws that would be changed altered with the passage of the ERA.[16]

The net result was that pro-ERA organizers found themselves, like Schlafly, exaggerating the more radical effects of the passage of the ERA. When Schlafly raised fears that such passage would mean that women would be drafted and sent into battle, pro-ERA forces defended the drafting of women and their equal roles in combat. They also claimed far-reaching effects on wage equity in the workplace, even though the ERA was defined only as promoting equality in legal status, and thus would have had no direct impact on wages in the private sector. It was difficult for feminists to argue that Schlafly's threats of radical change were baseless when they themselves were not prepared to back away from the ideal of women's equality in work in a way that might mollify the fears of those committed to the role of the economically dependent wife.[17]

The claims on both sides tended toward hyperbole. A successful ERA would not have caused an immediate change in the sex-segregated draft law, for example, though such a change might have happened eventually. But the War Powers provision would always have allowed the military to exempt women from combat if it so chose, according to its standards for combat effectiveness. The intervening two decades have seen increasing integration of women into the military combat roles, without the ERA, as technology has made hand-to-hand combat less and less a part of modern warfare.[18]

Principles of privacy, meanwhile, would have prevented integrated toilets, while laws mandating husbands' support for wives while their marriage was intact had never been enforced in any case. In sum, then, the ratification of the ERA in 1979 would probably have had no immediate effect on any law, though it would have strengthened the disposition already under way to examine the impact of laws on gender discrimination and prevented the passage of any new laws that were explicitly gender-discriminatory. Rather, the passage of the ERA in the 1970s would have been largely symbolic, though importantly so, given the coterminous backlash against women's rights.

The crusade against the Equal Rights Amendment allowed the Right not only to enshrine a negative caricature of feminism but also to mobilize new constituencies of women on behalf of a politics of the traditional family. This included both those whom Schlafly had already organized under her Eagle Forum and fundamentalist Protestant women who were more disposed to see the traditional family as divinely mandated and unchangeable.[19] By the late seventies, conservative evangelical Protestants as well as Mormons, right-wing Catholics, and Orthodox Jews would join the anti-ERA coalition.[20]

BUILDING THE CHRISTIAN RIGHT

The building of the Christian Right as a political force did not happen overnight. Already in the 1920s evangelicals had recognized the potency of the mass media (that is, radio) for evangelism. Older evangelicals such as Billy Graham would go on to hold mass televised rallies in the fifties and sixties in which they would link conversion to Christ with anticommunism. Pat Robertson began to establish his own media empire, the Christian Broadcasting Network, in the 1960s, launching the "700 Club" in a 1963 telethon as a fundraising device, when he called for seven hundred viewers to pledge ten dollars a month apiece to support his TV ministry. By 1985 it had an annual budget of $230 million and was broadcast on two hundred U.S. TV stations, as well as in sixty other countries.[21]

Other influential Christian TV networks today are the Trinity Broadcasting Network and the Family Christian Broadcasting Network, both based in California. The PTL (Praise the Lord) network, once another major contender, unraveled with the revelation of sexual misconduct by its president, Jim Bakker, in 1987. It would eventually be taken over by Robertson's CBN. Christian evangelism also still depends on radio: James Dobson's Focus on the Family organization, for example, uses it to reach its adherents.[22] Beverly LaHaye organized the Concerned Women of America (CWA) in 1979 to oppose the ERA and then moved it to Washington in 1986 as a lobbying group, while continuing to build a grass-roots base that relies on chain-letter writing by housewives. CWA sponsors a radio show, *Beverly LaHaye Live,* that aired on 124 stations in 1996.[23]

Far from simply broadcasting pulpit sermonizing, Christian radio and TV attract audiences with multifaceted talk shows that feature call-ins and stories of miraculous healing. Much of their fundraising comes through grass-roots donations in response to these broadcasts. In 1997 there were 1,648 full-time Christian radio stations and 257 full- or part-time television stations, with programs also available on cable systems.[24] But the Christian mass media do not stop there; they additionally encompass book and magazine publication. Focus on the Family, for instance, publishes magazines for every age group and both genders, and other Christian groups also use periodicals to supplement their outreach.[25]

Christian print materials range from didactic tracts by Christian media stars such as Pat Robertson[26] to gripping novels like Charles Colson's *Gideon's Torch* and Tim LaHaye's *Left Behind.*[27] LaHaye's book explores the "rapture" of born-again Christians who disappear from the Earth, leaving the unconverted with a short window of opportunity in which to get on the right side before the final Armageddon.

Christian music is another major growth area, commanding 10 percent of all music sales. Christian bookstores provide outlets for printed matter, videos, and CDs as well as other items such as T-shirts and jewelry. Studies have shown that the mass media do not detract from either churchgoing or print media, but rather supplement them in the evangelical subculture.[28]

The politicization of the evangelical network took a major step forward in 1979, when evangelical leaders turned away from the human-rights-oriented Jimmy Carter to support conservative presidential candidate Ronald Reagan. New Right organizers such as Richard Viguerie and Paul Weyrich, who had built direct-mail fundraising networks and political action groups in the 1970s, joined with Jerry Falwell, whose *Old-Fashioned Gospel Hour* had established him as a major televangelist, to found the Moral Majority. Setting up chapters in each state, the Moral Majority embarked on a major voter-registration drive among evangelicals to help get Reagan elected in 1980.[29]

The Moral Majority sought to set an agenda for a Reagan presidency that would include attacks on abortion, gay rights, sex education in schools, and pornography, and support for school prayer and tax exemptions for Christian schools. Political candidates were then evaluated on how they measured up to this agenda. Liberals such as Senators George McGovern and Frank Church were targeted in "moral report cards" distributed to churches on the Sunday before the November election.[30]

During Reagan's two terms, however, much of the Moral Majority's agenda went unrealized in Congress. The energies of the Christian Right were instead recruited into major support for Reaganite foreign policies of anti-Communist intervention and a strong military. The ideology of supply-side economics, combined with the need to finance an expanded military, resulted in fewer cuts in taxes and government spending than the neoconservatives wanted. The spending cuts focused on social-welfare areas, while the top 5 percent of wealthy Americans and corporations were greatly enriched by the tax cuts that were introduced.[31]

Their backing of Reagan's militarist and anti-Communist agenda got Christian Right groups such as Robertson's CBN heavily involved in supporting the *contras* against the Sandinista revolution in Nicaragua, Ríos Montt's murderous presidency in Guatemala, and aid to the military in El Salvador. Christian Right leaders also lined up behind the evangelical vigilante death squads against the People's Liberation Army in the Philippines and behind the Pretorian government in South Africa against the African National Congress, as well as taking sides in the puppet wars in Angola and Mozambique.[32]

The Christian Right has also had an enduring alliance with Zionism, lobbying for continuing aid to the state of Israel, while ignoring unjust treatment of Palestinians, both Christian and Muslim. While this pro-Israel stance has cemented the Christian Right's bond with Zionist members of the secular neoconservative camp, the alliance has been fraught with suspicion due to the tendency among the Christian leaders to adopt a "dominion theology" that seeks to reestablish a Christian America in which only its type of evangelical Christians will rule, enforcing a "biblical morality" on all. Moreover, their pro-Zionism is rooted in a premillennialist apocalypticism that sees Israel as the place where the final battle between God and Satan will be waged.[33]

This theology preserves traditional Christian religious exclusivism. Jews who adhere to Judaism will remain unsaved; as evangelist Bailey Smith, president of the Southern Baptist Convention, put it in a Religious Roundtable national-affairs briefing in Dallas in 1980, "God Almighty does not hear the prayer of a Jew."[34] Any hope for Jews must lie in a future millennium when elect groups of them are destined to convert to Christ in the final conflagration and join in the redeemed world. This will happen only as Jews return to the Middle East, refound a Jewish state, and rebuild the temple. The role of Jews in the Christian Right's redemptive vision thus invokes enduring support for the state of Israel among evangelicals—but on a basis that can only make Jews themselves uncomfortable.[35]

With the departure of Ronald Reagan and the collapse of the Soviet Union in the late eighties, the Christian Right's involvement in anticommunism lost its major impetus, and the movement's leaders turned back toward their still largely unrealized domestic agenda. Although Pat Robertson lost his 1988 bid for the Republican presidential nomination, his campaign succeeded in strengthening Christian Right political organizing within the Republican Party. Jerry Falwell disbanded the Moral Majority, but it was replaced by the Christian Coalition, which paired Robertson with a young political organizer named Ralph Reed.

Under Reed's leadership, the Christian Coalition would target local campaigns for school boards and town councils, nominating as candidates conservative evangelicals whose ideological complexion was often concealed to prevent liberal counterorganizing. While many such local "stealth campaigns" succeeded in the early nineties, liberals were soon alerted and often managed to defeat the coalition's candidates in ensuing elections.[36]

By 1996 Reed himself had begun to grow restive with the narrow political agenda of the Christian Right and sought to cast a "broader net" that would catch other fish, such as black and Latino evangelicals concerned about urban poverty issues. This effort brought only superficial support from Christian Right leaders, whose movement has remained overwhelmingly white. Reed resigned to start his own consulting firm in 1997.[37]

However, in the second half of the nineties, the Christian Right remained a major political force with an uneasy relation to the Republican Party. It has continued to deliver solid blocks of voters for conservative Republican candidates who embrace its agenda, but it has also acted to prevent any watering-down of the attack on abortion and gay rights on the part of Republican "moderates." A major new area of organizing in the nineties was the foundation of Christian Right legal firms, including Robertson's American Center for Law and Justice, the Home School Defense Council, and a funding arm called the Alliance Defense Group. Designed to defend homeschooling parents against the requirements of teacher certification, parents who objected to sex education or liberal textbooks in public schools, and Operation Rescue groups that blocked access to abortion clinics, these firms also stood behind the legal assaults on the Clinton presidency that culminated in the impeachment crusade.[38]

"PRO-FAMILY" ISSUES: SCHOOLS, FEMINISM, ABORTION, AND GAYS

The overall profile of "pro-family" issues has remained constant over the last quarter century, though coalitions and foci have varied according to the thrust of particular campaigns on local, state, or national levels. The issues coalesce around three major points. The first of these is actually a constellation of issues related to "parents' rights" to exclude their children from the influence of what is seen as the immoral "secular humanist" culture, connected most especially with public schools but also with government agencies, such as Children and Family Services, that might intervene against parents who are deemed abusive or neglectful.

These concerns are animated in campaigns to mandate prayer in public schools, to prevent the use of "secular humanist" textbooks, and to defend campus access and funding for evangelical student groups. But also defended are parents' rights to withdraw their children from public schools, made possible through either the extension of state funding for Christian schools in school vouchers or by permitting home schooling.[39]

A second constant of the Christian Right's agenda is opposition to abortion, with the ultimate goal of outlawing all abortions from conception on by means of a human-life amendment; in the interim, a variety of tactics may be employed to limit women's access to the procedure.

The third item on the agenda is the battle against homosexuality. Here the aim is to block any legislation that would either include sexual preference in antidiscrimination language referring to access to housing or employment (also schools and the military) or allow gays the legal rights of marriage.

Throughout these debates, an overarching issue is the defense of traditional gender hierarchy in patriarchal marriage. Fundamentally, the Christian Right wants to preserve the headship of the male over the female in monogamous marriage, with the husband as breadwinner and the wife as full-time housekeeper and mother, according to the divinely created family order that is supposed to be the foundation of social order.[40] But the presence of strong female leadership in the movement, as well as the preponderance of women among its grassroots troops, means that any language suggesting the inferiority of women must be muted in favor of terms that emphasize differences in God-given roles between equals.[41]

In 1980, conservatives sought to codify much of this "pro-family" agenda in law through the passage of an omnibus Pro-Family Act introduced into the Senate by Paul Laxalt, Ronald Reagan's campaign manager. The bill contained titles on education, welfare, religious institutions, taxation, and domestic relations. Under the heading of education, it proposed to deny federal funds to any public school or school district that did not make provision for prayer in the classroom. Other proposals in this section sought to inhibit union organizing by teachers, forbid sex-integrated sports activities, and ban textbooks that promoted the equality of women.

In the section on welfare, the act endorsed tax deductions for those supporting elderly relatives, but would deny food stamps to low-income college students and impose tax penalties on day-care centers. Through taxation, the bill sought to encourage the nuclear family with a working husband and a nonworking wife. Under domestic relations, it discouraged the promotion of shelters for battered wives and abused children, implying that such aid was deleterious to "the family." Shelter staff would be forbidden to provide women or teens with contraceptives or abortion counseling.

The bill also aimed to choke off federal funds for liberal social activism. It proposed to deny federal legal assistance to any program that advocated labor organizing, boycotts, picketing, strikes, or demonstrations or offered training for such activities. Legal assistance was likewise to be refused to programs that provided counseling on abortion, divorce, desertion from the armed forces, desegregation of schools, or the rights of homosexuals. The final section of the bill stated that federal antidiscrimination statutes should not be construed to protect homosexuals against discrimination in employment.[42]

This omnibus bill never made it out of committee for a Senate vote, but the Christian Right and its conservative allies have tried to attach parts of this agenda to a variety of other bills over the years. In May 1995 the Christian Coalition unveiled its Contract with the American Family, a document intended to buttress and extend Newt Gingrich's Contract with America. The Contract with the American Family was moderate by Christian Right standards, seeking only a ban on late-term abortions rather than a human-life amendment, and failing to mention gays at all.[43]

Instead, the Family Contract focused on the need for a "religious equality" amendment to protect student-led prayer in schools, and called for the elimination of the Department of Education and the end of funding for the National Endowment for the Humanities and the Corporation for Public Broadcasting, both seen as bastions of liberalism and "pornography." With Gingrich's demise, the omnibus approach of the midnineties faded. But the agenda contained in it, together with other key items on the Christian Right's wish list, particularly opposition to gay rights, continue to surface in new local, state, and national efforts.

The antiabortion initiative remains the emotional center of the "pro-family" movement, but it is blocked from achieving its ultimate goal of banning all abortions because a majority of Americans are still marginally pro-choice when faced with the prospect of a reversion to making all abortion illegal. This popular ambivalence in turn makes Republican leaders unwilling to back pro-lifers because in doing so they would risk alienating their own pro-choice wing.[44]

The result of this dilemma is that pro-life activists, though stymied at the national level, have nonetheless succeeded in passing a variety of legislation on the state level that restricts access to abortion. Such legislation may include a twenty-four-hour waiting period for women requesting abortions; mandatory counseling on health problems and alternatives to abortion; mandatory parental consent for women under eighteen; restrictions on Medicaid and/or insurance coverage for abortions; and prohibition of the use of public facilities for abortions. In its 1989 decision in *Webster vs. Reproductive Health Services,* the Supreme Court upheld the legality of such state restrictions. Yet abortions have not been banned altogether.[45]

Frustrated by the failure to achieve their goal, some antiabortion activists have turned to direct action. Inially this was to be nonviolent, taking the form only of picketing clinics, though often in a highly harassing manner, with protestors' shouting at the women who enter and displaying grisly posters. In 1988 Operation Rescue founder Randall Terry resorted to civil disobedience, using activists to block access to clinics and courting arrest. This sparked dozens of such blockades and thousands of arrests between 1988 and 1990. But the pro-choice movement fought back by suing Operation Rescue for damages and surrounding clinics with protective cordons. As prison terms lengthened and fines increased, Operation Rescue's activist ranks dwindled, though those who remained grew even more militant.[46]

There had been clinic bombings before, in the 1980s. Terry had promoted his actions as an alternative to such violence, but when his approach failed to deliver the hoped-for closing of all clinics, some militants from Operation Rescue, as well as new groups such as Lambs for Christ, began to engage in direct harassment of doctors, publishing their names, addresses, and phone numbers. In March 1993 things went even further, when a doctor was murdered by an antiabortion militant.[47]

As other doctors and clinic personnel were killed or injured and clinic bombings escalated, antiabortion leaders debated the question of "justifiable homicide." The defense of such killings by the militant wing, even though they were not approved of by the majority of the movement,[48] further discredited the antiabortion crusade. With the endorsement of President Clinton, Congress in 1993 passed the Freedom of Access to Clinics Act, which made clinic violence a federal crime.

Backing away from more violent tactics, moderates began to focus on creating their own clinics to counsel pregnant women—helping them carry their fetuses to term and find adoptive parents—and offering "healing" counselling for women who regret having had abortions. Thus though abortion remains a legal right at the dawn of the twenty-first century, in practice many women who desire abortions cannot find funds to pay for them or clinics with doctors licensed to perform them. Safe, legal abortion has become de facto inaccessible for many.[49]

A second major emotional center of Christian Right organizing has been the battle against gay rights. Condemnation of homosexuality is hardly new for Christian evangelicals, and such denunciations can also be seen in conservative literature of the 1950s. But the antigay agenda expanded in the 1970s as the gay and lesbian movement was organized politically and as sexual orientation began to be included in city and state antidiscrimination statutes. Major Christian Right groups such as Focus on the Family, as well as local coalitions, concentrated on repealing these statutes or preempting them by passing initiatives that forbade the inclusion of sexual preference in antidiscrimination laws.

An early example of such conflicts occurred in 1977, when the Dade County, Florida, board of commissioners passed an ordinance protecting gays against discrimination in housing, employment, and public accommodations. Singer Anita Bryant, an evangelical Christian and associate of Phyllis Schlafly in the anti-ERA campaign, became the spokesperson for a ballot initiative to repeal the Dade County ordinance, which was approved by a wide margin. The struggle was then carried to California, where one of Bryant's allies, state Senator John Briggs, placed an initiative on the 1978 state ballot to ban gays from teaching in the public schools. In this case the initiative (opposed by then California Governor Ronald Reagan) was defeated.[50]

Throughout the eighties, Christian Right groups continued to oppose or seek to roll back the inclusion of gays in antidiscrimination legislation. The late eighties and early nineties were the heyday for such efforts. In Oregon, in 1988, the conservative Oregon Citizens' Alliance succeeding in defeating an order issued by the governor banning employment discrimination based on sexual orientation in the executive branch of the state government. The Citizen's Alliance then drafted an "Abnormal Behaviors Initiative" for the 1992 election, lumping homosexuality together with pedophilia, sadism, and masochism and calling for a ban on the protection of all such "abnormal behaviors." The literature advocating the passage of this initiative portrayed gays as vicious "perverts." Oregonians voted it down.[51]

The next major proving ground for such ballot initiatives was Colorado, where antigay organizers learned from the Oregon defeat and crafted the legislation as a state amendment, avoiding extreme antigay language and dismissing as unnecessary antidiscrimination laws that included sexual orientation. The latter argument claimed that gays were not a minority group suffering from discrimination, and that legislation on their behalf thus constituted a "special right" not enjoyed by other citizens. The amendment passed, only to be ruled unconstitutional, first by a state judge in 1993, then by the Colorado Supreme Court, and finally, in 1996, by the United States Supreme Court. This ruling curtailed the use of ballot measures intended to prevent antidiscrimination laws from including gays, but struggles to repeal such laws or prevent them from being passed continue.[52]

In 2000, many rights enjoyed by heterosexuals are still denied to gay, lesbian, and transgendered persons. Some thirteen states have same- and opposite-sex sodomy laws on their books, while another five states proscribe only same-gender sodomy. In these states, gay and lesbian sex is illegal even in private, though such laws are seldom enforced. Only twenty-one states have hate-crime laws that include sexual orientation, while nineteen more have similar laws that do *not* protect gay people; ten states (including Wyoming) have no hate-crime laws at all. Since the late eighties, homosexuals have become a major target of such crimes.[53]

Only ten states and the District of Columbia have statutes prohibiting discrimination based on sexual orientation in any area (meaning
housing, public or private employment, education, or public accommodations). Where state legislation is lacking, 157 cities and counties
have passed their own such laws, but that leaves more than ten thousand cities and counties in which discrimination is legal. Gay and lesbian persons also face legal barriers in areas such as the adoption of
children. Only a few states, among them New York and New Jersey,
allow gay people to adopt, and only Vermont, Massachusetts, and
New York permit gay men and lesbians to adopt a partner's child. A
wide variety of privileges extended to married heterosexuals including rights to inheritances, pensions, and shared medical insurance, are denied to gay couples.[54]

In the mid- to late nineties, the right of gays to marry, and hence
to enjoy the legal privileges and social acceptance of marriage, has become a major focus of the gay-rights and antigay movements. To pre-
empt the possibility that the state of Hawaii might legalize gay marriage, antigay groups rushed to pass laws against it at both the state and
federal levels. During the 1996 presidential campaign, Bill Clinton
avoided having this issue used against him by signing a Defense of
Marriage Act passed by Congress. Thirty states have enacted similar
laws banning same-sex marriage.[55] In April 2000 the state of Vermont
approved civil marriages for homosexuals.

The blessing of same-sex unions has also become a major divisive
issue in the churches, even though such blessings do not constitute legal marriages and confer no legal benefits. The question of marriage,
and particularly of its relation to the church, nonetheless goes to the
heart of the Christian Right's antigay agenda. Central to this agenda
is the contention that gay sex is intrinsically sinful, regardless of how
loving or how committed is the relationship in which it takes place.

Traditional Christians believe that God founded the order of Creation that mandates monogamous heterosexual marriage as the only
legitimate context in which sex may take place. Same-gender sex (or,
in earlier views, nonprocreative, nonvaginal sex) is inherently "disor-
dered," not only personally sinful but also destructive of the heterosexual family as the foundation of social order. It therefore cannot be
the basis of any healthy or holy relationship that might enjoy the
blessing of the church or the legal sanction of the state.

The antigay ideology of the Christian Right alternates between two views of gay and lesbian people. One view, aimed mostly at gay males, sees homosexuals as sick and sinful perverts bent on spreading their "disease" by seducing children (hence the particular alarm over gay teachers), gaining social acceptance, and ultimately taking over American society. Gay males are pictured as being at once dangerously and repulsively orgiastic and yet secretive, wealthy, and powerful, plotting the takeover of key elements of society from the arts and education to the church and eventually the government. This "gay agenda" is depicted in apocalyptic terms in popular antigay literature and videos, as portending the impending doom of American civilization.[56]

The gay-takeover/doomsday scenario promoted by the Christian Right is buttressed by specific rhetoric against lesbians. While generally ignored in antigay literature, lesbians, when they are mentioned, are often identified with feminism. Feminism itself is depicted as a man-hating, child-rejecting perversion of women in rebellion against their proper attitude of submission to male authority in family and in society; its logical consequence is lesbianism. This feminism as lesbianism is in turn connected with demonic cult behavior such as witchcraft, paganism, and nazism.[57] An example of such rhetoric may be found in a fundraising appeal that Pat Robertson sent out in 1996 as part of a campaign opposing a state equal-rights amendment in Iowa. The letter accuses feminism of compelling women to "leave their husbands, kill their children, practice witchcraft, destroy capitalism and become lesbians."[58]

A second view of gays that alternates with the first makes them the tragic victims of bad parenting, having lacked proper gender modeling by neglectful fathers and dominant mothers who failed to develop the appropriate masculine or feminine gender identity in their offspring. Their homosexuality is seen as both a sickness and a sin, yet one that can be cured through therapy and conversion to Christ. The Christian Right sponsors counseling centers designed to help gays "overcome" their homosexuality, convert to "proper" gender identities, and enter monogamous heterosexual marriages. Antigay literature and media display success stories of happy ex-gays and ex-lesbians have been converted to Christ and heterosexuality, and are now blissfully married and behaving as normative dominant males and submissive females.[59]

MALE IDENTITY MOVEMENTS

The newly submissive Christian female demands as her partner a newly confident manly Christian male. Among the various "men's movements" founded to complement and/or counteract the women's movement, the Promise Keepers group of the 1990s has become the most prominent. Promise Keepers was established in 1990 by Bill McCartney, then the coach of the University of Colorado's football team, and held its first rally in 1991 for 4,200 men in the football stadium of that university. In 1996, twenty-two weekend rallies in sports stadiums gathered together a million men in all. The organization's national staff numbered 437 in 1997, 30 percent of them by mandate African American, Latino, or Native American.[60]

The Promise Keepers' agenda is to hold men to promises to be sexually monogamous husbands and responsible fathers in Christian marriages. The seven promises that a Promise Keeper takes are: 1) to honor Jesus and obey the Bible; 2) to help other men obey their promises; 3) to preserve spiritual and ethical purity (i.e., no sexual straying, pornography, or sexual fantasies about women other than one's wife); 4) to build a strong marriage and family; 5) to support one's church and pastor; 6) to overcome racial and denominational barriers in "biblical unity"; 7) to obey Jesus' great commandment to love God and one's neighbor and to participate in the Great Commission to evangelize the world.[61]

Although the Promise Keepers' agenda is undoubtedly concerned with men's taking charge as "heads" of their families, it is pitched to a nineties culture that recognizes the fact of multiethnicity as well as the need to help husbands communicate better with their wives as partners if spouses are really to work and stay together. Evangelicals are slightly more likely to divorce even than the rest of American society,[62] and evangelical churches with mostly male clergy have a predominance of female members. Promise Keepers is about getting more men to return to sexual monogamy and responsible fatherhood, so that they will not only provide for their families financially but spend more time with their wives and children. Promise keepers is also about getting these men back into church.

This agenda has been welcomed by many women, and not just those who ideologically support male headship. Many women who have jobs also would like a responsible, caring male partner, not a man who only fathers children with her and then leaves her to do both the parenting and the breadwinning. Consequently, many women have formed their own groups, such as "Promise Reapers," to support men's involvement in Promise Keepers.[63] Promise Keepers' leaders are themselves careful to insist that their emphasis on men's taking back their roles as heads of their families is based on a "servant" model of male leadership.

Doubtless many women have calculated that they can cope with a little male bravado about headship in exchange for restored "service." Yet in the last analysis, the Promise Keepers' model of family relations seeks to renew a male hierarchy, however softened it may be by talk of service and better communication. It undercuts the possibility of a real transformation of male-female partnership in both family and society based on genuine structural change in home-work relations.[64]

The same opportunities and limits apply to the Promise Keepers' theme of racial reconciliation. Evangelical churches, like most others, remain highly segregated. Yet black Christians and a growing segment of Latinos adhere to evangelical Christianity. A movement that succeeded in gathering together white, black, and Latino male evangelicals under one umbrella would have great potential power, especially if it harnessed their shared patriarchalism and hostility toward feminism, gays, and abortion.

Yet the Promise Keepers' model for racial reconciliation restricts itself to the goal of overcoming personal prejudice. This is not an unimportant task for whites, who may experience a profound transformation in renouncing such prejudice, but it ignores real links to poverty and recognition of the economic basis of race/class hierarchy in America. This narrowing of the race issue to the personal, individual level at the expense of any systematic social application will probably limit African American evangelical participation to token pastors on the platform at Promise Keepers rallies, rather than mass involvement at the base.

A parallel black male movement to restore manliness and responsible family headship held its own mass rally in October 1995. The Million Man March, so called by Black Muslim leader Louis Farrakhan, featured a very different form of religious reconciliation, and one that was highly unacceptable to both white evangelicals and most of the rest of white America—namely, a rapprochement between black Christians and black Muslims, the latter representing both heightened racial militancy and male dominance.

Like the evangelical Promise Reapers, many black women were willing to take their chances with a bit of patriarchal bluster if it was accompanied by greater male responsibility toward the family. Black women are generally sensitive to the ways in which racism has debilitated the dignity and economic prowess of black men, so they tend to support efforts to restore black male self-respect, while resisting having it acted out at their expense. But this is a difficult subject, and one that black women prefer not to debate before white audiences. Most black women ranged from open support to tactful silence in the face of the Million Man March. Yet here, too, the question of genuine partnership between men and women as economic and parenting equals was evaded.[65]

The April 19, 1995, bombing of the Federal Building in Oklahoma City by adherents of the right-wing militia movement focused the attention of the media and law enforcement on the armed, racist fringe groups of the radical Right. Many of these were part of a revival of earlier Ku Klux Klan and Nazi movements with links to the ideology of Christian Identity. This ideology claims that only white Europeans are true humans, the descendants of Adam and Eve; Jews are products of fornication in the Garden between Eve and Satan, while blacks are "mud" people without true humanity.[66]

Christian Identity and Aryan Nation groups link race hatred with the anti-semitic fantasy that America and the rest of the world have been taken over by a Zionist conspiracy. They call on white Christians to retreat into armed enclaves, refuse to pay taxes to the federal government, and seek to "take back" sovereignty over an America that will thenceforth be limited to white Christians. This ideology appeals to alienated white males, particularly in rural areas and towns where the farm crisis and deindustrialization have caused a massive erosion of traditional employment for white men.[67]

Such Christian Identity movements should not be conflated with the "mainstream" of the Christian Right, though they may share common themes of Christian dominion and the rebuilding of a Christian America. The militia and Christian Identity movements represent no more than a few hundred thousand mostly disenfranchised whites, whose antigovernment stance reflects their withdrawal from political participation.

The Christian Right, by contrast, counts among its number some thirty million Christians who have become active political organizers and voters. Although it claims victimization in the struggle against the evil forces of feminism, homosexuality, and "secular humanism," it is in fact thoroughly system-supporting in its pro-capitalist commitment to traditional class hierarchies. Even as it diverts attention by crusading for the reestablishment of sex/gender hierarchy, it plays an integral role in the effort to build a conservative political majority that will ratify the growing concentration of wealth in the upper 20 percent of American society and the impoverishment of working-class and unemployed people. It needs to be met on that latter ground by those with other political agendas.[68]

CONFLICT IN THE CHURCHES

In the 1990s the deep cultural and political split between liberals and progressives on the one hand, with roots in the egalitarian movements of the 1960s, and the Christian Right–conservative alliance on the other was reflected in a sharp polarization within mainstream Protestant denominations and within Catholicism. Conservative and liberal Christians now have more in common with their counterparts in other denominations than with fellow communicants whose views differ from their own. As we noted in the previous chapter, in some cases conservative and progressive factions have even organized to counteract each other's power within the same churches.

There are several flashpoints of conflict within churches. Although the ordination of women is generally accepted in mainline Protestantism, it is still resisted by both Roman Catholic and right-wing evangelical leaders. The Vatican and American bishops have virtually interdicted discussion of women's ordination, even though popular support for this reform continues to grow among American Catholics. Southern Baptists, for their part, have sought to roll back the ordination of women. Since ordination is congregationally based for Baptists, this retrogression takes the form of refusal of fellowship and monetary support to those congregations that ordain women.[69]

Inclusive language and feminist theology are another point of contention in the churches. Conservative churches boycott inclusive-language lectionaries, hymnals, and Bible translations produced by liberals. This antipathy becomes particularly volatile when it comes to female imagery for God. Exemplifying this conflict was the orchestration of reaction by conservatives against the Reimagining Conference, held in November 1993. More than two thousand

Christian women and a few men convened in Minneapolis to mark the Decade of the Churches in Solidarity with Women. The gathering was international and multiethnic, celebrating the emergence of women's leadership and theology around the world. The main hymn of the conference featured the biblical image of Wisdom, a female personification of God.

A right-wing think tank, the Institute for Religion and Democracy, sent undercover agents to the conference to tape-record the speeches and songs. Taking phrases out of context, staffers created a press packet that "proved" that conference attendees were worshiping a "pagan Goddess, Sophia" (Wisdom) and aiming to infiltrate the churches with pernicious antibiblical "paganism." The results of this negative campaign were formidable: conference organizer Mary Ann Lundy lost her job in the Presbyterian Church (though sympathizers found her another with the World Council of Churches), and veritable inquisitions took place in Presbyterian, Lutheran, and Methodist churches as conservatives sought to oust women ministers who had attended the conference, and thus to remarginalize the growing presence of feminist women clergy.[70]

Homosexuality is another divisive issue for many churches. A movement named Reconciling Congregations has undertaken to create welcoming churches for gays and lesbians.[71] The question of ordination for homosexuals has become especially problematic, with major denominational studies on the issue usually ending in deep conflict. Majority votes generally run against such ordination in national assemblies, though some local churches continue to support gay or lesbian pastors.

The blessing of gay and lesbian marriages took center stage in the late nineties. In the United Methodist Church, such "holy union" ceremonies had been performed by some pastors for two decades, but conservative Methodists now sought to put a stop to the practice by inserting into the Methodist Book of Social Principles a statement condemning it. While the mandates in this book had traditionally been regarded by Methodists as being merely advisory rather than compulsory (it includes support for pacifism and social justice), the Judicial Council of the United Methodist Church ruled in 1998 that this particular statement was legally binding where the other mandates of the Social Principles were not.

In April 1999 Gregory Dell, a well-respected Methodist pastor in

Chicago, was subjected to a church trial for performing a holy union and convicted under the new ruling. The court moved to relieve him of his pastoral duties.[72] In another protest against the restriction, a group of more than ninety Methodist pastors conducted a holy union for a lesbian couple in Sacramento, California. Sixty-seven of them were indicted under the church judicial system, though their cases were eventually dismissed. Gregory Dell now heads a new Methodist organization named In All Things Charity, formed to fight the new ruling and change it in the Methodist General Conference of June 2000.[73]

These latter events reflect a deep division within the churches over the understanding of marriage, sexuality, and family. The focus in these church trials on the purely legal issue of whether Gregory Dell and the other Methodist pastors broke church law, and in so doing violated their oaths of ordination, seems suspect, especially since the law itself is new and appears to have been enacted for the specific purpose of entrapping such pastors. The real question for religious institutions is, What kinds of marriages, families, and sexualities are holy and to be blessed, and which are not? In chapter 9 I will return to this point.

CHAPTER 8

The Many Faces of American Families in the Year 2000

American families are increasingly diverse. It is no longer possible to speak of one predominant "normative" model of family. The efforts of the Christian Right to hark back to a nostalgic myth of male bread-winners and full-time housewives are becoming ever more unrealistic both culturally and economically. Two-earner families, with a working wife and husband, now comprise the majority of house-holds, for reasons having to do more with economic necessity than with feminism (though feminism certainly helped encourage women to aspire to better-paying professional positions and escape the job niches of low-paid secretarial and service work).

COMPONENTS OF FAMILY DIVERSITY: A POSTMODERN VIEW

A look at contemporary American Society shows that the "modern" family constructed in the Victorian era and reaffirmed in the 1950s is no longer the predominant form of American household—if indeed it ever was. A postmodern perspective calls for an acceptance of this reality of diversity of family models. The 1996 census counted 267 million Americans, of whom 13 percent were black, 11 percent Hispanic, 4 percent Asian or Pacific Islander, and 1 percent native American.[1] Hispanics constitute a growing percentage and are projected to surpass African Americans in the 2000 census. Non-Hispanic whites make up a dwindling majority of 71 percent. These Americans live in about a hundred million separate households, 70 percent of which, or seventy million households, are listed as families, defined as two or more people living together and related by blood, marriage, or adoption. The other 30 percent, or thirty million households, consist of single persons (about twenty-five million) or "unrelated" people (five million households).

These figures indicate that a startlingly large number of Americans live alone as single householders. This status can stretch across the life cycle: a person living alone may be an unmarried male or female worker in his or her early twenties, a man or woman of thirty to sixty who has never married or is divorced or widowed, or an elderly person subsisting on a pension and Social Security. Those five million households of "unrelated" people encompass various configurations, including gay and lesbian couples, cohabiting heterosexual couples, and other nonrelatives living together, such as members of religious orders.

The seventy million households counted as "families" consist predominantly of two-earner married couples with or without children. These now make up about 47 percent of American families. Another 30 percent of families have a male breadwinner and an economically dependent wife. Female-headed families, where the woman is both the primary economic provider and the parent, account for another 18 percent; only 5 percent have male head without a spouse. The figures for white and black households differ markedly: where white families are 49.3 percent two-earner, 32.1 percent male-breadwinner, and 14.1 percent female-headed, black families are 46.8 percent female-headed, 30.8 percent two-earner, and only 15.3 percent male-breadwinner.[2]

Increasingly, those households defined as families, whether with one male earner, one female earner, or two earners, are themselves part of a complex kinship network shaped by divorce and remarriage. Some 90 percent of Americans eventually marry, with the average age of marriage now in the midtwenties for women and the late twenties for men. This is close to the normative pattern for much of American history (the 1950s average of twenty for women and twenty-two for men was actually an aberration).[3]

Childbearing, however, now occurs later than at any period in American history. American women on average have two children, born when they are in their late twenties or early thirties. As women wait to marry and bear children until after completing their college and professional educations and establishing careers, more and more are having children in their mid- to late thirties. What these figures conceal is a bifurcation between two groups of women, which in turn corresponds to the increasing split between two classes of Americans: the educated who aspire to a middle-class income through education, the establishment of a profession, and delayed marriage and child-bearing, and those who drop out of high school and bear children in their teens, thereby lessening their prospects for escaping poverty.

The reconfiguration of households through divorce is now a major part of American family patterns. Divorce is not entirely new in American life: 12 percent of American marriages ended in divorce in 1900, and 30 percent in 1950. The divorce rate rose steadily in each decade of the twentieth century to peak in 1980, when some 5.2 per thousand marriages were dissolved each year. Since 1980 the rate has declined somewhat, to 4.3 per thousand in 1996.[4] About 80 percent of all of those who divorce ultimately, remarry, though more men do so than women (85 percent versus 75 percent).[5]

This latter gap reflects the larger income of divorced men as compared with divorced women, and the greater economic and social status that enables them to marry younger women. The divorced woman is likely to experience a sharp economic decline (about 40 percent) as she moves to support herself rather than be supported either by a male income or as part of a two-earner household.[6] The divorced woman's diminished economic power and the lower social status of female—as reflected in the custom of men marrying younger women—make it difficult for her to find an eligible man her age or older to marry.[7]

The high divorce rate and the large number of women as well as men who remarry mean that about a third of American households include divorced persons. The divorced may join the ranks of the single householders if they have no children or are noncustodial parents (usually men), or the women may become female heads of households. The majority will recouple and rejoin the ranks of male-headed or two-earner married households. In any case, the diversity of single-person, female-headed, and married-couple households embody a complex network of kinship relations.

If American families are looked at not in terms of households but in terms of kin networks, what emerges is a web of relationships created by blood, marriage, and remarriage, often maintained over great geographical distances. Thus the person listed as a single householder may be connected to parents who are themselves living in separate households created by divorce and remarriage, and to a network of siblings, half-siblings, and stepsiblings linked by these transfigurations.

Likewise, a woman living as part of a married couple may be raising her own children by a previous marriage, who may spend part of their time living with their father in another part of town or another city. The father's household may in turn contain a stepmother and children produced by this second marriage. The stepparents in the first and second households may themselves have been married before and may have children who visit, or visit them from, yet a third and a fourth household.[8]

Thus American kin networks can stretch across many households and are often maintained by long-distance communication and travel. E-mail, phone calls, and trips to or part-time stays in a second household may keep this kin network together. Family gatherings at weddings, funerals, or graduations may see several sets of parents, siblings, stepsiblings, and half-siblings, along with grandparents, aunts, and uncles across all these connections, assemble in all their startling complexity. Such complexity is not entirely new. As we saw in chapter 1, divorce and remarriage were common in Roman culture, while earlier European families were often reshaped by the early death of a spouse (usually the mother) and the remarriage of the father. Stepmothers, usually seen as "cruel" toward the children of the previous marriage, are a common theme in European folk tales.

SEX, CHILDBEARING, MARRIAGE, AND DIVORCE

If we look at American women across the course of their lives, it becomes evident that they will be a part of several households in sequence, part of that time as self-sufficient adults. For the first twenty years they will be supported primarily by their parents, which may increasingly mean by income earned by their mothers as well as their fathers. Women may want to graduate from college and even earn a postgraduate degree in order to establish a lucrative career before marriage and childbearing. But to achieve this goal, they will have to negotiate the complex relation of sexuality to marriage and procreation.

About half of all American women (and three in four males)[9] begin sexual relations by eighteen years of age, but most will not marry for another six to ten years after that. If they are to avoid early unwed childbearing with its disastrous implications for their economic and social wellbeing, young women must become adept in the use of contraception. Teen births, including births to black teens, have been declining since 1970.[10] Contrary to popular myth, more teenagers are not getting pregnant today than in earlier generations.[11] But most sixteen- or eighteen-year-olds who got pregnant a hundred years ago were married, engaged to be married, or quickly forced to marry. The fathers of their children could expect to earn their living without the benefit of a college or even a high school degree, through on-the-job training.

It is true that large numbers of teenage slaves and servant girls were seduced or forced into sexual relations and impregnated by powerful men who had no intention of marrying them. But such young women were viewed as simultaneously disgraced and victimized, while the men were seen as the sexual aggressors. Today's unwed pregnant teenager is assumed to have willingly made herself sexually available and thus to be blameworthy, despite the fact that the majority of girls who have their first intercourse before the age of fifteen describe it as coerced or unwanted.[12]

These days, jobs are scarce for young men without or with only a high school degree, and what jobs there are will not pay a family-supporting wage. This is a major reason for white women's and, even more, black women's becoming unwed mothers and female heads of households if they become pregnant as teenagers.[13] Thus the enormous anxiety around teenage sexuality today is both moral and economic. The adult world foments teen sexuality through its sex-saturated culture, then claims to be shocked by its consequences. Opposition to abortion only complicates this dilemma. Teens must quickly learn about effective contraception if they are to negotiate the divide between sexual relations and the need to delay childbearing until after education and marriage. Access to contraception and accurate knowledge of how to use it are crucial if there is to be a real reduction in the number of unwed teen mothers and also an abatement in the recourse to abortion. (My assumption here is that abortion should be "legal, safe, and rare"—that is, it should be available to those who want it, but should optimally be rendered unnecessary by successful birth control, which prevents women from having to make this difficult "choice" to being with.)[14]

The young woman who is able successfully to cross the divide and to attain a college degree and an income-producing skill will likely marry in her midtwenties and then decide in a conscious and planned way to have a family. Such a planned family is the other side of the proper use of contraception, which allows a woman not only to avoid unwanted pregnancy but also to choose childbearing at the time of her life when it is most economically appropriate—that is, when she is married to a man with a family-supporting income and she herself can continue to work full-time or part-time and afford to pay for child care.

Almost half of all American marriages dissolve in divorce at some point. About 40 percent of those end within the first four years, particularly among those who marry in their late teens and early twenties. Another 40 percent of divorcing couples are in their thirties or early forties, and some 20 percent in their late forties or beyond.[15] For American women, divorce may thus occur at several stages in their life cycle: after a few years of marriage, usually without children; at midcareer, with children who are still dependent; or at the point when children are completing college and/or about to become independent.

Divorces that take place after twenty years of marriage often reflect the feelings of women or men that they have discharged their responsibilities to their children and can at last dissolve a bond that has long been unsatisfactory. But the aftermath of such late divorces is frequently different for men than for women. Men more often divorce during a midlife crisis, to marry another, much younger woman and even start a second family, while women divorce to enter more fully into their careers.[16]

Although joint custody is becoming a normal pattern in American divorce, this still means that children usually reside with and are primarily supported by their mothers and merely visit their fathers. Only about 40 percent of divorced fathers comply with child-support payments in the first year of separation, and the figure drops to 13 percent after ten years.[17] The more involved men are in coparenting, the more likely they are to pay child support.[18] But that child support will not be sufficient to enable the divorced woman to care for her family; she will need her own income as well. The assumption that divorced women with children can be largely self-supporting through their own employment has become the operating assumption of American divorce law.[19]

The majority of divorced women remarry. This means in most cases that the woman will join her income to that of her new husband to form a two-earner family. This will greatly boost the economic status of the new household. The average employed white woman makes $24,000 a year; combining that with the male median income of $34,000 will move the new family into a comfortable economic range. But the two-earner family with children—perhaps "hers," "his," and "theirs,"—will experience additional stress in the form of long hours of work for both spouses. This can make for acute tensions between time spent at work and time needed for unpaid housework and nurture of family relations. Despite an increased willingness on the part of men to do housework and child care in the American family today, most of this "second-shift" work will still fall on the woman.[20]

Even if a woman's first, or second, marriage lasts into old age, she can nonetheless expect to live an average of seven years longer than her husband (eight years longer if she is black).[21] Thus, when she gets old, a woman will likely again be a single person, living either by herself or in a retirement home. Few grandmothers today live in households with their children, and those who do are primarily members of ethnic communities that maintain earlier patterns of extended families. Thanks to Social Security, pensions, and Supplemental Security Income (SSI), few elderly Americans are destitute, but elderly women are more likely to be poor than elderly men.[22] The margin of a woman's comfort in her old age will depend very much on her own work trajectory during her lifetime, as well as what she may have inherited from a husband's work.

This excursus into a typical American woman's life span indicates that no American woman can safely be socialized as a teenager or young adult into a future based on the expectation of being supported by a husband for the rest of her life. Most American women—some 80 percent—will work for some period of their life, part of that time as independent, self-supporting adults who may also be the primary supporters of children, and part as one half of a two-earner couple. The "promise keepers" who idealize the lifelong economic dependency of women on men are setting those women up to be unprepared for self-support in future crises.

The high divorce rate among Americans is often blamed by conservatives on a "decay" of moral values. This plaint is often couched in terms of a false historical dualism: in some mythical past, it is claimed, people married "for life" and stuck it out through thick and thin, whereas today people marry on a whim and quickly break up when the relationship goes sour. This is a partial truth at best, both about the past and about contemporary realities. All industrialized nations have seen rising divorce rates, though the United States is significantly higher than other countries'—almost twice as high as the rate in Sweden (4.3 per thousand compared with 2.5 per thousand),[23] a nation that Americans often see as morally lax. As we noted in chapter 7, born-again Christians and, even more, fundamentalist Christians have a divorce rate slightly higher than the average for the United States.[24]

If divorce is hardly new to western society, divorced women were nonetheless deeply stigmatized in the past and likely to be economically destitute. The Christian tradition forbade divorce until the Reformation, when some small allowance was made for it under certain conditions. Unhappy marriages, domestic violence, premarital sex, and adultery (especially for men)—all these are old stories. Three major changes shaped the pattern of divorce between 1900 and 2000: first, economic production virtually disappeared from the home, and so couples no longer functioned as a team in a household economy; second, women became autonomous legal persons who could vote and own property, and their earning capacity greatly expanded; and third, legal independence allowed women to be economically self-supporting without husbands.

The first of these changes happened in the mid–nineteenth century; the second developed more slowly, toward the end of the nineteenth century, and culminated in the passage of the Nineteenth Amendment in 1920 (with some fine-tuning in the 1970s); and the third change took place gradually over the twentieth century, particularly its last thirty years. Taken together, these changes have recast marriage as a love relationship to be entered into primarily for companionship and only secondarily for child rearing. Because many women can be self-supporting, unhappy marriages need no longer be endured. It is now more often women than men who make the decision to divorce.[25]

This is not to say that divorce is a decision taken lightly. Even no-fault divorce (in which neither spouse has to prove that the other has been guilty of a fault, such as abuse or adultery) is extremely stressful personally and difficult economically for both women and men. Precisely because American couples invest so much in the hope of deeply bonded, lifelong companionship, divorce represents a time of deep disappointment and even traumatic conflict. If children are involved, the working-out of equitable coparenting may not be easily achieved.

While men emerge economically better off than women from divorce, both suffer economic losses. The cost of the divorce itself may be considerable, and men lose a second earner in the family, while women must become the primary household earner, usually on a lower salary. The whole experience is sufficiently painful that few couples would undertake it did not the alternative in terms of the unhappiness of staying married seem worse. Making divorce more difficult—for example, by going back to fault-finding—would not lessen its occurrence, but only make the process itself more stressful and expensive.[26]

A better means of inhibiting divorce would be to require more careful preparation for marriage. Marriages that are entered into after a year or more of preparation, in which differences in views on vital matters such as economic and legal issues are worked through, may be more likely to survive. Indeed, the decline in the divorce rate over the last twenty years may itself reflect the trend toward marriage at older and more mature ages.

While lifelong monogamy continues to be an ideal, but serial monogamy has become an established reality for many people in modern industrial societies, and that is not likely to change. One reason for this, again, is that women are no longer economically and legally dependent on men and can support themselves. Another reason is that both men and women now live twice as long as they did in centuries past and thus go through more stages of life development. A relationship that was satisfactory for one stage of life may become deeply hampering in another. Not only men but now also women are outgrowing former companions. The very demand that marriage offer fulfilling companionship itself creates the need for divorce, as Milton realized in the seventeenth century.[27]

GENDER, RACE, AND THE ECONOMY

As indicated above, a major reason for the delay of marriage and childbearing, besides the likelihood that a woman who becomes pregnant in her teen years will remain an unwed mother for some years, is the economic difficulty men face in achieving a family-supporting wage without a college or even a postgraduate degree. Shifts in the postindustrial economy have driven down incomes for those with only a high school degree, while escalating the salaries of the top 20 percent of Americans in the managerial and high-tech areas.

Jobs in America are increasingly polarized between two strata of workers: those who make hourly wages at the minimum rate ($5.15 an hour in 1996) or a few dollars more, and those with high credentials who receive full-time, full-year contracts at $30,000 to $50,000 annually. A wage of $8.20 an hour would be necessary even to attain the 1997 official poverty level of $16,400 for a family of four. Thus many families with one full-time worker or even one full-time and one part-time worker at minimum wage cannot rise from poverty.

Although the minimum wage has been steadily raised over the last half century, it has failed to keep up with rising costs of living. In 1969, a full-time minimum-wage job took a worker to 120 percent of the poverty level for that year, but since 1980 the ratio of minimum-wage income to cost of living has continually fallen, reaching 70 percent of the poverty level in 1990 and 1997.[28]

The reasons for this declining wage for low-credentialed workers are complex. One major cause that is often cited is the deindustrialization of America and the consequent loss of high-wage, unionized manual labor. Heavy industrial production in steel, automobiles, railroad cars, and the like has all but disappeared from the United States due to globalization of production and the movement of such factories to lower-waged Third World areas, even as the offices of production managers remain in this country.[29]

Low-skilled manual-labor jobs have also been eliminated by technological advances. Computerization has rendered obsolete many jobs based on human labor, while creating a few better-paid positions for the computer-skilled.[30] Work itself has also become more unstable for all but the very wealthy. Downsizing can put even well-paid managers and engineers out of work on short notice, with little promise of replacing their jobs with others of comparable status and income.[31] Today's workers, at the beginning of the twenty-first century, have had to become mobile and flexible, harboring no loyalty toward companies that have no loyalty toward them after years of service, and ready to "jump ship" at any moment to relocate from workplaces that seem to be about to cut jobs. Many have created their own forms of self-employment to respond to a high-tech market.

Jobs have grown in the United States primarily in the service areas, which are low-paid, part-time, part-year, and without benefits. This is a major cause of both poverty and the lack of medical insurance and pensions for the working poor. But deindustrialization and the expanding service economy only partly explain the two-tiered work structure. Another important factor is the rising demand for high credentialing even for entry-level positions. The term *credentialing,* as opposed to skills, is used to differentiate between that which may be obtained through on-the-job experience and which is demanded before a candidate will even be considered for a job, despite the fact that a college degree may have little connection with the specific abilities needed.

In earlier generations, men's jobs allowed a longer ladder of upward mobility through work experience. A man might start in an office as an errand boy without a college or even a high school degree and make his way up to the management level through hard work, ingenuity, and (usually) good connections. Today men's jobs are much more segmented, with little upward mobility between one category and another. A man who starts as an office boy will never become a manager; to become a manager, he must enter at the management level with a college degree, and more often than not, an M.B.A.[32]

As we saw in the shift of clerical work from men to women in the late nineteenth century, women's work has always been more segmented, without upward mobility from clerical to management levels, which have generally not been open to women.[33] In this sense we can say that there is now less differentiation between male and female work, because although low-paid, female-identified work persists in the areas of clerical, nursing, personal, and domestic service, men today also have much less chance of moving up on the basis of on-the-job skills, experience, or connections. College and professional degrees are the gatekeepers that afford entry into higher job categories.[34]

A second cause of declining affluence for the middle 60 percent of Americans is the rising cost of living, and especially the increased expenses of education, housing, property taxes, and cars, the biggest household expenditures. The widening economic gap between the middle sector and the wealthiest 20 percent—and most particularly the top 1 percent—of Americans has created a sharp cultural dissonance between two key generations: those born in the 1920s and '30s, who experienced the belt-tightening of the Depression and the patriotism of World War II, and established their families and rose to middle-class comfort amid the expanding economy and government subsidies of the 1950s; and their children, the "baby boomers," who were born in the 1950s and sought to enter the job market and start families in the 1980s and '90s.[35]

A major part of this dissonance can be traced to a U.S. culture that lacks a critical education on economic and class structures and conceives of wealth and poverty primarily in individualistic and moralistic terms, as a matter of hard work and personal discipline versus laziness and the wrongful expectation of "getting something for nothing." This individualist and moralist culture renders older generations of middle-class white Americans blind to the roots of their own success (e.g., the extent to which it was based on government subsidies such as the GI Bill, which supported education and housing) and uncomprehending of the difficult times faced by their own children, as well as the endemic poverty of those seen as "other"—that is, the nonwhite poor. This myopia underlies the punitive responses to the dilemmas of those nonwhite poor, who are presumed to be the cause of their own poverty due to their lack of moral discipline.[36]

But cultural fracturing is not limited to survivors of the Depression and World War II and their children. There is another, similar division between the early baby boomers, who grew up in the 1960s and early '70s, when an expanding economy created an expectation of expanding justice for all, and the later, more conservative generation that reached college in the Reagan years and got the message that they had better secure their own affluence at the expense of other, less privileged Americans.[37]

A quick review of the rising costs of education, transportation, and housing reveals the economic crunch faced by young adults of the 1980s and '90s. In 1950, a college education at a state university cost only a few hundred dollars a year, while elite private colleges might run $1,000 to $2000 annually. Today these costs have increased tenfold: state universities average over $6,500 a year for tuition, with many charging twice that amount, and elite private universities range from $20,000 to $30,000.[38] Even allowing for inflation, this is a major escalation of costs for what has become the indispensable entryway to better jobs.

Whereas in the 1950s the GI Bill covered much of the expense of higher education, the last two decades have seen college grants virtually disappear in favor of college loans. Many graduates now enter their first jobs with tens of thousands of dollars in debts to pay off.[39]

The costs of housing have likewise increased tenfold. A three-bedroom starter house in a pleasant suburb that cost $15,000 to $20,000 in the 1950s may now be worth $250,000 or even more, depending on the region of the country. The GI Bill eased house purchases in the 1950s, enabling young people who were starting their families in their early twenties to become homeowners. The ownership of a home whose value has increased ten times over the last thirty years has become the major asset of many older Americans, something they can trade for a comfortable retirement supplemented by income from pensions and Social Security.[40] However, rising property taxes can also force older owners to sell such homes and move to smaller quarters.[41]

The same rising housing cost that has become a windfall for older-middle class Americans is making it more difficult for their children to buy their own homes. The average age at first purchase of a house had risen to age thirty-five by 1991, compared with age twenty-seven as recently as 1980.[42] About half of all Americans are unable to clear enough of their debts and accumulate sufficient savings for a down payment that would allow them to move from being renters to being buyers of homes. This means they are spending more for housing as renters (around 44 percent of their income)[43] and are unable to deduct taxes and amass equity through homeownership. Many will enter their own older years without this key asset.

Transportation costs have also escalated. In the 1950s, a new car cost about $2,000; in 1999 even a small car went for around $15,000.

The decision of the U.S. government in the 1950s to suburbanize America through the private car and to allow mass transit to erode means that some form of transportation is needed to commute among work, home, and shopping. The private car is the preferred and often the only convenient means of connecting these vital parts of modern life.[44] A car is the first major purchase of most young adults and the first source of debts to be paid off through installment buying.

While higher education is the entryway to better jobs for young adults, it is also both their major expenditure and their major source of debt. Its economic benefits, meanwhile, vary by race and gender. More education raises all boats, but some more than others. In 1996 the median annual wage of white men with a high school education was $30,764, while for white women with high school degrees the mean was $20,285. With a college degree, white men averaged $60,858 and white women $37,275. White men who had graduate degrees made $113,997, while white women earned $60,099.[45] Black men's and women's incomes also rise with education, but on a scale that is closer to that of white women than that of white men. The overall median income of white men is $33,515, while black men's median is $24,799, and white women's $24,264. Black women average only $21,079,[46] though this figure rises sharply for those with post-graduate professional degrees.[47]

The relations among education, rising wages, and gender have also changed over the last twenty years. Between 1979 and 1993 the average wage for males without a high school degree, for full-time, full-year work, dropped 22.5 percent (to $400 a month). Male high school graduates saw their wages fall 11.9 percent (to $542 a month), while males with some further education lost 5.3 percent (to $645 per month). Only men with college degrees gained in wages (9.8 percent, to $1,004 a month).

Women's wages for full-time, full-year work during the same period rose for all educational levels except those without a high school degree. These women lost wages, but only 6.3 percent, down to $287 a month. Female high school graduates gained 5.7 percent, to $385 a month, while those with some further training saw their wages rise 11 percent, to $456 a month. Those with a college degree gained 27.1 percent, rising to $677 a month. Men still average more than women across the educational spectrum, but the gap has narrowed for all but the female lacking a high school degree.[48]

Women in all ethnic groups achieve more education than men, and this raises their incomes, but not to the levels of the top earners, white men. Twenty-five percent of Americans graduate from college, with women earning 55 percent of the college degrees. Women also receive 55 percent of the master's degrees. The education gap is wider between black and Hispanc men and women: blacks earning bachelor's degrees are 63 percent female and only 37 percent male, while Hispanics are 57 percent female and 43 percent male.[49]

However, women's college majors and graduate fields of specialization are more likely to be in low-paying areas such as secondary-school education, nursing, health, or social work, while men predominate in earning college and graduate degrees in science, engineering, and business. In 1995 women received 39 percent of the doctorates, 38 percent of the medical degrees, 43 percent of the law degrees, and 14 percent of the engineering degrees.[50] But women encounter greater difficulty than white men in translating these degrees into equally well paying jobs with equivalent upward mobility. In college teaching, women made up 43.7 percent of the faculties, but tenured faculty were 73 percent male.[51]

Although women's employment has significantly expanded in the prestigious professions, they are still the minority. In 1996 women were 12.3 percent of the ordained clergy, 13.7 percent of the dentists, 26.4 percent of the doctors, 29 percent of the lawyers, and 30.8 percent of the computer programmers. Women's work continues to be clustered in the traditional female professions and service areas, where they comprise 68.5 percent of social workers, 82.7 percent of librarians, 83.3 percent of primary-school teachers, 93.3 percent of nurses, and 99.1 percent of dental assistants.[52]

In both the professions where they are the minority and those where they are the majority, women are paid less than men in the same fields, both because men are concentrated in the top managerial levels and because they earn more in jobs at the same level. For example, while women predominate in the area of sales, they earn only 59 percent of what men in sales earn,[53] largely because of sex segregation of the goods sold. Men who sell cars, televisions, computers and washing machines make almost twice as much as women who sell women's clothes. Even among doctors, women earn only 58 percent of the average wage of male doctors.[54]

Overall, however, the gap has narrowed between women's median wage and men's. In the 1960s, data showed that women earned only 59 percent of what men earned. By the 1990s, women averaged about 75 percent of male wages,[55] but that approximation of female to male was due primarily to the falling income of lower-credentialed males, and only secondarily to women's own rising wages. More women are now making more money thanks to their greater access to elite professions, but male wages in those professions have risen even more than those of women.

THE GROWING GAP BETWEEN WEALTH AND POVERTY

The year 1973 was a key moment in the American economic U-turn toward greater polarization between wealth and poverty. From 1960 to 1973, the proportion of Americans whose income was below the poverty level fell from 22 percent to 11 percent; from 1973 to 1994, the figure rose again, to 14.4 percent. The Reagan years saw a significant shift of wealth from the middle and lower 80 percent of Americans to the upper 20 percent, and especially top 1 percent. In 1950 the top 1 percent had 28 percent of the wealth; by 1996 it had 38 percent.[56] The top 20 percent earned 43.7 percent of all income in 1950; by 1996 this latter figure had grown to 48.9 percent. Over the same period, the middle 60 percent lost 4.9 percent of the income, falling from 52.3 percent to 47.4 percent, while the income in the hands of the poorest 20 percent fell from 4.0 percent to 3.7 percent. This means that the top 20 percent of Americans now earn more than the middle 60 percent, and almost as much as the other 80 percent combined.[57]

The polarization between riches at the top and diminishing assets for the lower 80 percent of Americans is greater at the level of wealth ownership than income. The top 20 percent own 76 percent of the productive wealth in the form of businesses, stocks, bonds, and money-market accounts, with two thirds of it concentrated in the richest 1 percent. At the pinnacle of this elite are the "Forbes 400," the wealthiest Americans who collectively possess about 40 percent of the fixed capital. The bottom 80 percent own only 24 percent of the wealth, most of it in the form of houses and consumer durables such as cars. The lowest 27 percent have debts that exceed their assets.[58]

The major cause of poverty, as we have seen, is the low wages paid in jobs available to the low-skilled and low-credentialed. This situation will not be solved by forcing women who are raising children alone to get off "welfare" and into work, since the jobs available to them will not lift them out of poverty, even if they are able to work full-time and full-year. Not only are the jobs open to unskilled, low-credentialed woman low-paid, with wages reaching only 80 percent of the poverty level for full-time work, but such work is generally available only on a part-time basis and without benefits. Moreover, such women incur additional expenses by working, particularly for child care and transportation. This means that a job may bring in less income than AFDC (Aid to Families with Dependent Children) subsidies. The costs and difficulties associated with child care and transportation often defeat such women's efforts to retain jobs even when they have managed to secure them.

This is not to suggest that "welfare" payments ever supported such women handsomely. The image of a "welfare queen" who produces many children in order to live in comfort at government expense has always been at extreme variance with reality. Welfare payments were never intended to bring poor families above the poverty level, only to diminish the extremes of that poverty. White middle-class Americans have long been hostile to the nonworking poor, insisting, for example, on means- and morals-tested aid that both demeans those who receive it and excludes many of the poor, historically nonwhites.

Aid to Dependent Children started as a small program for those euphemistically called "widows"—actually any single mothers with dependent children—as part of the Social Security Act of 1935.[59] Although the number of women receiving such aid grew over subsequent decades, black and Hispanic women were largely excluded through the discretion allowed the welfare intake worker. A racial subtext was assumed for the "worthy mother" who should be home full-time, typically a white woman who properly ought to be dependent on the "family wage" of a white man. When such a male wage was lacking the woman due to the absence of a male wage-earner, the government functioned much like a stingy uncle to permit such women to fulfill their duties as mothers.

Black women with children had never, from slavery times on, been seen as appropriately homebound to tend to their own children. Instead, it was presumed that they (and other nonwhite women) could work even if they had infants or toddlers; nonwhite children could get along without full-time mothering. Black women should make themselves available for low-waged jobs such as sharecropping and domestic work. Put simply, white women should stay home and raise their children, while black women should go out to work to take care of white women's children.

Between 1968 and 1973, a lively movement named the National Welfare Rights Organization (NWRO) developed among female welfare recipients, with the aid of civil-rights lawyers and activists. Its aim was to construct welfare as a right rather than a stingy means- and morals-tested "handout." Handbooks were compiled to make information on the criteria for receipt of welfare benefits available to the poor. The welfare rolls burgeoned in those years as more and more people, particularly black women, were encouraged to apply and to claim their rights to aid on the basis of their economic need.[60]

The image of the typical welfare mother was now transformed from a deserving poor white widow frugally caring for her children to a bossy black matriarch who "emasculated" black males and caused them to be dysfunctional; then it shifted again, to a lazy, sexually promiscuous black teenage mother.[61] This construction of who the poor are who receive subsidies has facilitated an ongoing assault on welfare, from the Reagan years through the 1996 Welfare Reform Bill, passed by Congress and signed by President Clinton.

Those who have sought a better reform of welfare have long tried to correct this picture, often pointing out that since the New Deal, the federal government has actually erected a three-tiered system of government subsidies.[62] The first tier goes to the corporate wealthy, subsidizing oil companies and corporate farmers and bailing out failed savings-and-loans at public expense. The huge U.S. military budget is itself a government-subsidized form of state capitalism.[63] These subsidies are not recognized as such, but are instead defined as necessities for national defense and economic prosperity.

The second tier of subsidies goes to the elderly through the Social Security system. These, too, are defined not as subsidies, but rather as forced savings for old age. The elderly are seen as only getting back what they have earned through a lifetime of work (though the funds in fact come from current workers). Unemployment insurance is likewise viewed as an entitlement, to tide over those who have worked and will work again. Aid is also provided to handicapped people who are not expected to work, such as the blind and the physically and mentally impaired, who have been gradually included in guaranteed subsidies through SSI (Supplementary Security Income). These subsidies are not morals-tested, supervised, or stigmatized. They are underwritten entirely by the federal government, rather than being shared in by the states.[64]

By contrast, AFDC has long been a stigmatized stepchild of the government system of subsidies, and its recipients have been treated as morally questionable, in need of constant supervision to prevent "cheating." Funding for the program is shared between federal and state governments and has varied considerably from state to state. Since 1970, AFDC benefits for women with dependent children have regularly been cut back. In 1970 they averaged almost $800 a month for a family of four (in 1995 dollars), but by 1994 they had fallen to about $440, with Connecticut giving the highest benefit, at $680 a month, and Mississippi the lowest, at $120. Even the highest benefit yielded an annual income of only $8,160, a little over 50 percent of the poverty level.[65]

It is often pointed out that the poor are not primarily unemployed black single mothers living in high-crime ghettos. This group accounts for only about 12 percent of the poor. Poor people (i.e., those whose income falls before the official poverty level, itself a low figure) live in all regions of the country, in rural and suburban as well as urban areas. Poverty affects all ages: 40.8 percent are children, 49.8 percent are between eighteen and sixty-four years old, and 9.4 percent are over sixty-five. The majority are white (48.1 percent), with blacks' making up 27.1 percent and Latinos 20.1 percent. Asians and Native Americans account for the remaining 4.7 percent.[66]

Some 34.9 percent of the poor live in married-couple families, and 42.8 percent in families headed by single adults (mostly females). About 38 percent of white female-headed families, 55 percent of black female-headed families, and almost 60 percent of Hispanic female-headed families are poor. Sixty-three percent of the poor work at least part-time, and many have full-time, full-year jobs.[67] Most of the poor do not stay poor all their lives but go through a period of poverty and then escape it through a rise in income. For women, this period of poverty is often caused by getting a divorce and becoming a single mother with dependent children.

In 1991, 74.3 percent of white Americans had never been poor, while 16.6 percent had been poor for one to three years, another 6.4 percent for four to nine years, and only 1.8 percent for more than ten years. Among African Americans, 36.4 percent had never been poor, 18.9 percent had been poor for one to three years, 28.1 percent for four to nine years, and 16.7 percent for more than ten years.[68] Only 25 percent of all poor families had received any AFDC payments, and most of those only for short periods of time: 52.2 percent for one to three years (over a lifetime), 25.1 percent for four to nine years, and 22.7 percent for more than ten years. Those who had been continuously on welfare for over ten years comprised only 6.7 percent of recipients.[69] Thus the image of the chronic "welfare-dependent," unemployed black single mother living in the ghetto is a misleading one.

Nevertheless, explanations of how diverse, how white, and how hardworking the poor actually are have an unfortunate apologetic cast to them. It seems to go without saying that white middle-class Americans should regard as totally unworthy black single mothers who live in ghettos with chronic unemployment and deteriorated business, housing, and school institutions. In order to evoke feelings of concern, the poor must be seen as a white married couple that works, lives in a rural area or small town, and is impoverished due to temporary misfortune. But this can only suggest renewed ways of discriminating between the worthy and the unworthy poor based on race, work, and marital status. The real question is how to get most Americans to feel that black women and men living in endemic poverty in deteriorated inner city areas are part of "us," not a "them" to be cut off from the body of citizens.[70]

THE FALSE PROMISE OF THE 1996 WELFARE REFORM
The 1980s heard a rising call from social conservatives to drastically cut, if not altogether eliminate, welfare (i.e., AFDC and other subsidies for the poor, such as food stamps). Welfare was said to *cause* poverty rather than help the poor overcome it, creating a pathological personality (colored black and gendered female) that was chronically dependent, shiftless, and lacking the moral discipline for work thanks to these government "handouts."[71] The preferred solution to this problem was to force as many poor women as possible off the welfare rolls by making them get jobs. Work was assumed to be the answer to poverty and to the problems of the welfare recipient.

This rhetoric was largely specious and fostered endemic misunderstanding of the issues of poverty. As Rebecca Blank has shown in her 1997 book, *It Takes a Nation: A New Agenda for Fighting Poverty*, welfare programs such as AFDC, food stamps, and Medicaid have not failed; they have basically done pretty much what they were designed to do, which was not to get poor people out of poverty but to lessen that poverty and assure the poor of minimum nutrition and medical care.[72]

If such subsidies do not solve the problems of poverty, neither have they created them. By the same token, forcing poor women to work at low-paying jobs will not raise them out of poverty, since the pay level of the jobs available to them is insufficient to achieve that. Moreover, work for single mothers with dependent children is not a solution to the main problem that the AFDC was intended to solve—namely, how to enable these mothers to be fully available to take care of their children. It simply poses the question anew, Who will take care of the children when their mothers are working?

The work open to such mothers is not sufficient to pay for day care, and all efforts to organize an adequately funded day-care program for the poor have been rejected by American lawmakers—on the ground that it would allow women to work and hence not be available to take care of their children![73] American poverty policy suffers from a chronic contradiction in its views of women's roles. Popular thinking holds that women with small children should not work but instead should stay home to care for these children; by extension, day care is bad because it permits mothers to work and not take care of their children themselves. But poor (black) mothers are supposed to work and become self-supporting without day care for their children.

This misguided approach to welfare and poverty culminated in the 1996 Welfare Reform Law, which rescinded AFDC as a federally funded entitlement and turned it into a state-run program with restricted block grants (TANF, or Temporary Assistance to Needy Families) carrying lifetime limits (generally five years, though Indiana voted to allow only a two-year limit).[74] The receipt of grants depends on the applicant's compliance with various forms of behavior modification, including attending programs of work preparation and training, finishing high school, not having any more children, and taking whatever job is offered him or her.

In the four years since the passage of the law changing AFDC to TANF, there have been many claims on the part of government leaders, such as President Clinton, that it has "worked." From August 1996 to July 1998, the caseload of families dropped 31 percent, from 4.4 million to 3 million, and that of individuals 32 percent, from 12.3 million to 8.4 million.[75] But statistics showing how many people have been dropped from the welfare rolls have little to do with raising such persons out of poverty through adequately paid work.

Nor will efforts to force people into jobs actually reduce costs per person. The more training and supervision a program requires, the more costly it will be. Training people for jobs will cost far more than simply subsidizing those who fall below a certain income and leaving them to find their own way to improve their income above the level of the subsidy. Demands that persons attend job-training courses in order to get assistance require that such courses be organized and administered; likewise, demands that people stay in school call for monitors to regularly survey and report on school attendance.[76]

Evidence of what is happening to those who have been removed from the welfare rolls is incomplete (no provision was made for follow-up studies on these people), but partial studies done in the two years after the passage of the Welfare Reform Law suggest that poverty has increased rather than the reverse. Some 50 to 60 percent of those who left the welfare rolls found jobs, but only at the $5.50- to $7-an-hour level, which is not sufficient to lift a family out of poverty—particularly given the added costs of child care and transportation.[77]

Job tenure for those forced off the rolls is unstable. Many find jobs only to lose them again a few months later, for a variety of reasons that include lack of adequate preparation for work, unreliable day care, transportation problems, the health of the worker or family members, and family violence. With falling incomes and no health benefits, many of those forced off the rolls have to forgo needed medical and dental care, and some must resort to food pantries and soup kitchens to feed their families.[78]

A study conducted in six states used as criteria a number of hardships—having to go without food for one or more days, having the heat shut off, having to move because of an inability to pay the rent, doubling up housing to save money, and having to go without needed health and dental care—to test whether life had gotten worse for those who had left welfare. Overall, such hardships had increased for those removed from the rolls, by an index of 48 percent compared to 33 percent for those currently on assistance.[79]

The welfare-reform discourse about getting single mothers out of "welfare dependency" and into work has been framed by a peculiar set of assumptions that need to be examined rather than merely accepted. The underlying presumption is that every adult, male or female, should be "independent" and self-sustaining through wage labor. This view represents the culmination of a long set of historical shifts about the meaning of "dependents" and "dependency."

In feudal and early modern Christian societies, almost everyone was a dependent of someone else, with the exception of a small group of ruling-class males. In America, feudal relations and then slavery were abolished, ending that particular form of dependency of one subjugated group on another, dominant one. Although in fact all workers are highly dependent on their employers and the owners of their companies, wage labor has been construed as economically "independent," leaving only nonworking women, children, paupers, the elderly, and the infirm as "dependents."

As women have increasingly joined the work force, it has become more common to assume that they, too, are not to be "dependents," but should support themselves by their work. Only children under eighteen (who in earlier centuries were seen as workers at a young age) are "natural" dependents who should not work but should instead go to school in order to prepare themselves to be "independent" workers. Even the elderly are seen not as dependents, but as "independent" through their past work. The infirm alone are exempted from this demand to be "independent" wage workers.[80]

With most women now working outside the home, staying home to care for dependent children is no longer seen as a natural and honored role whereby women do socially valuable and necessary, if unwaged, work; instead, it is viewed as a form of pathology and immaturity, a failure to become an adult (i.e., a self-supporting worker). This judgment, as we have noted, is contradictory, however, for it is applied only to poor single mothers, not to white middle-class married women with children, who are encouraged to be "dependent" on their husbands' income.

Dependency in order to care for children is thus individualized and pathologized for poor (black) women who depend on government assistance, even as it is idealized for middle-class (white) women who depend on husbands. This disparity is mystified by the failure to recognize its economic base. Only upper-middle-class women can afford to stay home with small children, and only because of their high-waged husbands; most of the rest of the middle class maintains its standard of living only through the two-earner family. Poor women are faced with the impossible double tasks of mothering and providing economic support for their families at poverty wages; then they are blamed for failing to do both adequately.

The individualizing and pathologizing of dependency must be deconstructed by critiquing their antithesis, the notion of "independence" through wage labor. Only those who own large shares in corporations are "independently" wealthy, and they do not actually have to work. Wage workers, even high-wage workers, are dependent on an economic system over which they have little control. We need to recognize the webs of interdependency that define all of our lives—between men and women, parents and children in families, families and work, workers and employers. The question is not how to juxtapose a demeaned dependency with a fictitious independence, but how to ensure that these many forms of interdependence can become more just and more life-enhancing for those on both sides of the relation.

American society is increasingly polarized today, not only between the richest few and the rest, but also between the middle class and the poor. A three-tiered class system divides America into a wealthy owner class, an overworked middle class, and an underemployed and underpaid poor. In both the middle and the lower class, men and women are stretched to the breaking point, as they struggle to support families that they have little time to nurture or enjoy.

For middle-class Americans, both men and women, work expectations have expanded from an eight- to a ten- or even a twelve-hour day. The more one aspires to a high-paid profession, the longer the hours one is expected to work. Women who seek well-paid professions are on the same treadmill, while also carrying the primary burden of "family time."[81] The situation is even more extreme for the poor single mother trying to do both jobs at poverty wages. It is this contradictory tension between work time and family time that defines the greatest problem facing families today—for women particularly, but also for men. Its solution cannot be found in minor adjustments, but requires deeper transformations of the whole system of relationships between work and family and between men and women within and across all these divisions.

CHAPTER 9

Reimagining Families:
Home, Work, Gender, and Faith

A black and white bumper sticker, given to me by a gay male friend, adorns the back bumper of my car. It reads "Hate is not a family value." The slogan is a critique of the failure of the Christian Right's "family values" campaign to embody an ethic of justice and reconciliation in American society in the late twentieth century. That failure is rooted in the underlying premises of the Christian Right's views of family and society, which turn on a view of the "order of Creation" that (divinely) mandates patriarchal hierarchy of men over women, Christians over non-Christians, rich over poor.

Underlying patriarchal hierarchicalism is exclusivism. There is one superior race: white Western Europeans. There is one exclusively true religion—Christianity—and one right kind of Christian: a born-again evangelical Protestant. There is one right family model: a heterosexual, monogamous marriage with a male breadwinner and a female housewife. There is one right economic system, free-market capitalism, and one chosen nation, the United States of America. Those who are the leaders of this elect group have a God-given right and duty to impose it on everyone else and to sanction those who do not conform to one or another of its aspects—for example, gays, feminists, non-Christians, nonevangelicals, nonwhites, non-Americans.

These "biblical" mandates for society dovetail neatly with right-wing American views of the supremacy of the individual, unregulated rights of business, and of U.S. military superiority over the rest of the world. Class hierarchy, with its concentration of wealth at the top of American society, is seen as the appropriate reward for hard work and divine favor, while the poor have no one but themselves to blame. The assumption that the male-headed nuclear family is normative and God-given justifies a fierce rhetoric of homophobia and misogynism, spilling over into physical violence against family-planning clinics and gay people in a gun-saturated culture.

AN ECOFEMINIST FAMILY ETHIC

The reimagining of families by progressive people of faith demands more than just protest against these consequences of Christian Right views. It calls for the articulation of alternative values that promote a more authentic ethic of human relationships. The alternative ethic for postmodern family social values that I will propose in this chapter may best be defined as an "ecofeminist" ethic, one based on the equality and partnership of men and women in family, work, and society, and on the reconfiguring of work-family relations and economic and political hierarchies to foster a more equitable sharing of wealth within sustainable communities.[1]

This ethic calls for limits on the workaholic life-style that assumes that one is "justified" in spending longer and longer hours on the job. It seeks harmonization of the different spheres of life through fuller time for cultivation of our gardens, our relations with one another, our spouses, children, friends. In the ancient Hebrew vision, work time must be balanced by sabbath time.[2] All creation must regularly pause, rest, be restored, and celebrate God's presence with us. Working all the time is not a virtue but a sin, a grave violation of our relation to God and to one another in the life-sustaining rhythms of creation and re-creation.

In this concluding chapter I will explore the implications of an ecojustice feminist ethic for work-family relations, for supporting diverse forms of familial community, for sex and reproduction, and for fairness in the sharing of wealth. In the final section I will turn explicitly to the theological and biblical roots of this ethic. Does the anti-family eschatological ethic of the Gospels harbor a recoverable message for the understanding of diversity and sustainability in familial community today? How are nature and grace, creation and redemption related? On what side of this relation do marriage, reproduction, and family fall? And how does this relate to the sacramentality or non-sacramentality of marriage?

Basic to an ecofeminist ethic is the full and equivalent humanity of women in partnership with men. A feminist ethic rejects both gender hierarchy and gender complementarity as distortions of the full humanness of women and men, and sources of the unjust relationship between them. Men are neither natural nor divinely mandated "heads" over women, to whom women are called to submit and subordinate themselves. Nor is the relationship appropriately one of complementary differences, of "masculine" rationality and agency and "feminine" intuition and altruism.

Whatever nuances of differences in style may exist through biology and socialization, men and women each possess the full range of all human capacities. We need to see a social development through the life cycle by which men and women, women and women, men and men across generations can be friends and partners in mutual agency and self-giving, in interdependent flourishing through and with one another, rather than at the expense of one another. Good families are families that nurture this kind of mutuality in self-giving and receiving.

What this means in terms of family relations is an ethic of sharing that is truly equivalent. One should not flourish at the expense of the other. Committed relationship also means an acceptance of self-limitation. One decides to commit oneself to particular relationships, to building particular communities, by forgoing infinite possibilities. Each partner gives up some options for the sake of the wellbeing and development of the other, but in a way that is equitable and shared, rather than rooted in a gender hierarchy in which women do most of the deferring and men have a right to most of the flourishing. This can never be a fixed and finalized format, but must be one that calls for constant reformulation in a process of growth and change.

Patriarchal family systems have been based on male hierarchy and the separation of public and private—the public political sphere of ruling-class men and the subordinate private realm of women, children, and servants. Victorian patriarchy reformulated this in a softened way that concealed hierarchy under a language of complementarity. This corresponded to a new alignment of the public sphere of men with paid labor and the domestic sphere of women with unwaged housework.

This nineteenth-century middle-class family system was based on the attainment of a male "family wage," by which the male head could support the rest of the family without their waged labor. This, as we have seen, worked only for a short period of time, and only for the white midddle class; it never worked at all for blacks or indeed for most of the white working class, though the white male labor movement made it an ideal and goal.

This pattern has broken down due to economic, social, and legal shifts, as we have noted in the course of this study of family history. Women's legal equality and expanded education promise equal access to income-producing work, as well as to cultural and political development in the larger society; at the same time, the rising cost of living at the expense of wages demands that households have two earners for economic comfort. Most wives work for some part of their marriage, and more and more do so even when they have preschool children. Rather than deploring the loss of a family pattern of male breadwinning, which never worked for long or for everyone, we need to renegotiate the work-home partnership of men and women, and of other kinds of domestic partners who share homes and incomes.

Ideally, each partner would do half of the work of the home, and both partners would work in the paid economy. But more important is that in both areas the partners seek to shape fulfilling lives for each other. The old division of labor, with women at home and men at work, must shift to a new sharing of both home and work. This does not necessarily mean, however, doing exactly the same thing either at home or beyond the home, in the paid economy, culture, or politics.

In our home, for example, I cook and wash some dishes; my spouse washes most of the dishes, and does the vacuuming and repairs. In the garden I do more vegetables, and he does more grass. We complement each other by each doing what we like and can do better. In the paid work world, we have both been teachers. We have been privileged to have our paid work coincide with our vocation and the arena of our personal growth. In the early years of our marriage, when we had small children, both of us went to graduate school to complete our degrees. We shared caring for the children, and for about twenty hours a week had paid child care.

As we both began our careers, I taught part-time when the children were young, while he worked full-time. In our later years he has been more part-time, while I have worked full-time. I have had an extensive career as a writer and teacher, and he has been my enthusiastic supporter in this expansion of my creativity. We both have pursued our political interests and involvements on a volunteer basis.

Both of us, in turn, came from families that expected both education and work from both women and men. My mother graduated from a liberal-arts college in 1916, and my father earned a master's degree in engineering. My mother worked for a decade before marriage and traveled abroad to imbibe culture; she grew up bilingual in English and Spanish and added French to her languages through travel, pursuing lifelong learning. She did not work during her twenty years of marriage, from 1928 to 1948, but worked for another twelve years as a widowed single parent.[3]

My husband's parents followed an immigrant working-class pattern of survival through a two-earner household—his father was a housepainter and his mother a nurse—both working full-time (when possible) but spelling each other by his mother's working the night shift. His father had had only a few years of primary-school education in Germany. His mother finished high school and went on to graduate from nursing school, a lofty ambition for a woman in her context. He did more of the housework, repaired things, and tended the garden; she was the reader and the keeper of accounts.

I recount these family histories simply to illustrate that American couples of our parents' generation did not necessarily reflect the presumed "traditional" model of a male family wage and lifetime female dependency. Those of our own generation and, even more, of our daughters' generation have already adjusted to a pattern of mutually supporting two careers and shared home and family care. What is needed now is a shift in cultural ideology and in political, legal, and economic policies that will recognize and support this pattern of shared family, shared work, and shared social life. At present, the dominant cultural ideology, as well as the dominant economic and legal models, are rooted in a late-nineteenth-century home/work as female/male split that is dysfunctional and causes great tension and injustice for most households, particularly those with a low-income single earner.

BETTER POLICIES TO SUPPORT FAMILIES

The ideology of the modern nuclear family as a monolithic model needs to give way to a postmodern view of family—that is, one that recognizes a diversity of forms of partnering.[4] Policies that would provide legal, economic, and political support for the postmodern reality of family diversity have been on the table for more than thirty years, but they have been consistently resisted and rejected by U.S. policymakers, who have been largely unwilling to accept the obsolescence of the late-nineteenth-century family ideology. The social policy needed today is one that would ease the tensions between home and work for men and women alike and allow time for the genuine sharing of both spheres by both partners.

The tensions of the male/female as work/home split are intensified when children are involved. Child-raising now comprises only a third of most people's lives, and significant numbers of Americans choose not to have children at all. Yet family policy focuses particularly on families with dependent children because it is for them that the time and money crunch is most fraught.

Sustainable family policy for all couples, especially those with dependent children, means 1) shorter and more flexible work hours for jobs that pay an adequate wage; 2) paid maternity and paternity leave of at least three months for one partner (male or female) and at least two weeks for the other; 3) subsidies for that partner who cuts back to a shorter work week in order to do more of the parenting in the first four years of a child's life; 4) subsidized day care during the time when both parents are working; 5) after-school programs for children during the hours between the end of school and the return of their parents from work; and 6) full medical insurance and pensions for all adults, regardless of whether or not they work full-time and whatever the level of their income.

Effective policies would allow each parent of small children to continue to earn an income and maintain a career trajectory. But at the same time, work would take up fewer hours of the day for both partners, leaving them space to parent and to cultivate relations with each other as spouses. To these ends, we should consider 1) instituting a thirty-five-hour work week as the normative limit for all jobs;[5] 2) mandating flex time—so that one spouse could choose to start work at seven in the morning and end at three in the afternoon, and the other could work from ten to six—or four-day work weeks that would free partners to be home three days a week; 3) offering state subsidies of reduced hours for a parent who cuts back on work to care for his/her children; and 4) providing affordable day care subsidized by both employer and state and located either where people live or where they work.

These changes would enable two-earner couples to spell one another in their work and home responsibilities. They would have more time for parenting, and their children would spend less time in day care—perhaps twenty to twenty-five hours a week for preschool children, rather than the fifty or more that many parents are forced to resort to today. Subsidies would be increased for the single parent to make up somewhat for the lack of a second earner—at least to the level of a minimum income to meet basic needs.

Such policies have long been accepted by industrialized nations in Europe.[6] But the greater attachment of Americans to a certain ideology of race, class, and gender hierarchy, buttressed by religion, has blocked serious consideration of these reforms in this country. A concerted educational campaign is needed to reopen the discussion in American public discourse.

A second key "family value" for today involves acceptance of and support for a diversity of family forms. The family with a female homemaker and a male breadwinner is not the normative pattern, but it is one that should be available and honored when it is truly chosen, in a way that allows both the woman *and* the man to develop their best talents. A woman may, for example, want to be an artist or a writer and to do such work at home together with child care, without the demands of gaining a living wage from her work. The option of a man's staying home as the primary parent while his wife holds the main income-producing job should also be honored.[7]

We need to support a variety of family and household patterns. These include the single householder; the gay or lesbian couple, including partners raising children by adoption, former marriages, or artificial insemination; the single parent, male or female; the two-earner heterosexual couple; the three- or four-generation family; families blended through divorce and remarriage; and cohabiting partnerships of two, three, or more people that may or may not include a sexual pair. This diversity is already the reality of American life.

The exigencies of life in America at the dawn of the third millennium A.D. mean that people must support one another through a diversity of relationships. In all of these they should be encouraged by religious bodies to be as mutual, sustaining, and life-affirming as possible. These values of mutuality and commitment to flourishing life are not lessened but rather expanded when they are affirmed in many forms, and not in one form only that marginalizes and denigrates all the other forms by which people are sustaining their lives in community. We need to unmask the rhetoric that claims that the affirmation of "holy unions" for gay couples somehow demeans marriage for heterosexuals. All of our unions are made holier by expanding the options for faithful relationship and taking seriously their careful preparation and joyful blessing.

Both the church and the state have a stake in stable, committed partnerships that provide the framework for child-raising, sustaining the wellbeing of related people over a period of time, and caring for others in crisis, illness, and old age. But I submit that the role of the state and that of the church in affirming such relationships differ. It is time to uncouple the legal role of the state in defining domestic-partner contracts from the role of the church as the preparer and blesser of covenants.

As we have seen in the history of family recounted in this book, the merger of church and state to define marriage as both legal contract and church ceremony occurred slowly in Christianity, with different forms; fully emerging in Protestant and Catholic contexts only in the Reformation era. Divergent views of how nature and grace, creation and redemption met in marriage split Catholics from Protestants and still persist, though they have gone largely unexplored theologically on either side. Distinguishing the legal from the sacramental, and contract from covenant, would provide a new opportunity to examine and clarify the theological issues.

The church should get out of the business of being a legal agent for the state in making marriage contracts through the performance of weddings. Domestic-partnership contracts belong to the state and should be available in a variety of forms, covering not only heterosexual couples but also homosexual couples; single parents who wish to appoint other persons legal guardians of their children in case of crisis; single persons who wish to designate friends as responsible for their medical needs in time of illness; and those who want to name others as receivers of their medical benefits or property.

Such options should be available for a wide range of legally contracted partnerships, without privileging only one type of relationship as the sole legitimate type. The person one lives with as a beloved may or may not be the same person one wishes to be responsible for one's medical needs or the primary heir of one's estate. Many of these options already exist, but they need to be regularized in such a way that a certain package of legal privileges and responsibilities does not automatically belong to one kind of relationship—that is, heterosexual marriage—without being available in whole or in diverse part to those in other kinds of relationships.

HALLOWING COVENANT RELATIONS

Once the church is out of the business of being a surrogate for the state in making legal contracts, it can be freed to focus on its more important roles as preparer and blesser of covenants and healer of those who need to move away from covenants that have broken down, moving on to new lives and new kinds of relationships with former partners. It is the church's job to guide the spirituality and ethics of deepening relationship into sacramental bonding and redemptive promise.

The life-cycle ceremonies that have been available to Christians have focused on three moments: monogamous heterosexual marriage for life, baptism, and confirmation of children (as well as sickness and death). While surely important, these are no longer adequate to the complex realities of society, including the more diverse forms of family, such as homosexual couples; the ten- to fifteen-year gap between puberty and marriage for many people, occupied by experimental sexual relations; and the breakdown of marriages in divorce. We need to find pastoral and liturgical forms that can help people in these diverse situations and stages of life, which are currently ignored by the church or rejected as sinful and without redeeming value.

I can only touch on these more expanded expressions of covenanting in a schematic way here; they could fill a whole book in themselves. I suggest the creation of covenant celebrations that can hallow and heal us in these many stages of life and types of relation. The first two have to do with the entering into of a sexual relation by two people, heterosexual or homosexual, who seek to integrate sex with the covenant of friendship and mutual support of each other's development. These covenants aim to unify three forms of love— *eros, philia,* and *agape*—by first bringing together erotic love and friendship; then, on a more mature level, the third form of love develops, service in self-giving to one another and to the larger society and creation, as the couple grows into union in and through the love of God.

We might think of sexual-friendship covenants as allowing for two stages of entry: temporary vows and life vows. Temporary vows would allow younger couples in particular, not yet ready for permanent commitment personally or economically, to make a commitment to each other that is exploratory, perhaps to be evaluated and renewed on a year-to-year basis. The vows could be simple, without great public ceremony. A few friends and mentors could gather together to confirm the new relationship and help those entering into it to talk it through. This recognition would give the relationship a legitimacy and seriousness without the partners yet having to make a decision for permanency.

Such temporary vows by cohabiting couples would recognize the transitional stage between teenage sexuality and permanent commitment that is already a fact of life for many people, but that is denied or covered up by parents and youth because there exists no means of affirming it as its own stage of life. This crucial period of early sexuality between the teens and midtwenties would no longer need to be veiled in lies, with dangerous consequences for the future of both the youth and any possible offspring. Temporary sexual covenants would explicitly exclude child-creation, helping young people to learn how to bring together *eros* and *philia* while precluding impregnation by the effective use of contraception.

A second type of covenant would allow a couple to enter into a permanently committed relationship that seeks a fuller unity of *eros, philia,* and *agape* over the course of many years, with or without the expectation of creating and raising children together. I believe that these covenant vows should take place only after some period of preparation in which the legal, economic, social, and sexual aspects of the relationship are worked through by the couple, and only when both partners feel firm in their decision to commit themselves to a lifelong effort of covenantal bonding. A larger public ceremony and celebration are appropriate for these covenantal vows, as a way to link the couple with other members of a community who will vow to be their supporters in their journey.

A third type of covenant ceremony would belong to the time shortly after the birth of a child. This could be thought of as a naming ceremony or a baptism, depending on one's theology of baptism. The welcoming and naming of a child should involve the parents' vowing to remain faithful to the parenting of the child through his or her dependent years and to continue in a relationship with the child to the end of their lives, regardless of whether they themselves remain in relation as a couple.

The naming ceremony should also link the child to other adults, "godparents" or, as in the Latin American tradition, *co-madres* and *co-padres*. These spiritual parents should promise to support the parents in raising their child (both socially and economically), to help mentor the child as he or she grows, and to be ready to assume a fuller responsibility for the child if the parents' ability to carry out their parental duty is diminished through death or a break in their relationship. This role also can allow those who choose not to parent themselves to nonetheless participate in parenting through broader godparent relationships.

A fourth covenanting ceremony should take place at some point during the midteen years, as the child moves toward becoming a young adult. This ceremony would correspond to the bar or bat mitzvah for Jews, to confirmation for some Christians, or to baptism-confirmation for Christians of believer-baptism traditions. At this time the youth should choose one or two people who will mentor him or her over a year's time, helping work through the issues involved in the transition from childhood to adulthood, with all its conflicting messages about sexuality, economics, and relationship to adults and peers.

A formal covenanting ceremony should be embedded in a community of friends, parents, and children who have already been journeying together. The child would read a faith statement of his or her understanding of this transforming moment between childhood and young adulthood, and then would mark the moment by moving from the circle of children to that of the adults. In doing this, he or she would begin to leave the life stage of being primarily the recipient of nurture from parents and other mentors, and begin to enter another stage, of being a nurturer of others—peers and younger children and eventually parents as well.[8] The young person might take an additional name at this time to signify his or her entry into a new stage of self-defined identity.

The preparation for the coming-of-age ceremony should include education in sexuality. Young people need to know how to separate sexual play from intercourse. They need to begin the cultivation of an *ars erotica* that integrates sexuality with friendship and responsible relationship. As they move toward a more committed but not yet permanent sexual friendship, they need education in contraception, and they need to learn how to separate mutual sexual pleasuring from pregnancy. Such education was once a part of many cultures' indigenous puberty rites, rites that were repressed by missionaries as immoral—with the effect of reproducing the Western pattern of unwed teenage pregnancies.[9]

In addition to these four covenant ceremonies related to sexual friendship, child raising, and coming of age, a fifth form of covenanting for community is needed. This type of covenanting would bring adults together in spiritual friendship that is not physically sexual. They would vow to build community together to support both their own spiritual journeys and their service to others. It would correspond to the Christian tradition of spiritual covenant communities, but it could be shaped in more flexible ways, not necessarily excluding other—for example, sexual—forms of relationship. It might be limited to particular ministries and/or time periods, but it might equally involve building more permanent institutions intended to carry their members across a longer part of the life cycle, perhaps comprising education, ministry, and support in old age, as in religious orders.

Every covenanting relationship, particularly those envisioned as long-term, must deal with failure, with the possibility of brokenness, the outgrowing of a relationship, or the inability to shape the sort of deeper union to which one may aspire but which nonetheless finds oneself unable to attain. This is the moment when those who have covenanted together to be partners often find themselves most abandoned by community, most isolated and silenced.

Here the spiritual community must find forms of healing ceremony that can help partners who are dissolving a relationship work through the transition to new lives, new ways to be friends, ways to continue to parent their children together even if they themselves are no longer a couple. The covenant with children continues and is not dissolved by changes in the relations of parents. We need new forms of liturgy to express and help heal this painful transition through divorce, so that former partners can still retain some elements of friendship with each other, of continued community with friends, and of sustained parenting of their children.[10]

RETHINKING SEXUAL AND REPRODUCTIVE ETHICS

This discussion of covenants for sexual friendship demands a discussion of sexual ethics. Sexphobia has been a powerful force in Christian society, and its legacy continues in America today. The Christian tradition made sex sinful in its very nature and sought to limit it as much as possible, both by separating out a clerical and religious celibate elite and by attempting to subjugate lay people to a severe discipline that restricted sex solely to purposes of childbearing in the context of lifelong marriage. Sexual pleasure outside this context was "mortally" sinful, and the (male) orgasm was defined as the means by which sin was transmitted from generation to generation.

The lasting effect of this antisexual tradition has been not to make Christian societies sexually abstemious, but rather to create a deep split within the Christian personality between puritanism and prurience. One can see this split in some of the Christian evangelical leaders, not to mention in the supposedly celibate priests who are revealed to have engaged in sexual abuse of children, both male and female. On the level of the Superego, sex is disdained, feared, and treated as an obscene subject. On the Id level, covert sexual activity takes an exploitative and often violent form that is implicitly, if not explicitly, misogynist. Women are both despised and seen as objects to be used and discarded.

To overcome this fissure between puritan and prurient views of sex, both of which despise women, we need a new *ars erotica* that will teach people how to deepen their sexual pleasure, integrating eros and friendship. This humanizing of sex—that is, the linking of it to friendship, to a caring relationship between partners—seems to be more of a female tendency than a male one. This has partly to do with socialization and the deeper threat that women face through sexual use without friendship, with the concomitant possibility of becoming pregnant and being abandoned to bear a child alone. But it may also be rooted in biology in the sense of physical structure, of women as penetrated and men as penetrators, which may allow men to externalize the sex act while women internalize it.

The humanizing of sex thus carries an element of socializing the male to the female point of view on sex and relationship, and controlling the male tendency to view sex, and hence woman, as a casual conquest. In some cases the sexual revolution of recent decades has been exploited in an attempt to force women to accept the male view of sex and make themselves available for casual "romps" without relationship. We have seen how some young women of the 1960s New Left tried to be "politically correct" by acceding to this male view of sex, only to revolt against it in anger and disgust when they recognized its deep violation of their persons. Significantly, this revolt became a major root of the radical feminist movement.

With the renewal of a misogynist Christian Right, American dominant culture has recommitted to its puritan-prurient split personality. This means that young people in their teens to mid- or late twenties—those who have become sexually active but are not yet ready or able to marry—are largely left to deal with sex on their own, without moral guidelines. An *ars erotica* that cultivated the integration of sex with friendship would allow all of us to imagine sex as a maturation process. Early dating with sexual play but not intercourse moves naturally to a going-steady relationship and then to a decision to form a temporary covenant that might include living together, cultivating eros in friendship, but not yet in permanent commitment or readiness for child-raising.

Fidelity and commitment are essential to the integrating of eros and friendship, but such integration needs to be seen as a process of maturation rather than a single leap from "virginity" to marriage. Traditional sexual ethics were based on the legal boundary between sex inside the institution of marriage and sex outside it. Outside of marriage, all sex was sinful, regardless of its quality of care and friendship. Inside it, it was "anything goes," including the "right" of the husband to rape his wife. Since the wife had a "duty" to submit sexually to her husband, no amount of force used to make her do so within marriage was seen by the church as sinful.[11]

A sexual ethic rooted in friendship would judge as immoral sex that is casual, violent, abusive, or without care for or relationship to the partner. Sex becomes moral as it moves increasingly to integrate eros and friendship, to inspire partners to be faithful and committed to one another's wellbeing. A sexual relationship that is on a for-the-time-being footing yet has those qualities of friendship is more moral than a legal marriage in which sex is abusive and uncaring. Sexual morality and immorality thus cease to be a question of a fixed institutional boundary between marriage and nonmarriage and become, rather, a process of growth toward relationality and away from exploitative use.

This guideline for sexual ethics allows a common moral standard to be applied to heterosexual and homosexual relations. Homosexual relations are not sinful just because they are not heterosexual or procreative, but homosexuality, like heterosexuality, can be judged as sinful to the extent that it is abusive and uncaring of the other. Gay people (and again, men seem to have more difficulty with this than women) need to mature in their sexuality, integrating it with friendship and a commitment to one another's wellbeing. This is a matter not of homosexual relations imitating heterosexual marriages—a much-debated question in the homosexual community[12]—but of both developing a more genuine ethic of mutuality.

This discussion of sexual ethics as rooted in the quality of friendship allows for a different approach to reproductive ethics, a major area of controversy in the United States. The present impasse over abortion has spilled over into hostility toward contraception and sexual education for the young and unmarried. Here again there is a male subtext of misogyny. Women are not trusted to make decisions about procreation even though, and precisely because, impregnation, gestation, and birth are processes of the female body. In order to control childbearing, men feel they must control women, and not allow them to make decisions about whether or not to be impregnated by the male or bear the resulting child. To deny women the right to control their bodies is basically, then, to refuse them the right to control male sexual acts upon them, and the resulting effects of those acts on their bodies.

A better approach would be to recognize that women can be trusted to want to have children at the appropriate time, and that child-raising is a life-term commitment of parents to children. This relationship is changing with advances in reproductive technology. Some lesbian women are using artificial insemination to conceive, with a female partner as the child's second, or "social," parent. But however intent the social parent may be on committing equally to the child, it is hard to confirm this psychologically or socially without having any legal status. The "use" of surrogate mothers also shifts the relationship between the social and the biological parent.[13]

Yet it is vital to the wellbeing of children to have the assurance of a permanent, lifelong relationship to those who both create and raise them. The decision to parent is a social one that must entail a commitment to a permanent relationship between the parents and the children they raise. Effective contraception is not a threat to childbearing. (Although the worldwide population crisis provides a compelling argument for holding the level of childbearing to below the replacement rate in America today.)[14] Rather, it is a means of rendering the decision to parent *intentional*. Being able to avoid unchosen pregnancy allows couples to make childbearing fully intentional, undertaken in that social context and and at that stage of life which will enable a child to be raised with optimum conditions of wellbeing.

This possibility of intentional choice to bear a child when appropriate, as well as not to bear one when not appropriate, ensures the wellbeing of both women and children and hence of society as a whole. The more effective such choice becomes at the level of the decision to conceive or not to conceive, the more abortion as a second and unfortunate choice to terminate an unchosen pregnancy can be eliminated, remaining as a medical option only in difficult cases such as those involving severely deformed fetuses or ectopic pregnancies. It needs to be made clear once and for all to the antiabortion crusaders that abortion is reduced not by criminalizing it, which only makes it illegal and unsafe, but by limiting the risk of unchosen pregnancy *before* conception.[15] This means accepting the primacy of women's moral agency in reproduction, with men collaborating with women in decisions about parenting.

This exploration of the basic principles of sexual and reproductive ethics calls for some attention to issues related to the polarization of wealth and poverty in contemporary America. Any discussion of the contradictions between women's roles in work and family, and how they relate to the creation of partnerships and child-raising, must begin by assuming an adequate income, something that is still lacking for some 20 percent of the American population. This burden falls hardest on poor women raising children alone, whose lot is worsening through a draconian "welfare reform" that takes as its main criterion of success a reduction in caseloads.

In the conclusion to her major study, *It Takes a Nation,* Rebecca Blank dismisses any hope of effecting a more comprehensive solution to poverty in the United States, given the present climate of hostility toward the poor, especially the poor single mother. She sees the best option for alleviating poverty as lying in the expansion of a complex package of supports for the poor. This package would bring together earnings (full- or part-time), an earned-income tax credit, remitting taxes to the poor under a certain income, food stamps, subsidies for child care, direct grants for dependent child care, and Medicaid. If appropriately expanded, these programs could together bring the low-income household up to the poverty line. Blank believes this should be the goal of antipoverty workers.[16]

I believe that Blank's approach is realistic, and that it may be the best that can be done in the short term. But the limits of this strategy must be recognized. The effort to reduce assistance to single mothers by demanding that they take any job offered them, no matter how low-paying, is merely the latest manifestation of a long-standing American pattern—namely, forcing the poor to have no other recourse than to take unjustly low-paid jobs. Adding a series of subsidies to this low pay in order to bring the family income to the poverty level actually represents government subsidizing of businesses that pay below-poverty wages.[17]

A simpler approach would be to raise the minimum wage to a level that would translate at least to the official poverty line. At the current poverty line for a family of three, this would mean a $6.40 minimum wage for one earner working a forty-hour work week. This could then be supplemented by a negative-income system similar to that outlined by Milton Friedman twenty years ago and almost passed by the Nixon administration. The system would be based on the government's collection of taxes on a progressive scale from those whose incomes fall above a certain level, and the concomitant subsidy of those whose incomes fall below that level.

Friedman's scheme calls for a 50 percent work incentive above a minimum income level, with recipients getting one dollar for each two they earn up to a certain cutoff point where families begin to pay taxes rather than receive tax benefits. If the floor for this system was set at the poverty line for a family of three ($12,800), a family with no income at all would receive at least that much aid. For each dollar it earned it would receive two back, up to double the poverty line ($25,600).[18] The complex system of trying to force people to work, punishing them for their failure, and constantly having to monitor them could be eliminated, at considerable saving.

This means trusting people to make their own decisions about how much to work in the paid labor force. The poor could be treated with dignity, as citizens who have a right to have their basic needs met and to make decisions about their own lives. Medicaid, food stamps, and other such forms of nonmonetary aid should also be available to those at a certain level of low income. Blank may be right that Americans find it untenable to provide assistance to the poor without monitoring and controlling them. But the growing failure of the present effort at "reform" may open the way for a rethinking of the issue of poverty on a broader, national basis.

Ultimately, however, no comprehensive plan for alleviating poverty can have a chance of political success if it does not address the problem of the superrich, those owners of corporations who largely dominate the American political system, determine its policies, and define the hegemonic culture by control of the mainstream media. The power of the rich to dictate who is elected to government needs to be curbed by an insurgent democratic movement, one that uses the electoral might of the majority to strip the rich of the power to set policies that favor them rather than the majority.

A detailed discussion of this problem is beyond the limits of this book. But it must be noted here as the determining framework for any economic reforms toward a more just balance of family responsibilities and the demands of work.[19] Moreover, economic justice should be integrated into an all-encompassing vision of ecologically sustainable communities. Clean air, water, and soil, more organic communities in which homes, jobs, shopping, and educational, religious, and cultural institutions are linked together by public transportation—all need to brought together in one vision.[20]

REIMAGINING FAMILIES AS REDEMPTIVE COMMUNITIES

We must not only make the state useable for an inclusive justice, but also make the church useable for prophetic and life-enhancing ministry to support communities of faith. At this moment all the Christian churches, Catholic and Protestant, are in deep internal schism. They are split between fundamentalists on the one hand, who seek to shore up an absolute worldview of fixed certainties that support patriarchal hierarchy, militarism, and free-market capitalism, and progressives on the other, who have accepted the diversity of cultures and religious perspectives and seek egalitarian justice.

My sense is that no reconciliation is possible between these two poles because their outlooks are based on irreconcilably different presuppositions. Progressives are being stalemated in every church as they try to concede to the fundamentalists in order to keep their national church or local congregation together. I do not advocate formal institutional separation in most cases if it would mean abandoning the institution to the conservatives. I think progressives should contest the territory and seek to communicate with and educate those who are open to change. They should cease ceding key terms such as "family," "life," "faith," "truth," "Jesus Christ," and "the Bible" to the fundamentalists, and clarify and express the intellectual and ethical principles underlying their own perspective.

If fundamentalists and progressives are irreparably split *within* denominations, the progressive wings of the various Christian churches hold very similar views *across* demominations. They have a common faith and share similar ethical principles. This is also true beyond the Christian church, where progressive Jews, Muslims, and Buddhists have much in common with their Christian counterparts, as has become evident to me through interreligious dialogue. Progressive people of faith in the different traditions are now developing networks. Among Catholics, Call to Action seeks to unite the progressive wing via a newsletter and annual regional and national conferences. A number of Protestant churches also have one or more progressive networks, including the Witherspoon Society and Semper Reformanda among Presbyterians and the Methodist Federation for Social Action and the Consultation network among Episcopalians.[21]

A new ecumenism is needed to link the progressive wings of the churches in supporting social policies of egalitarian justice and sustainable development. We need ecumenical organizations—councils of religious communities on local, national, and international bases —to bring together the progressive wings of the world's religions, as well as issue-based alliances working in the areas of peace, justice, and ecology. Together these groups can also make available forms of religious nurture and celebration for people seeking covenantal community. The kinds of creative covenant ceremonies I proposed earlier in this chapter require such alliances of progressive religious leaders and communities to support new thinking and practice.

I turn in the concluding pages of this text to the question of

Christian faith and its relationship to the sacramental status of marriage. The Christian Right has assumed that its views are "profamily" and that the type of family such views promote is biblical and divinely ordained. These assumptions must all be contested. The "values" they have championed have been largely deleterious to the social needs of most real families in the United States. They have exacerbated rather than eased the contradictions between work and home—women's double shift—particularly for poor women, who carry these burdens under the most difficult conditions.

As we have seen in this study, the family model promoted by the Christian Right has its origins in the ideology of Victorian white middle-class America, not in the Bible. The Bible, comprising Hebrew Scripture and the New Testament, reflects a variety of family patterns common in its era(s), all quite different from the model of the Victorian nuclear family. In fact, if there is a normative view of the family to be found in the New Testament, based as it is on the teachings of Jesus, it is the antifamily perspective of the Jesus movement and the early Pauline churches, a perspective later challenged by the deutero-Pauline strata that tried to reinstate the family of patriarchal slavocracy.

The New Testament's antifamily stance cannot be appropriated literally today, no more than can any other biblical view. Rather, a critical and creative rereading is necessary to suggest possible insights for us. This in turn demands a reevaluation of the historical Christian tradition on the meaning of family, as it evolved from New Testament antifamily views into the patristic and medieval perspectives and then into those of the Reformation and modern eras. Let me attempt a brief recapitulation of this trajectory as already recounted in this volume.

The antifamily tradition of the New Testament was rooted in a critique of the family systems of the day as an expression of the demonic powers and principalities of a fallen world. Family was seen as a locus of pride, power, and possessions by elites that marginalized most poor people (particularly in the urban world of empires) and denied them the benefits of family. Family systems constructed a hierarchy of men over women, masters over slaves, the old over the young, ruling nations over conquered ones. Real community was proscribed between these separated categories of people.

The Christian church, by contrast, defined itself as a new family that broke down such separations and brought together men and women, former masters and slaves, Jews and Greeks, the "clean" and the socially despised in table fellowship and a new kinship in Christ. This new family set itself against the existing family systems from which its members had come. It saw itself as awaiting a final transformation of the world in the Kingdom of God, when all Creation could feast together at the messianic banquet and all oppression would be overcome.

The subversive character of the church in undermining both the family and the state was recognized and denounced in attacks made on Christianity by spokesmen of classical society. The Christian leaders themselves also became worried about the potential of such views to overturn the social hierarchy and to erode control of women, youth, and slaves. They thus sought to spiritualize the antifamily and new-family themes of the Jesus movement and to reinstate patriarchal slavocracy as normative for the present order of Creation, to be dissolved only in the Kingdom of God.

Some Christian movements continued into the third century to cleave to the socially subversive antifamily themes to found new egalitarian communities. But patristic Christianity followed the course of spiritualizing antifamily views and identifying them with a platonic sublimation of sexuality into asceticism and the pursuit of contemplative wisdom. What evolved from this synthesis of asceticism and patriarchalism was a three-tiered system of Christian society comprising a celibate male elite of superior holiness and rule; a marginalized female celibate elite that was conceded holiness but deprived as much as possible of rule; and a second-class married laity whose very participation in sex and procreation marked it as belonging to the lower, sinful world. Only the celibate elites belonged fully to the church's anticipation of heavenly holiness.

This view of sex even in marriage as venially sinful and inferior to celibate holiness made the definition of marriage as sacramental ambiguous. Augustine identified the three "goods" of marriage as the production of children, the curbing of concupiscence, and the sacramental imaging of the union of Christ and the church. That the first two "goods" lay in the sphere of original nature and fallen sinfulness served to cast the real status of the third "good" into doubt.

Producing children was defined as a good of nature, necessary to remedy mortality. For Augustine it could now be put aside for a celibacy that anticipated the Kingdom of God, in which there would be no more marrying or giving in marriage, and no more need for reproduction. The remedy for concupiscence was not its cure; it merely curbed the sinful impulse and put it to good use in procreation, which nonetheless remained the means of transmitting sin from one generation to the next.

How then did these two functions of procreation and remedy of concupiscence, which belonged to the realms of nature and sin, relate to marriage as a sacrament, as the image of the redemptive union of Christ and the church? Sacramentality meant that the relationship was holy, a means of grace and an anticipation of redemption. The symbolism of Christ and the church was drawn from the Jewish messianic tradition of redemptive communion between the Messiah and the New Jerusalem as his bride. It reflected God and Israel in marital union. But the Christian tradition denied that sex was holy, and allowed no place for marriage and procreation in the Kingdom of God.

The result of this contradiction was that the Catholic tradition never succeeded in creating a positive spirituality of sexuality. Marriage as a sacrament pointed toward an ascetic denial of sex and toward its sublimation into the spiritual union of God and the soul. Actual sex could not even be a humble, fleshly mirroring of this spiritual union, as in the Jewish tradition,[22] but must be rejected in order to make such a union possible. One can safely read the Song of Songs as a hymn of the divine union of the soul and God only when the actual practice of sex and even the erotic urges to physical sex have been eliminated.[23]

The Reformation recognized the contradiction inherent in the three "goods" of marriage, as well as their evil subversion in the hierarchy of the celibate over the married. Reformers chose to reject both celibacy and the sacramentality of marriage based on the split between creation and redemption. Instead, marriage was confined to the realm of creation and sin. As an ordinance of creation it was mandated for all, and as a remedy for sin it was necessary for all. Thereby patriarchy was ratified as an ordinance of nature, and women's subjugation within creation reinforced as a punishment for sin. The Christian Right's insistence that its view of the family is biblical and divinely mandated is based on this notion that the patriarchal family is an ordinance of creation instituted by God.

By denying the sacramentality of marriage, Protestantism opened the way for its dissolution in divorce, representing a more realistic and more practical recognition of the limits of human ability to make perfect or even tolerable unions all of the time. But it also denied that marriage could be a means of grace or an anticipation of the union of Christ and the church in messianic communion. Nature itself, and all bodily things, were thus refused the possibility of being means of grace.

Classical Protestantism rooted itself in a harsh division between fallen nature incapable of embodying the divine and a "wholly other" God radically transcendent over finite creation. The dynamic relation of creation to redemption, the notion of the bodily world transmuted and perfected to become a sacramental manifestation of the divine, anticipating the redeemed communion of God and creation—so compelling in the writings of the sacramental theologians of the patristic and medieval traditions—were cast aside.

Yet Protestantism has nonetheless largely ignored this denial of the sacramental nature of marriage, even as Catholics have failed to reconcile marriage as a sacrament with the sin of sex. Both Protestants and Catholics of the nineteenth century romanticized marriage, home, and family. The home now took the place of the church as the anticipation of Heaven, with the wife as its angelic minister. The holiness of home and of women was defined by their separation from the public world of paid labor as the sphere of "the world"—that is, the realm of power, pride, and sin. Here, too, sex was sublimated: women were angelic only so long as they remained asexual, "virgin mothers" who were maternal but not sexual.

Today we face the breakdown of this Victorian pattern of the idealized family, with its segregation of male and female in separate spheres of work and home. The question now becomes, Is there some new way of reading marriage, family, sex, and procreation theologically that can support a more just and more sustainable harmony of women and men, home and work?

A new vision of family, of home and work, needs to be based on the mutuality of whole human beings, not on the truncation of such beings into separate parts, home for women and work for men. Women and men as whole human beings participate in the entirety of life, sharing in family nurture as well as in the larger paid economy, culture, and politics. We need to imagine new ways to knit these together in more organic wholes, allowing for better harmony and balance between areas of life in which men and women both participate as equals.

Theologically, this requires first of all a clear and explicit rejection of the doctrine that holds that the patriarchal family of male headship and female subordination is the "order of creation," mandated by God. The patriarchal family in its various forms, from the slavocracy of antiquity to the Victorian nuclear family, is a human construct, not a divine mandate. In antiquity it was founded on an oppressive power that benefited dominant men at the expense of women and the servant/slave classes, while the Victorian version of the patriarchal ideal was achievable only by a well-paid male elite that denied women full human development. Maintaining this family model today spells poverty for those women who lack a male "breadwinner," and economic struggle for many families with only a single, male earner.

These family systems, then, not only are not of God, but partake of demonic distortions that impede justice and wellbeing for many. They manifest the powers and principalities of an alienated "world." This judgment of family as alien to God and contrary to redemptive community underlay the antifamily tradition of the Jesus movement and the early church. Today, as in the early church, we need to realize that becoming a redemptive community means reimagining the family. The church, God's messianic people, is a new family, an alternative, liberated community of chosen kin through which we can taste the messianic banquet.

Reimagining families as redemptive communities does not mean setting creation against redemption, sex against holiness, or the reproduction of bodies against the cultivation of souls. These dualisms defeated the early Christian critique of family, as well as its sacramental promise in Catholic theology. Rather, we need to reimagine a dynamic interrelation of creation and new creation, of the reproducing and renewing of life. *Eros* needs to be integrated into *philia*, and *philia* into *agape*, in deepening relationships among lovers, friends, and partners seeking to shape life-enhancing communities.

Making love will then indeed become sacramental, a means of grace for redemptive life. The union of Christ and the church, messianic hope and redemptive community, is anticipated and prefigured in the union of lovers becoming friends, builders of nurturing families, and partners in the effort to bring about the reign of God's peace and justice on Earth.

1. Families in Jewish and Greco-Roman Worlds and Early Christianity

1. Keith R. Bradley, *Discovering the Roman Family* (New York: Oxford University Press, 1991); Cheryl Cox, *Household Interests: Property, Marriage Strategies and Family Dynamics in Ancient Athens* (Princeton, N.J.: Princeton University Press, 1998); Suzanne Dixon, *The Roman Family* (Baltimore: John Hopkins University Press, 1992), and *The Roman Mother* (London: Routledge, 1990); Jane Gardner, *Women in Roman Law and Society* (Bloomington, Ind.: Indiana University Press, 1991); Judith Hallett, *Fathers and Daughters in Roman Society: Women in the Elite Family* (Princeton, N.J.: Princeton University Press, 1989); Richard Hawley and Barbara Levick, eds., *Women in Antiquity: New Assessments* (London: Routledge, 1995); Walter K. Lacey, *The Family in Classical Greece* (Ithaca, N.Y.: Cornell University Press, 1984); Beryl Rawson, *Family in Ancient Rome* (Ithaca, N.Y.: Cornell University Press, 1986); Richard Saller, *Patriarchy, Property and Death in the Roman Family* (New York: Cambridge University Press, 1994); and Philip Slater, *The Glory of Hera: Greek Mythology and the Greek Family* (Boston: Beacon Press, 1968).

2. See Shaye J. D. Cohen, ed., *The Jewish Family in Antiquity* (Atlanta: Scholar's Press, 1993); Tal Ilan, *Jewish Women in Greco-Roman Palestine* (Peabody, Mass.: Hendrickson, 1995); and Leo G. Perdue, Carol Meyers, John J. Collins, and Joseph Blenkinsopp, *Families in Ancient Israel* (Louisville: Westminster/John Knox Press, 1997).

3. "Fictive kin" refers to the various ways in which societies link people who are not blood relatives into relations of "family-like" community and responsibility, thereby creating networks of mutual support and providing those without families with communities of caring. One such strategy in Christian tradition is the institution of godparents through baptism. This was seen as constituting such a kinlike relation that the laws of incest in medieval Christianity were extended to cover relations between godparents and godchildren (see chapter 2). In Latin American societies, the godparent relation is an integral part of the family system; see Roger N. Lancaster, *Life Is Hard: Machismo, Danger and the Intimacy of Power in Nicaragua* (Berkeley: University of California Press, 1993), 63–68.

4. See Jane Gardner, *Family and "Familia" in Roman Law and Life* (New York: Clarendon Press, 1998).

5. See Susan Treggiari, *Roman Marriage: "Iusto Coniuges" from the Time of Cicero to Ulpian* (Oxford: Clarendon Press, 1991).

6. Dixon, *Roman Family*, 4–5, and R. Saller, "*Familia, Domus* and the Roman Conception of the Family," *Phoenix* 38 (1984): 336–55. See also R. Saller's definition of these terms in his *Patriarchy, Property and Death in the Roman Family* (Cambridge: Cambridge University Press, 1994), 74–101.

7. Treggiari, *Roman Marriage*, 32–36.

8. For the illegality of marriage for slaves, see Keith R. Bradley, *Slaves and Masters in the Roman Empire: A Study in Social Control* (Brussels: Latomus, 1984), 47. It was also illegal for a Roman citizen to marry a noncitizen, or for a soldier to marry during his twenty years of service. See Treggiari, *Roman Marriage*, 44; and Dixon, *Roman Family*, 53–57.

9. See "Children in the Roman Family," in Dixon, *Roman Family*, 98–132; also Thomas Wiedemann, *Adults and Children in the Roman Empire* (New Haven: Yale University Press, 1989).

10. For the practice of marrying off girls shortly after menarche, see Treggiari, *Roman Marriage*, 39–43. See also Keith Hopkins, "The Age of Roman Girls at Marriage," *Population Studies* 18 (1965): 309–27; and Brent Shaw, "The Age of Roman Girls at Marriage: Some Reconsiderations," *Journal of Roman Studies* 77 (1987): 30–46. For the age of males at marriage, see David Herlihy, *Medieval Households* (Cambridge, Mass.: Harvard University Press, 1985), 17–18.

11. Herlihy, *Medieval Households*, 483–502. On the practices of adoption, particularly of adults, see Dixon, *Roman Family*, 112–13; also Mireille Cornier, "Divorce and Adoption as Roman Familial Strategies," in Beryl Rawson, ed., *Marriage, Divorce and Adoption in Ancient Rome* (New York: Oxford University Press, 1991).

12. For a description of the structure of the Greek and Roman upper-class house with its public front area and office (*tablinum*), see Carolyn Osiek and David L. Balch, *Families in the New Testament World: Households and House Churches* (Louisville: Westminster/John Knox Press, 1997), 9–11.

13. For the *salutatio* as a formal function in the day of an elite Roman male, see Treggiari, *Roman Marriage*, 420.

14. For the sleeping and slave quarters in a Roman house, see Osiek and Balch, *Families in the New Testament World*, 6.

15. Ibid., 18–19.

16. For the sexual use of slaves, see Bradley, *Slaves and Masters*, 116–18.

17. See Dixon, *Roman Family*, 109, 123; also K. R. Bradley, "Child Labor in the Roman World," *Historical Reflections* 12 (1985): 311–30.

18. For the slave family, see Bradley, *Slaves and Masters*, 49–80.

19. See Carol Meyers, "The Family in Early Israel," in Perdue et al., *Families in Ancient Israel*, 1–47. For women's roles in the ancient Israelite family, see Carol Mey-

ers, *Discovering Eve: Ancient Israelite Women in Context* (New York: Oxford University Press, 1988).

20. See Joseph Blenkinsopp, "The Family in First Temple Israel," in Perdue et al., *Families in Ancient Israel*, 49–51.

21. Ibid., 85–92.

22. See Dale B. Martin, "Slavery and the Ancient Jewish Family," in Cohen, *The Jewish Family in Antiquity*, 113–29. Rabbinic laws allowed five wives to a man who could afford them, and eighteen to kings. It has been assumed that polygamy had all but disappeared in the first century A.D., but recently discovered marriage contracts indicate that polygamy (primarily bigamy) was still practiced in this period. See John L. Collins, "Marriage, Divorce and Family in Second Temple Judaism," in Perdue et al., *Families in Ancient Israel*, 107–9, 121–22.

23. See Miriam Peskowitz, "Family/ies in Antiquity: Evidence from Tannaitic Literature and Roman Galilean Architecture," in Cohen, *The Jewish Family in Antiquity*, 28–34.

24. Marriage contracts from the Jewish community in Elephantine indicate that Jewish women could initiate divorce, but this seems to have been due to Egyptian influence and conflicted with general Jewish law at the time. See Collins, "Marriage, Divorce and Family in Second Temple Judaism," in Perdue et al., *Families in Ancient Israel*, 115–21.

25. See Michael Satlow, "Reconsidering the Rabbinic *Ketubah* Payment," in Cohen, *The Jewish Family in Antiquity*, 113–51.

26. See John M. G. Barclay, "The Family as Bearer of Religion in Judaism and Early Christianity," in Halvor Moxnes, ed., *Constructing Early Christian Families* (New York: Routledge, 1997), 67–68. See also D. G. Orr, "Roman Domestic Religion: The Evidence of Household Shrines," in *Aufstieg und Niedergang der romanischen Welt* 2 (1978): 1557–91; and J. R. Clarke, *The House in Roman Italy, 100 B.C.–A.D. 250: Ritual Space and Domestication* (Berkeley: University of California Press, 1991).

27. Barclay, "The Family as Bearer of Religion," in Moxnes, *Constructing Early Christian Families*, 68–72. See also O. Larry Yarbrough, "Parents and Children in the Jewish Family in Antiquity," in Cohen, *The Jewish Family in Antiquity*, 39–59.

28. For the myth of the archaic Roman family, see Dixon, *Roman Family*, 19–24.

29. For Augustan family law, see Eva Marie Lassen, "The Roman Family: Ideal and Metaphor" in Moxnes, *Constructing Early Christian Families*, 107–8. The Roman historian Livy was one of the primary exponents of these myths of the archaic Roman family, as well as a promoter of Augustan social reforms. Suetonius, in his life of Augustus, says that the emperor's wife, Livia, and daughters wove his clothes: *Divus Augustus*, chaps. 64, 73. See Elizabeth Bartman, *Portraits of Livia: Imaging the Imperial Woman* (Cambridge: Cambridge University Press, 1999), 96.

30. Treggiari, *Roman Marriage*, 183–204.

31. Ibid., 215–16, on the Stoic philosopher Seneca's views of marriage partnership.

32. For the Greek patterns of meals, the modification of female exclusion in Roman elite families, and the ambiguity, for Christians, of the association of women at formal meals with courtesans, see Kathleen E. Corby, *Private Women, Public Meals: Social Conflict in the Synoptic Tradition* (Peabody, Mass.: Hendrickson, 1993).

33. Both Plato (in the *Symposium*) and Aristotle (in *Nichomachian Ethics*) assume that true friendship is possible only between equals. Men and women, being essentially unequal, therefore cannot be friends. That friendship is possible only between male peers is repeated by Augustine and Thomas Aquinas. However, the practice of Christian celibacy suggested to some that this inequality had been dissolved in Christ and hence male and female celibates could be friends. See Rosemary Rader, *Breaking Boundaries: Male/Female Friendship in Early Christian Communities* (New York: Paulist Press, 1983).

34. See Treggiari, *Roman Marriage*, 243–61.

35. See particularly Proverbs 31:10–31, the ode to the capable wife.

36. The modeling of divine wisdom after the capable wife is found particularly in Proverbs 8–9 and the Wisdom of Solomon 6–8.

37. Prov. 27:15–16.

38. E.g., Prov. 5:3–6. The word translated as "loose" was a typical reference to the foreign woman; see Phyllis Bird, "The Image of Woman in the Old Testament," in Rosemary R. Ruether, ed., *Religion and Sexism: Images of Women in the Jewish and Christian Traditions* (New York: Simon and Schuster, 1974), 58–59 and 82n. 44.

39. See Ross S. Kraemer, *Maenads, Martyrs, Matrons and Monastics: A Sourcebook on Women's Religions in the Greco-Roman World* (Philadelphia: Fortress Press, 1988), 218–20. Also see Kraemer's *Her Share of the Blessings: Women's Religions among Pagans, Jews and Christians in the Greco-Roman World* (New York: Oxford University Press, 1992), 117–22.

40. Kramer, *Her Share of the Blessings,* 98–99. See also David Goodblatt, "The Beruriah Traditions," *Journal of Jewish Studies* 26 (1975): 68–85.

41. Greek philosophical asceticism practiced austerity in food and sex but not abstinence, with adherents usually marrying. Although a kind of sectarian communal life is attributed to Pythagoreans, they were not celibate; see Iamblichus, *On the Pythagorean Life.* Cynics rejected marriage as part of their general rejection of civilization for a radical life of anarchy, but they were not communal. Thus monastic or communal celibacy in the Mediterranean world seems to be attested first in Philo, rather than among the Greeks. For the protest element in asceticism, see James Francis, *Subversive Virtue: Asceticism and Authority in the Pagan World of the Second Century C.E.* (University Park, Pa.: Pennsylvania State University Press, 1994).

42. Platonic asceticism was based on a dualism of soul and body and a view of spirituality as "mortification," or preparation for the final freeing of the soul from the body in death; see Plato's *Phaedo.* But this did not necessarily imply celibacy. See John M. Dillon, "Rejecting the Body, Refining the Body: Some Remarks on the

Development of Platonic Asceticism," in Vincent L. Wimbush and Richard Valantasis, eds., *Asceticism* (New York: Oxford University Press, 1995), 80–87.

43. See Stephen C. Barton, "The Relativization of Family Ties in the Jewish and Christian Traditions," in Moxnes, *Constructing Early Christian Families,* 86–87, 93–94.

44. Philo, "The Contemplative Life," F. H. Colson, trans. in vol. 9 of the Loeb Classical Library (Cambridge, Mass.: Harvard University Press, 1954), 104–69. English quotes are taken from Nahum N. Glatzer, ed., *The Essential Philo* (New York: Schocken Books, 1971), 311–30.

45. Glatzer, *Essential Philo,* 125.

46. Ibid., 155.

47. Philo sees the Therapeutae as a contemplative expression of the larger Essene movement, whose way of life he regards as "practical" rather than intellectual; see the beginning of "The Contemplative Life" and also his treatise "On the Virtuous Being Also Free," Glatzer, *Essential Philo,* 311, 331.

48. Josephus, *Jewish Wars* 2:124–63, trans. G. A. Williamson (Baltimore: Penguin Books, 1959), 125–28.

49. Ibid., 125.

50. Ibid., 129.

51. The excavation of the Qumran cemetery uncovered some eleven hundred graves, all containing men, except for a few on the margins that held women and children. See Geza Vermes, *The Dead Sea Scrolls in English* (Baltimore: Penguin Books, 1962), 30.

52. The two community rules are the *Manual of Discipline,* or *Community Rule,* and the *Zadokite Document,* or *Damascus Rule.* Theodor H. Gaster, *The Dead Sea Scrolls in English* (Garden City, N.Y.: Doubleday Anchor Books, 1956), uses the former names, while Vermes, *Dead Sea Scrolls,* uses the latter.

53. This fragmentary document is called the *Manual of Discipline for the Future Congregation of Israel* by Gaster (pp. 307–12), and the *Messianic Rule* by Vermes (pp. 118–21).

54. Christian apologists typically conceal the apocalyptic tradition when addressing the gentile world. Josephus and Philo seem to follow a similar pattern, speaking in philosophical terms to Gentiles and referring to apocalyptic thought, which the Romans would have seen as subversive and revolutionary, only in veiled terms, if at all.

55. Jewish law prescribed periods of abstinence from sex for males in preparation for an encounter with the Holy (see, for example, the giving of the Law on Mount Sinai, Exodus 19:15) and in preparation for and during Holy War. It is likely that the celibacy practiced by the Qumran community was undertaken in this light of prepa-

ration for Holy War and the advent of God, rather than in the philosophical mode, as it was understood by Philo.

56. See Risto Uro, "Asceticism and Anti-Familial Language in the Gospel of Thomas," in Moxnes, *Constructing Early Christian Families,* 216–34.

57. Jane Schaberg, *The Illegitimacy of Jesus: A Feminist Theological Interpretation of the Infancy Narratives* (San Francisco: Harper and Row, 1987).

58. For the various options in interpreting the matronymic "Son of Mary," including illegitimacy, with preference for the view that Joseph is dead, see Raymond Brown, Karl P. Donfried, Joseph A. Fitzmeyer, and John Reumann, *Mary in the New Testament* (Philadelphia: Fortress Press, 1978), 61–64.

59. On fictive kin in earliest Christianity, see Lareta H. Finger, *An Investigation of Communal Meals in Acts 2:42–47 and 6:1–6: A Socio-Historical and Gender Analysis of Commensality in the Jerusalem Church* (Ph.D. diss., Northwestern University, 1997), 142–50; also K. O. Sandes, *A New Family: Conversion and Ecclesiology in the Early Church with Cross-Cultural Comparisons* (Bern: Peter Land, 1994).

60. Col. 3:9–11. This formula of the new humanity in Christ notably omits the gender terms *male* and *female,* used in Galatians 3:28.

61. Lone Fatum, "Brotherhood in Christ: A Gender Hermeneutical Reading of 1 Thessalonians," in Moxnes, *Constructing Early Christian Families,* 183–97.

62. Paul integrates three metaphors from contemporary Roman family practices: the manumission of a slave (who takes the family name of his former master as a client of that master, not as his adopted son), the adoption of a son (usually from a related elite family), and the coming of age of a boy into manhood and possession of his inheritance (and thereby into freedom from subjugation under his former guardians). It was possible but very rare for a slave to be manumitted and then adopted by the master as a son; this may have happened when the slave was actually the master's son by a slave woman.

63. The term *skeuos* can mean "vessel" or "tool." It is being used metaphorically in 1 Thessalonians 4:4–5 to refer to the body as the vessel of the soul, the penis as the male sexual "tool," or the wife as "vessel" owned and used by the male in sexual intercourse. Contemporary translations (e.g., The New Revised Standard Version) understand the term as "body"—that is, the bodies of male and female persons addressed by Paul—while older translations (such as King James) took the phrase to refer to the wives of males addressed by Paul. J. Whitton suggests the possibility of the second meaning in "A Neglected Meaning of *Skeuos* in 1 Thessalonians 4:4," *New Testament Studies* 28 (1982): 142–43. See also the discusssion in Fatum, "Brotherhood in Christ," in Moxnes, *Constructing Early Christian Families,* 190. Fatum reads the word as meaning "wives."

64. Vincent L. Wimbush, *Paul the Worldly Ascetic: Response to the World and Self-Understanding according to 1 Corinthians 7* (Macon, Ga.: Mercer University Press, 1987).

65. See Dale B. Martin, "Paul without Passion: On Paul's Rejection of Desire in Sex and Marriage," in Moxnes, *Constructing Early Christian Families*, 201–15.

66. Daniel Boyarin suggests that Paul understands freedom from the law specifically as freedom from the law mandating procreation. See his "Body Politic among the Brides of Christ: Paul and the Origins of Sexual Renunciation," in Wimbush and Valantasis, *Asceticism*, 459–78.

67. Gathering at the family tomb on the anniversary of the death of a relative was a key family ritual; see D. P. Harmon, "The Family Festivals of Rome," *Aufstieg und Niedergang der romanischen Welt* 2 (1978): 1600–3. Although Christians were encouraged to dispense with such festivals, Augustine in the late fourth century was dismayed that some Christians in North Africa continued to observe this rite; see his Epistle 22; also Peter Brown, *Augustine of Hippo* (Berkeley: University of California Press, 1967), 207.

68. David L. Balch understands the family codes of the Pauline and Petrine letters as an effort to appear respectable to Gentiles who saw Christians as subverting family hierarchies. But since it is unlikely that these pagan critics would have read this Christian literature, the codes seem to be concerned more with internal conflicts over continued patriarchal relations in the church. See Balch, *Let Wives Be Submissive: The Domestic Code of 1 Peter* (Chico, Calif.: Scholar's Press, 1981.

69. This passage from Celsus, "True Word," is preserved in quotations embedded in Origen's refutation of it; see Henry Chadwick, *Contra Celsus* (Cambridge: Cambridge University Press, 1953), 165–66.

70. "The Martyrdom of Perpetua and Felicitas," in *Ante-Nicene Fathers*, vol. 3, ed. Alexander Roberts and James Donaldson (Grand Rapids: Eerdmans, 1951), 697–706.

71. "The Acts of Paul and Thecla," in *Ante-Nicene Fathers*, vol. 8, ed. Alexander Roberts and James Donaldson (Grand Rapids: Eerdmans, 1951), 487–92.

72. Stevan L. Davies, *The Revolt of the Widows: The Social World of the Apocryphal Acts* (Carbondale and Edwardsville, Ill.: Southern Illinois University Press, 1980).

73. See Christine Trevett, *Montanism: Gender, Authority and the New Prophecy* (Cambridge: Cambridge University Press, 1996).

74. For a discussion of the conflicts in 1 Timothy over gender and family relations, see Rosemary Ruether, *Women and Redemption: A Theological History* (Minneapolis: Fortress Press, 1998), 40–43.

2. Asceticism, Sex, and Marriage in Patristic and Medieval Christianities

1. Although historians of the early church have assumed that most Christians of the second century were married householders, that assumption underestimates the importance of Syriac Christianity, with its view that celibacy was a requirement for

baptism. See A. Vööbus, *Celibacy: A Requirement for Admission to Baptism in the Early Syrian Church* (Papers of the Estonian Theological Society in Exile 1: Stockholm, 1951). The large number of Encratite, gnostic, and apocalyptic movements of the second century that advocated separation from sexual relations constituted major expressions of Christianity; the fact that many would later be declared heretical by the emerging Catholic church should not obscure the fact that they saw themselves as normative Christianity and were so seen by many Christians. On the "myth of orthodoxy" that has veiled for many historians the reality of the situation, see Walter Bauer, *Orthodoxy and Heresy in Earliest Christianity* (Philadelphia: Fortress Press, 1971).

2. Peter Brown, *The Body and Society: Men, Women and Sexual Renunciation in Early Christianity* (New York: Columbia University Press, 1988).

3. Modern theologians who celebrate the theme of "incarnation" as central to Christian doctrine assume that it refers to an embrace of finite, material embodiment and thus contradicts the Christian history of negation of such embodiment; they fail to see that the early Christian reading of incarnation in fact promoted this repression. See Sallie McFague, *The Body of God: An Ecological Theology* (Minneapolis: Fortress Press, 1993), 163–64.

4. For example, Athanasius, *On the Incarnation of the Word* (London: Religious Tract Society, 1903).

5. For the relation between famine and fasting in Egyptian monasticism, see Brown, *The Body and Society,* 218–20. For the relations among fasting, women, and sexuality, see Teresa M. Shaw, *The Burden of the Flesh: Fasting and Sexuality in Early Christianity* (Minneapolis: Fortress Press, 1998).

6. Tatian's Encratite writings advocating the rejection of all sexual relations are preserved only in quotations from Clement, Irenaeus, and others who seek to refute him; see "Fragments of Lost Works of Tatian," in *Tatian, Theophilus and the Clementine Recognitions,* vol. 3 of the Ante-Nicene Library, (Edinburgh: T. and T. Clark, 1867), 46–48.

7. See note 1 above; also A. Vööbus, *A History of Asceticism in the Syrian Orient* (Louvain: CSCO, 1958).

8. Marcionite churches flourished up to the end of the third century, when many were absorbed into Manichaean communities. Small groups continued to exist into the sixth century. See Eusebius, *Ecclesiastical History* 4:30 for the third century; for reports of Marcionites in the 430s, see Theodoret of Cyrrhus, letters 81 and 145.

9. For the Marcionite view of the church, see R. Joseph Hoffmann, *Marcion: On the Restitution of Christianity* (Chico, Calif.: Scholar's Press, 1984). For a revised interpretation of Marcion's view of the Jewish God and people, see Heikki Räisänen, "Marcion and the Jewish Roots of Christianity," in *Marcion, Muhammad and the Mahatma: Exegetical Perspectives in the Encounter of Cultures* (London: SCM Press, 1997), 64–80.

10. For Montanist imminent apocalypticism and worldly renunciation, see particularly Christine Trevett, *Montanism: Gender, Authority and the New Prophecy* (Cambridge: Cambridge University Press, 1996).

11. For an interpretation of Valentinian cosmogonic myth, see Hans Jonas, *The Gnostic Religion: The Message of the Alien God and the Beginnings of Christianity* (Boston: Beacon Press, 1958), 29–99, 174–205.

12. For Valentinian understanding of spiritual marriage, see Brown, *The Body and Society,* 105–17; also Michael Allen Williams, "Uses of Gender Imagery in Ancient Gnostic Texts," in C. W. Bynum, S. Harrell, and P. Richman, eds., *Gender and Religion: On the Complexity of Symbols* (Boston: Beacon Press, 1986), 196–227.

13. Clement of Alexandria, *Stromateis,* book 3; see the English translation in Henry Chadwick, *Alexandrian Christianity* (Philadelphia: Westminster Press, 1954), 40–92.

14. See particularly Tertullian's treatises "To His Wife," "Exhortation to Chastity," and "On Monogamy," in vol. 4 of *Ante-Nicene Fathers,* ed. Alexander Roberts and James Donaldson (Buffalo: Christian Literature Publishing Company, 1885), 39–73. For an evaluation of Tertullian's views on marriage and continence, see Brown, *The Body and Society,* 77–82; also Timothy D. Barnes, *Tertullian: A Historical and Literary Study* (Oxford: Clarendon Press, 1971), 136–40.

15. For Origen's interaction with Christian gnostics of the School of Valentinius, see Elaine Pagels, *The Johannine Gospel in Gnostic Exegesis: Heracleon's Commentary on John* (Nashville: Abingdon Press, 1973), 16–19, 35, 36, 109–113.

16. Origen, *On First Principles* 1:1–5, ed. G. W. Butterworth (New York: Harper and Row, 1966), 7–51.

17. Ibid., 2:2 (Butterworth, 81–82).

18. Ibid, 1:6 (Butterworth, 53–58).

19. Gregory of Nyssa, "On the Making of Man," in *Library of the Nicene and Post-Nicene Fathers,* 2d ser., vol. 5, ed. W. Moore and H. A. Wilson (Grand Rapids: Eerdmans, 1954), 387–427.

20. For the interpretation of "coats of skin" in Genesis 3:7 (Septuagint: *dermatinous chitonas*), see Nyssa, "On the Making of Man." For the same idea in Gregory of Nazianzus, see Rosemary Ruether, *Gregory of Nazianzus: Rhetor and Philosopher* (Oxford: Clarendon Press, 1969), 135–36.

21. Gregory of Nyssa, "On Virginity," in *Ascetical Works,* trans. Virginia W. Callahan, vol. 58 of *The Fathers of the Church* (Washington, D.C.: Catholic University of America Press, 1967), 3–75.

22. See Gregory's dialogue "On the Soul and the Resurrection," with his sister Macrina cast as spiritual mentor, in *Ascetical Works,* 198–272. Note especially, on page 266, the definition of the term "skin" as the finite aspects of the body that were assumed in the fall into sin and will be discarded on the resurrection.

23. See Brown, *The Body and Society,* 223–40.

24. Peter Brown, "The Rise and Function of the Holy Man in Late Antiquity," in *Society and the Holy in Late Antiquity* (Berkeley: University of California Press, 1981), 103–52.

25. For holy men as village patrons, see Peter Brown, "Town, Village and Holy Men," in *Society and the Holy,* 153–65.

26. Jerome, "On the Perpetual Virginity of the Blessed Mary against Helvidius," in *Dogmatic and Polemical Works,* trans. John N. Hritzu, vol. 53 of *The Fathers of the Church* (Washington, D.C.: Catholic University of America Press, 1965), 3–43.

27. This theme of Mary's virginity *in partum* is defended in the apocryphal Gospel, the Proevangelium of James.

28. Jerome, "On the Perpetual Virginity of Mary" 21 (Hritzu translation, 42–43).

29. David G. Hunter suggests that Jovinian's arguments indicate that he had Manichaeanism as his target and viewed ascetic enthusiasts such as Augustine and Jerome as Manichaeans; see his "Resistance to the Virginal Ideal in Late-Fourth-Century Rome: The Case of Jovinian," *Theological Studies* 48 (1987): 45–64.

30. Jovinian's four propositions were as follows: 1) Virgins, widows, and married women, who have once been washed in Christ, if they do not differ in other works, are of the same merit; 2) Those who have been born again in baptism with full faith cannot be overthrown by the Devil; 3) There is no difference between abstinence from food and receiving it with thanksgiving; 4) There is one reward in the kingdom of heaven for all who have preserved their baptism. See Jerome, *Adversus Jovinius: Patrologia Latina,* vol. 23, col. 224, ed. J. P. Migne (Paris, 1845). For the correlation of these propositions with a critique of Manichaeanism, see Hunter, "Resistance to the Virginal Ideal."

31. For the fourth-century fathers' use of Mark 4:20 to signify the differentiated rewards of virgins, widows, and married people, see Jerome, Epistles 22:15, 48:3, 66:2, 120:1,9, and *Adv. Jov.* 1:3; also Augustine, *De Sancta Virg.* 45; and Ambrose, *De Virg.* 1:60.

32. Jovinian was condemned by synods at Rome in 392 under Pope Siricius and at Milan in 393 under Ambrose.

33. Jerome, *Adv. Jov.* 7.

34. Augustine, *De Bono Conj.*, English, "On the Good of Marriage," in *Treatises on Marriage and Other Subjects* (New York: Fathers of the Church, 1955).

35. Augustine, *Two Books on Genesis against the Manichees* and *On the Literal Interpretation of Genesis: Unfinished Book,* ed. Roland J. Teske, vol. 84 of *The Fathers of the Church* (Washington, D.C.: Catholic University of America Press, 1991), 76–78.

36. Augustine, *The Literal Meaning of Genesis,* in *Ancient Christian Writers,* vols. 41–42, ed. J. H. Taylor (New York: Newman Press, 1982), and *The City of God* 14:10, 22–26. For the evolution of Augustine's anthropology, see Elizabeth Clark, "'Adam's Only Companion': Augustine and the Early Christian Debate on Marriage," *Recherches Augustiniennes* 21 (1986): 139–62.

37. Augustine, *De Pecc. Merit. et Remiss.* 1:29; *De Grat. Chr. et de Pecc. Orig.* 1:27, 2:41–44; *De Nupt. et Concup.* 1:13, 22; *Adv. Julian* 3:7, 5:14.

38. Augustine, *Civ. Dei* 14:26. For the medieval belief that loss of virginity and menstruation would not have occurred before the Fall, see Charles T. Wood, "The Doctor's Dilemma: Sin, Salvation and the Menstrual Cycle in Medieval Thought," *Speculum* 56 (1981): 710–27.

39. Augustine, *De Bono Conj.* 17–20; *De Nupt. et Concup.* 1:9–10.

40. Augustine, *De Nupt. et Concup.* 1:14–15; *De Bono Conj.* 13; *De Bono Viduit.* 8:11; *De Sancta Virg.* 9:16; also Jerome, *Adv. Jov.* 1:36.

41. See Samuel Laeuchli, *Power and Sexuality: The Emergence of Canon Law at the Council of Elvira* (Philadelphia: Temple University Press, 1972).

42. "Bishops, presbyters and deacons and all other clerics having a position in the ministry are ordered to abstain completely from their wives and not to have children. Whoever, in fact, does this, shall be expelled from the dignity of the clerical state": canon 33, ibid., 130.

43. In the 380s, Augustine identified baptism with conversion and retirement from worldly to monastic life, but by the early fifth century he was promoting infant baptism. His view of the transmission of original sin to the infant through sexual generation was a major factor in his endorsement of this practice, long the custom of the African church. See Augustine sermon 294 and letter 64.5.

44. See Peter Brown, *Augustine of Hippo: A Biography* (Berkeley: University of California Press, 1967), 125–45, for this period of Augustine's life.

45. Bernard Verkamp has shown not only the centrality of the argument of cultic purity as the basis for the fourth- to twelfth-century insistence on priestly celibacy, but the continuaton of this as the primary emphasis through the 1950s. Only with the Second Vatican Council was there a turn away from this argument and an attempt to find another basis for priestly celibacy. See his "Cultic Purity and the Law of Celibacy," *Review for Religious* 30 (March, 1971): 199–217.

46. For the Trullan Council in 692 and the Western rejection of its rulings on clerical marriage, see Anne Llewellyn Barstow, *Married Priests and the Reforming Papacy: The Eleventh-Century Debates* (Toronto: Edwin Mellen Press, 1982), 54, 204–5 n. 29; Also Petro Bilaniuk, "Celibacy and the Eastern Tradition," in *Celibacy: The Necessary Option,* ed. George H. Frein (New York: Herder and Herder, 1968), 32–72.

47. For the importance of the division over celibacy in the final break with the Eastern church, see Barstow, *Married Priests,* 213 n. 16.

48. The Council of Agde in 506, convened by Caesarius of Arles, a strong advocate of mutuality in marriage, required the wife to consent to her husband's vow and to take a vow herself (canon 16): see Susan Wemple, *Women in Frankish Society: Marriage and the Cloister, 500–900* (Philadelphia: University of Pennsylvania Press, 1981), 131. See also Jean Paul Audet, *Structures of the Christian Priesthood: A Study of Home,*

Marriage and Celibacy in the Pastoral Service of the Church, trans. R. Sheed (New York: Sheed and Ward, 1968), 3–67.

49. The Didascalia Apostolorum, a Syrian church order of the early third century, distinguished between those widows who were objects of the church's charity and an order of widows who were appointed, took a vow of continence, could not remarry, and had a particular office of prayer. Deaconesses were differentiated from the order of widows and linked with the clergy. Presbyters represented the apostles, and deaconesses the Holy Spirit. They were charged with anointing women for baptism and visiting them in their homes, an office parallel to but more limited than that of the male deacon. The Apostolic Constitutions, a collection of church law from the second half of the fourth century, includes the material of the Didascalia. Here the deaconess is described as being given an ordination of laying-on of hands and prayer by the bishop that she will receive the Holy Spirit and worthily discharge her work (8:20, 1–2). In the Latin church of the fourth to sixth centuries, by contrast, deaconesses were conflated with the order of widows. Latin synods repeatedly denied that such women were ordained—for example, the Council of Orange (441): "Deaconesses are absolutely not to be ordained" (canon 25). See Roger Gryson, *The Ministry of Women in the Early Church* (Collegeville, Minn.: Liturgical Press, 1976), 35–43, 62, 102.

50. The Council of Orleans (541) commanded married priests and deacons to sleep in separate rooms from their wives, while the Council of Tours (567) added that wives must be always in the presence of a slave girl, and bishops should maintain a separate residence and have lower clergy with them at all times, even when they slept: see Wemple, *Women in Frankish Society,* 133.

51. See Verkamp, "Cultic Purity," for the centrality of this concept to church legislaton of the early Middle Ages.

52. A synod at Auxerre at the end of the sixth century declared that because women were impure by nature, they had to be veiled in the presence of the sacraments and could not touch anything consecrated; Frankish bishops extended these decrees to say that women could not receive the Eucharist in their hands, must be veiled when they took communion, and could not touch the altar cloth. See Wemple, *Women in Frankish Society,* 141.

53. Church synods not only showed no concern for the wives and children of clergy who were to be discarded, but vituperated against them as if they were evil. Several decrees suggested that they were to be punished by being sold into slavery. Wives were threatened with denial of church burial, being barred from divine worship, and having their heads shaved in public. See Verkamp, "Cultic Purity," 207, 211.

54. Pope Zachary's reply to Boniface declared that priests and deacons "having more than one wife" should not be allowed to perform priestly duties, citing the apostolic exhortations to "let my priests marry once" and be "husband of one wife": see Barstow, *Married Priests,* 34.

55. For the text of the synod convened by Boniface in which priests "falling into car-

nal sin" were threatened with imprisonment on bread and water and flogging, see ibid., 35.

56. In the tenth century, Rather, the bishop of Verona, complained that married priests married off their daughters to other priests, as well as having their sons ordained and providing them with benefices. Such patterns of intermarriage in clergy families, as well as the handing-down of benefices to ordained sons, were common into the twelfth century. Even at the time of the Protestant Reformation, some of the reformers came from priestly families or married the daughters of priests: see ibid., 37–45. Also Marian U. Chrisman, "Women and the Reformation in Strasbourg, 1490–1530," *Archiv für Reformationsgeschichte* 63 (1972): 150–54.

57. For example, the Council of Elvira decreed that a man who committed the sin of fornication, repented and carried out the required period of penance, and then committed the sin again, was not to be readmitted to communion even at the end of his life. In contrast, a woman who left her husband and took up with another man was not to receive communion "even at the end"; no first repentance was offered: canons 7 and 8, Laeuchli, *Power and Sexuality,* 127.

58. Bishop Ambrose in Milan carried on a series of struggles against the Empress Justina, who favored equal rights for Catholics and Arians, with an eye to the power of Germanic Arians. For an account of these conflicts, see W. H. C. Frend, *The Rise of Christianity* (Philadelphia: Fortress Press, 1984), 620–23.

59. Gregory of Tours, *History of the Franks* 2:21–22.

60. For the importance of women in the fusion of Gallo-Roman and German families and cultures, see Wemple, *Women in Frankish Society,* 9–25.

61. For Celtic and German family patterns before Christianization, see David Herlihy, "The Household in Barbarian Antiquity," in *Medieval Households* (Cambridge, Mass.: Harvard University Press, 1985), 29–55.

62. The basis for such incest taboos is uncertain; despite claims to the contrary, no such extensive taboos appear in the Bible. Herlihy sees these taboos as creating a broader circulation of women and equalizing households between poor and rich, rather than concentrating both women and the wealth of family networks in the upper class. He suggests that bishops may have intended these good social benefits: "Making Sense of Incest: Women and the Marriage Rules of the Early Middle Ages," in *Women, Family and Society in Medieval Europe: Historical Essays* (Providence: Berghahn Books, 1995), 96–112.

I am not sure I agree that these effects are so clear, and I am skeptical of the suggestion that they were intentional on the part of bishops. I see this more in the framework of Laeuchli's view that strict separation of clergy from sexual relations and strict control over the sexuality of the laity were two sides of a power struggle between the clergy and lay elites, by which clergy both defined themselves as superior and asserted their dominance through control of lay sexuality: see *Power and Sexuality,* 56–88.

63. Exemplifying this struggle is the duel between Lothar II (king of Lorraine,

855–869) and leading churchmen over Lothar's effort to divorce his wife, Theut-berga, and install Waldrada, the mistress of his youth, as his queen: see Wemple, *Women in Frankish Society,* 84–86.

64. The first texts of nuptial liturgies are from the seventh century: see Philip L. Reynolds, *Marriage in the Western Church: The Christianization of Marriage during the Patristic and Early Medieval Periods* (Leiden: Brill, 1994), 374–82. But this rite was not obligatory for a valid marriage, the essence of which was consent between the cou-ple. The Fourth Lateran Council (1215) demanded public announcement of the intent to marry, as well as public formalization, but did not require compliance as a condition of validity. Concubinage or common-law marriage was common in the Middle Ages; it was not clearly distinguished from marriage in canon law and not clearly forbidden by church law until the sixteenth century: see James Brundage, "Concubinage and Marriage in Medieval Canon Law," in Vern L. Bullough and James Brundage, eds., *Sexual Practices and the Medieval Church* (Buffalo: Prometheus Books, 1982), 118–28.

65. See the discussion on consummation in the theology of marriage in Reynolds, *Marriage in the Western Church,* 315–61. For the twelfth-century conflict over whether consent or consummation was key, and the decisive influence of the model of the marriage of Mary and Joseph, see Penny S. Gold, "The Marriage of Mary and Joseph in the Twelfth-Century Ideology of Marriage," in Bullough and Brun-dage, *Sexual Practices,* 102–17.

66. The hagiographic topos is well illustrated in the *Life of Christina of Markyate,* written in the twelfth century: C. H. Talbot, ed. and trans., *The Life of Christina of Markyate, a Twelfth-Century Recluse* (Oxford: Oxford University Press, 1959).

67. Common-law marriage rather than formalized church marriage was common in the medieval world among the members of the lower classes, who were less con-cerned about the legitimacy of their children for purposes of inheritance. There was also an assumption (still widespread among Latin American Catholics) that the unformalized marriage could be dissolved at will, while the church marriage was permanent and indissoluble. Thus laws forbidding divorce have worked against the contracting of formal sacramental marriages among Catholics.

68. See Wemple, *Women in Frankish Society,* 97–123.

69. See Brown, *The Body and Society,* 258–78.

70. Ibid., 278–84; also Rosemary Ruether, "Mothers of the Church: Ascetic Women in the Late Patristic Age," in *Women of Spirit: Female Leadership in the Jewish and Christian Traditions,* ed. Rosemary R. Ruether and Eleanor McLaughlin, (New York: Simon and Schuster, 1979), 71–98.

71. Gryson, *Ministry of Women,* 88–91.

72. See Elizabeth Clark, "The Life of Olympias," in *Jerome, Chrysostom and Friends* (Toronto: Edwin Mellen Press, 1979), 127–42.

73. See note 49 above.

74. For the life of Radegund, see Fortunatus, *De vita sanctae Radegundis;* also Gregory of Tours, *History of the Franks* 3:7.

75. For example the abbess of Remiremont, in the early tenth century, held the titles of "Abbatissa atque diachonissa": see Wemple, *Women in Frankish Society,* 173, 298 n. 188. Mitered abbesses, who claimed the ecclesial jurisdiction (but not the sacramental power) of bishops, were common among tenth-century Saxon heads of women's communities: see Lina Eckerstein, *Women under Monasticism* (Cambridge: Cambridge University Press, 1898), 203.

76. For sixth- to tenth-century female monastic life and learning, see Wemple, *Women in Frankish Society,* 175–88.

77. On the ambiguity of women's monasteries as family cult centers and places to put unwanted women, see ibid., 171–72.

78. For eleventh-century writings defending clerical marriage, see Barstow, *Married Priests,* 105–74.

79. The charge that the reformers were homosexual is canvassed by Barstow, ibid., 113–14. John Boswell accepts the thesis that many monastic reformers were homosexual and uses this as evidence for the relative tolerance of homosexuality in the earlier Middle Ages; see his *Christianity, Social Tolerance and Homosexuality* (Chicago: University of Chicago Press, 1980), 216–18.

80. For the development of a new type of marriage emphasizing male descent and primogeniture as a response on the part of the Northern aristocracy to the loss of control over church land, see Herlihy, *Medieval Households,* 82–88.

81. For the definition of children of clerics as bastards, or products of "fornication," see Bernhard Schimmelpfennig, "Ex fornicatione nati," *Studies in Medieval and Renaissance History* 2 (1979): 1–50.

82. For the forbidding of ordination to priest's sons, see Barstow, *Married Priests,* 78, 224 n. 69.

83. See ibid., 181–83.

84. Cicero, *De natura deorum* 2:10:28: Brown, *The Body and Society,* 27–28.

85. See Herlihy, *Medieval Households,* 118–20.

86. For the fusion of mysticism and erotic courtly love, see particularly Mechthild of Magdeburg, *The Flowing Light of Godhead,* trans. Christine Mesch Galvani (New York: Garland, 1991). For a discussion, see Rosemary Ruether, *Women and Redemption: A Theological History* (Minneapolis: Fortress Press, 1998), 97–104; also Barbara Newman, *From Virile Woman to Woman Christ* (Philadelphia: University of Pennsylvania Press, 1995), 137–67. For mystical visions of suckling the infant Jesus in Marie d'Oignies, and bridal mysticism in Hadewijch of Brabant, see Elizabeth A. Pertoff, *Medieval Women's Visionary Literature* (Oxford: Oxford University Press, 1986), 182, 196–97.

3. Family, Work, Gender, and Church in the Reformation Era

1. See the discussion in Merry E. Wiesner, *Gender, Church and State* (London: Longman, 1998), 1–5.

2. Lyndal Roper, *The Holy Household: Women and Morals in Reformation Augsburg* (Oxford: Clarendon Press, 1989), 8–9, 12–13.

3. Susan C. Karant-Nunn, *Zwickau in Transition, 1500–1547: The Reformation as an Agent of Change* (Columbus: Ohio State University Press, 1987), 20–55.

4. Merry E. Wiesner, "Women's Defense of Their Public Role," in *Gender, Church and State,* 6–29.

5. David Herlihy, *"Opera Muliebria": Women and Work in Medieval Europe* (New York: McGraw-Hill, 1990), 77–91.

6. For women as taxpayers in German cities, see Merry E. Wiesner, "War, Work and Wealth: The Basis of Citizenship in Early Modern Cities," in *Gender, Church and State,* 114–25.

7. See the discussion of the political context of Knox's attack on women rulers in Merry E. Wiesner, *Women and Gender in Early Modern Europe* (New York: Cambridge University Press, 1993), 241–42.

8. See Constance Jordan, "Feminism and the Humanists: The Case for Sir Thomas Elyot's *Defense of Good Women,*" in Margaret W. Ferguson, Maureen Quilligan, and Nancy J. Vickers, *Rewriting the Renaissance* (Chicago: University of Chicago Press, 1986), 242–58.

9. Henricus Cornelius Agrippa von Nettleheim, *On the Nobility and Preeminence of the Female Sex* (1529), ed. Albert Rabil (Chicago: University of Chicago Press, 1996).

10. See Nancy Roelker, "The Role of Noblewomen in the French Reformation," *Archiv für Reformationsgeschichte* 63 (1972), and "The Appeal of Calvinism to French Noblewomen in the Sixteenth Century," *Journal of Interdisciplinary History* 2 (1972): 391–418.

11. See Roper, *Holy Household,* 31–36.

12. In Paris in the late thirteenth and early fourteenth centuries, women worked in most trades and all economic sectors and dominated in silk making, wax selling, and candlemaking. In Cologne during this period the guilds of yarn makers, gold spinners, silk spinners, and silk weavers were exclusively female; see Herlihy, "*Opera Muliebria,*" 143–47, 173.

13. See Merry E. Wiesner, *Working Women in Renaissance Germany* (New Brunswick, N.J.: Rutgers University Press, 1986), 157–63, and *Gender, Church and State,* 143–45; also Roper, *Holy Household,* 49–54.

14. See Merry E. Wiesner, "*Wandervögel* and Women: Journeymen's Concepts of Masculinity in Early Modern Germany," in *Gender, Church and State,* 178–96.

15. For the marginalization of women's work in relation to guilds and their work in independent production, see Wiesner, *Working Women,* 168–85.

16. For the marginalization of women in healing, see ibid., 37–74.

17. For women as midwives, see ibid.; also Wiesner, *Women and Gender,* 66–69; and Hilary Marland, ed., *The Art of Midwifery: Early Modern Midwives in Europe and North America* (London: Routledge and Kegan Paul, 1993).

18. For women in public and domestic service, see Wiesner, *Working Women,* 75–97.

19. For women's work in rural areas, see ibid., 86–92. For the medieval peasant woman, see Shulamith Shahar, *The Fourth Estate: A History of Women in the Middle Ages* (London: Methuen, 1983), 220–50; also Barbara Hanawalt, *The Ties That Bound: Peasant Families in Medieval England* (New York: Oxford University Press, 1986).

20. See Roper, *Holy Household,* 31–41.

21. For the role of the Fugger family in early capitalism in Augsburg, see Lyndal Roper, "Stealing Manhood: Capitalism and Magic in Early Modern Germany," in *Oedipus and the Devil: Witchcraft, Sexuality and Religion in Early Modern Europe* (London: Routledge, 1994), 125–45.

22. See Roper, *Holy Household,* 18.

23. See Roper, "Prostitution and the Moral Order," in *Holy Household,* 89–131; also Wiesner, *Working Women,* 97–106.

24. Although women in the medieval and Reformation eras were seen as equally highly sexed as men, or even more so, it was assumed that they, unlike men, could and must control their sexuality until marriage. No brothels were set up to accommodate unmarried women's sexual needs, and arguments for closing brothels sometimes mentioned this double standard; see Roper, *Holy Household,* 107–8.

25. For Spain and Portugal, see "The Triumphant Church," in R. Po-Chia Hsia, *The World of Catholic Renewal, 1540–1770* (New York: Cambridge University Press, 1998), 42–59.

26. Ibid., 28–29; for the renewal of convents, see Lina Eckenstein, *Women under Monasticism* (1896; reprint, New York: Russell and Russell, 1963), 398–431.

27. For Catherine Zell's attack on Episcopal hypocrisy in profiting from fines on clerical children, see Miriam U. Chrisman, "Women and the Reformation in Strasbourg, 1490–1530," *Archive for Reformation History* 63 (1972): 150–54; also Elsie Anne McKee, *Katharina Schütz Zell: The Life and Writings of a Sixteenth-Century Reformer* (Leiden: Brill, 1999), 1:51.

28. Roper, *Holy Household,* 17.

29. See Hsia, *The World of Catholic Renewal,* 39.

30. For the Peasants' War and its impact on the magisterial reformation, see George Huntson Williams, *The Radical Reformation,* 3d ed. (Kirksville, Mo.: Sixteenth-

Century Journal Publishers, 1992), 137–74; also Karant-Nunn, *Zwickau in Transition,* 137–52.

31. See Williams, "Marriage, Family Life and Divorce in the Radical Reformation," in *Radical Reformation,* 755–88.

32. See Williams, "Münster, 1532–35," ibid., 553–88.

33. Luther's thought originally appeared to encourage such a peasant's claims of rights, but he would later vehemently denounce them in his infamous address "On the Murderous Hordes of Peasants." In *Luther's Works,* vol. 46, ed. Robert C. Schultz (Philadelphia: Fortress Press, 1967), 45–56.

34. See Wiesner, "The Reformation of the Women," in *Gender, Church and State,* 63–83.

35. See particularly Wiesner, "Ideology Meets Empire: Reformed Convents and the Reformation," ibid., 47–62.

36. See Roper, "The Reformation of Convents," in *Holy Household,* 206–51.

37. Caritas Perckheimer, abbess of a reformed convent in Nuremberg, is an important example of those who resisted efforts to forcibly remove their nuns and were allowed finally to remain in their convents but not take on new novices. See Paula Darsko Barker, *A Mirror of Piety and Learning: Caritas Perckheimer against the Reformation* (Ph.D. diss., Divinity School, University of Chicago, December 1990).

38. For the early history of Gandersheim, see Eckenstein, *Women under Monasticism,* 154–60.

39. See note 26 above.

40. See Karant-Nunn, "On the Fringe of Society: Treatment of the Unfortunate," in *Zwickau in Transition,* 215–32.

41. Roper, *Holy Household,* 221–22.

42. For discipline ordinances, see Roper, "The Politics of Sin," in *Holy Household,* 56–88.

43. See Roderick Phillips, *Putting Asunder: A History of Divorce in Western Society* (Cambridge: Cambridge University Press, 1988), 88.

44. See Roper, "Blood and Codpieces: Masculinity in the Early Modern German Town," and "Drinking, Whoring and Gorging: Brutish Indiscipline and the Formation of Protestant Identity," in *Oedipus and the Devil,* 107–24, 145–67.

45. See the analysis in Roper, *Holy Household,* 130.

46. See Roper, "Discipline and Marital Disharmony," ibid., 165–205.

47. Steven Ozment, *When Fathers Ruled: Family Life in Reformation Europe* (Cambridge, Mass: Harvard University Press, 1983).

48. See Rosemary R. Ruether, *Women and Redemption: A Theological History* (Minneapolis: Fortress Press, 1998), 116–20.

49. *Luther's Works,* vol. 3, ed. James Atkinson, (Philadelphia: Fortress Press, 1966), 202–3.

50. See Luther, "Treatises on Marriage," in *Works,* vol. 44.

51. For Luther's contributions on the rites of marriage, baptism, confirmation, penance, the Lord's Supper, and Extreme Unction, see Susan C. Karant-Nunn, *The Reformation of Ritual: An Interpretation of Early Modern Germany* (London: Routledge, 1997), 13–16, 50–53, 67, 94–99, 114–19, 145–50.

52. Ibid., 66–70.

53. For the rejection and curbing of clandestine or private marriage by Protestants and Catholics in the sixteenth century, see Joel F. Harrington, *Reordering Marriage and Society in Reformation Germany* (Cambridge: Cambridge University Press, 1995), 25–47, 197–214.

54. For the sacramentality of Creation in patristic theology, see Rosemary R. Ruether, *Gaia and God: An Ecofeminist Theology of Earth Healing* (San Francisco: Harper San Francisco, 1989), 235–37.

55. For the effort to purge Protestant life of sacramentals, see Karant-Nunn, *Reform of Ritual,* 131–32.

56. Zwingli's treatises on baptism and the Lord's Supper may be found in English translation in volume 24 of the *Library of Christian Classics* (Philadelphia: Westminster Press, 1953), 119–238. For the more "interiorized" and rationalist views on baptism and the Eucharist of Zwingli and Calvin, see Karant-Nunn, *Reform of Ritual,* 61, 133–34. Also Keith Thomas, *Religion and the Decline of Magic* (New York: Charles Scribner's Sons, 1971); and Edward Muir, *Ritual in Early Modern Europe* (Cambridge: Cambridge University Press, 1997).

57. Luther engaged in a series of conflicts with Carlstadt and then with Zwingli on the Eucharist, taking the side of a revised version of the Real Presence. This was a major source of the schism between Lutheran and Reformed churches. For the controversy with Carlstadt, the Anabaptists, and Zwingli, see Williams, *Radical Reformation,* 117–19, 175–211.

58. Karant-Nunn, *Reformation of Ritual,* 43–71.

59. Ibid., 114–24.

60. For the development of the consent doctrine in the Middle Ages, see James A. Brundage, *Law, Sex and Christian Society in Medieval Europe* (Chicago: University of Chicago Press, 1987), 236–38, 268, 273–75, and *passim.*

61. For German folk traditions in marriage, see Karant-Nunn, *Reformation of Ritual,* 22–32; for Italy, see Christiane Klapisch-Zuber, *Women, Family and Ritual in Renaissance Italy* (Chicago: University of Chicago Press, 1985).

62. For the Lutheran wedding rite, see Karant-Nunn, *Reformation of Ritual,* 13–22.

63. For the reluctance to surrender folk traditions for marriage, see ibid., 36–38.

64. Treatises on marriage abounded in this period; see, for example, Mennonite

Dirk Philips, *On Christian Marriage* (1568), and Swiss reformer Heinrich Bullinger's *The Christian State of Matrimony.* For English Puritans, see William Perkins, *Christian Oeconomie* (1590), and William Gouge, *Of Domestical Duties: Eight Treatises* (1622).

65. For an older but still-useful account of the Puritan concept of the Christian household, see Edmund Morgan, *The Puritan Family* (New York: Harper and Row, 1966); also John Demos, *A Little Commonwealth: Family Life in Plymouth Colony* (New York: Oxford University Press, 1970).

66. For example, William Perkins, *A Discourse of the Dammed Art of Witchcraft* (1596).

67. Misogynist broadsides with vivid pictures of women dominating or cheating on their husbands proliferated during this period, inspiring the popular "Marriage Devil" books that prompted severe discipline of rebellious and sharp-tongued wives; see Harrington, "Against the Marriage Devil," in *Reordering Marriage,* 216–72.

68. See Phillips, *Putting Asunder,* 45–52.

69. For Luther's and other reformers' approval of Landgrave Philip of Hesse's bigamous marriage in 1539, see ibid., 76.

70. For openness to plural marriage, following the example of the Patriarchs, among Humanists, magisterial reformers, and Anabaptists, see Williams, *Radical Reformation,* 781–84.

71. For divorce-court practices among Lutherans and Calvinists and in the Church of England, see Phillips, *Putting Asunder,* 50–94. Only the Church of England retained ecclesiastical courts for marriage cases and left in place the medieval laws that refused all divorce.

72. Martin Bucer's treatise "Marriage, Divorce and Celibacy" appeared in his commentary on Matthew, Mark, and Luke.

73. John Milton, *The Doctrine and Discipline of Divorce* (1643).

74. See Hsia, *The World of Catholic Renewal,* 47–48.

75. For Gallicanism in the sixteenth and seventeenth centuries, see ibid., 66–73.

76. Legal reforms in the early modern period tended to include those elements in both German and Roman law that justified female subordination, while excluding elements in either system that were more egalitarian: see Wiesner, *Women and Gender,* 30–35, and *Gender, Church and State,* 84–93.

77. On the seminary as a means of instilling a discipline of celibacy in priests, see Brundage, *Law, Sex and Christian Society,* 568–69.

78. Catholic women's struggles to found active orders against Catholic church regulations on cloister have been studied extensively, both in general and in terms of particular women leaders. For a general overview, see Ruth P. Liebowitz, "Virgins in the Service of Christ: The Dispute over an Active Apostolate for Women during

the Counter-Reformation," in *Women of Spirit: Female Leadership in the Jewish and Christian Traditions*, ed. Rosemary R. Ruether and Eleanor McLaughlin (New York: Simon and Schuster, 1979), 131–52.

79. For the Trentine decree on marriage, see Phillips, *Putting Asunder,* 35–39; also J. Waterworth, trans., *Canons and Decrees of the Council of Trent* (London: C. Dolman, 1848), 194–201.

80. See Roper, "Exorcism and the Theology of the Body," in *Oedipus and the Devil,* 226–48.

81. See Hsia on art and architecture as a reflection of the Catholic Reformation, in *The World of Catholic Renewal,* 152–64.

82. The identification of the patriarchal family as the base for patriarchal hierarchy in society is typical of political thought of the period; for an overview and a bibliography, see Wiesner, *Women and Gender,* 239–58.

4. The Making of the Victorian Family: 1780–1890

1. Lawrence Stone, *The Family, Sex and Marriage in England, 1500–1800* (New York: Harper and Row, 1977), 28–29.

2. Ibid., 224–25.

3. Ibid., 253–56; see also *Passions of the Renaissance,* ed. Roger Chartier, vol. 3 of *A History of Private Life* (Cambridge, Mass.: Harvard University Press, 1989), 6–7; also vol. 4, *From the Fires of Revolution to the Great War,* ed. Michelle Perrot (Cambridge, Mass.: Harvard University Press, 1990), 173, 341–47, 360–74.

4. Stone, *Family, Sex and Marriage in England,* 256–57.

5. Ibid., 42.

6. E. J. Hobshawn, *Industry and Empire: An Economic History of Britain Since 1750* (London: Weidenfeld and Nicolson, 1968), 15; also Edward P. Thompson, *Whigs and Hunters* (London: Allen Lane, 1975).

7. Louise A. Tilly and Joan W. Scott, *Women, Work and Family* (New York: Holt, Rinehart and Winston, 1978), 13, 74–75; also Gordon Wright, *Rural Revolution in France* (Palo Alto, Calif.: Stanford University Press, 1964), 6.

8. Ibid., 44–47.

9. Elinor Accampo, *Industrialization, Family Life and Class Relations: Saint Chamond, 1815–1914* (Berkeley: University of California Pres, 1989), 23–25.

10. On the idea of protoindustrialization, see Franklin F. Mendels, "Proto-Industrialization: The First Phase of Industrialization," *Journal of Economic History* 31, n. 1 (March 1972): 241–61; also Hans Medich, "The Proto-Industrial Family Economy: The Structural Function of Household and Family during the Transition from Peasant Society to Industrial Capitalism," *Social History* 3 (1976): 291–315.

11. For continuing domestic industry for women in late-nineteenth-century England, see Joan Perkin, *Victorian Women* (New York: New York University Press, 1993), 189–90; also Deborah Valenze, *The First Industrial Woman* (New York: Oxford University Press, 1995), 113–27.

12. Tilly and Scott, *Women, Work and Family*, 63.

13. Mary P. Ryan, *Cradle of the Middle Class: The Family in Oneida County, New York, 1790–1865* (Cambridge: Cambridge University Press, 1981), 9–10, 45–48.

14. See Catherine Clinton, *The Other Civil War: American Women in the Nineteenth Century* (New York: Hill and Wang, 1984), 24–29; also Thomas Dublin, *Women at Work: The Transformation of Work and Community in Lowell, Massachusetts, 1826–1860* (New York: Columbia University Press, 1979), and *Farm to Factory: Women's Letters, 1830–1860* (New York: Columbia University Press, 1981).

15. See Nancy F. Cott, *The Bonds of Womanhood: Woman's Sphere in New England, 1780–1835* (New Haven: Yale University Press, 1977), 35–40; also Katherine Sklar, *Catherine Beecher: A Study of American Domesticity* (New Haven: Yale University Press, 1973).

16. See Tamara K. Hareven, *Family Time and Industrial Time: The Relationship between Family and Work in a New England Industrial Community* (Cambridge: Cambridge University Press, 1982), 9–37, 85–119, 189–217.

17. For children as young as six or seven working in factories, see Tilly and Scott, *Women, Work and Family*, 113.

18. Ibid., 126–29.

19. Stone, *Family, Sex and Marriage*, 46–54; Accampo, *Industrialization*, 52.

20. See Andre Burguière and François Lebrun, "The One Hundred and One Families of Europe," in *The Impact of Modernity*, vol. 2 of *A History of the Family*, ed. Andre Burguière, Christiane Klapisch-Zuber, Martine Segalen, and Françoise Zonabend (Cambridge: Harvard University Press, 1996), 34–39.

21. Tilly and Scott, *Women, Work and Family*, 31–37, 106–16.

22. Ibid., 128.

23. Ibid., 23; also Accampo, *Industrialization*, 146–47. For the orphan asylum in Rochester, New York, see Nancy A. Hewitt, *Women's Activism and Social Change: Rochester, New York, 1822–1872* (Ithaca, N.Y.: Cornell University Press, 1984), 88–89, 94–95, 114–15.

24. Tilly and Scott, *Women, Work and Family*, 116–17.

25. The hospice in Chamond, France, run by nuns, was founded in the sixteenth century and took care of the elderly, the sick, and orphans; see Accampo, *Industrialization*, 146, 163–64. The Female Charitable Society of Rochester, New York, established a Home for Friendless Women, which was originally designed to house poor young women but eventually became a home for destitute elderly ones; see Hewitt, *Women's Activism*, 147–49, 191.

26. Accampo, *Industrialization,* 50–51.

27. Ibid., 58–61; also *From the Fires of Revolution,* 199–200, 599–601.

28. Stone, *Family, Sex and Marriage,* 64–81; Accampo, *Industrialization,* 61–68, 127–28.

29. Tilly and Scott, *Women, Work and Family,* 27–29; Stone, *Family, Sex and Marriage,* 68.

30. Stone, *Family, Sex and Marriage,* 54–60.

31. Ibid., 56; *From the Fires of Revolution,* 15, 21.

32. Stone, *Family, Sex and Marriage,* 159, 428–32; Accampo, *Industrialization,* 125–26.

33. Stone, *Family, Sex and Marriage,* 106–8; Tilly and Scott, *Women, Work and Family,* 13–14.

34. John Demos, *A Little Commonwealth: Family Life in Plymouth Colony* (New York: Oxford University Press, 1970).

35. Ryan, *Cradle of the Middle Class,* 18–43.

36. Ibid., 35–37.

37. Ibid., 62–65.

38. Ibid., 91–92; also Hewitt, *Women's Activism,* 64–66.

39. Whitney Cross, *The Burned-Over District: The Social and Intellectual History of Enthusiastic Religion in Western New York,* (Ithaca, N.Y.: Cornell University Press, 1950).

40. Ryan, *Cradle of the Middle Class,* 75–83.

41. Hewitt, *Women's Activism,* 17.

42. Ibid., 73.

43. Ryan, *Cradle of the Middle Class,* 105–44.

44. Hewitt, *Women's Activism,* 28; Ryan, *Cradle of the Middle Class,* 11.

45. Ryan, *Cradle of the Middle Class,* 116–25; Hewitt, *Women's Activism,* 102–3, 109–11, 126–27; also Clinton, *The Other Civil War,* 59–62; Nancy Woloch, *Women and the American Experience,* 2d ed. (New York: McGraw-Hill, 1994), 175–78; Mary P. Ryan, "The Power of Women's Networks: A Case Study of Female Reform in Ante-Bellum America," *Feminist Studies* 5, no. 1 (spring 1979), 66–85; and Carroll Smith-Rosenberg, "Beauty and the Beast: A Case Study in Sex Roles and Social Stress in Jacksonian America," *American Quarterly* 23 (October 1971): 562–84.

46. Ryan, *Cradle of the Middle Class,* 78–79, 111–12.

47. Hewitt, *Women's Activism,* 46.

48. Ibid., 49–50.

49. See Gerda Lerner, *The Grimké Sisters from South Carolina: Pioneers for Women's Rights and Abolition* (Boston: Houghton Mifflin, 1967); also Rosemary R. Ruether,

Women and Redemption: A Theological History (Minneapolis: Fortress Press, 1998), 161–66.

50. The Rochester Female Charitable Society voted not to extend any services to Catholics: Hewitt, *Women's Activism*, 175, 237. In Oneida County, Catholics began their own orphanage to prevent the Protestantizing of their children; see Ryan, *Cradle of the Middle Class*, 212–17.

51. See Mark Holloway, *Heavens on Earth: Utopian Communities in America, 1680–1880* (New York: Dover, 1966), 37–52.

52. For Shaker theology, see Ruether, *Women and Redemption*, 149–59. For Shaker history, see Edward Deming Andrews, *The People Called Shakers* (New York: Dover, 1963). For their celibate family organization, see Lawrence Foster, *Women, Family and Utopia: Communal Experiments of the Shakers, the Oneida Community and the Mormons* (Syracuse, N.Y.: Syracuse University Press, 1991), 17–42.

53. For Rappites, see Christina Knoedler, *The Harmony Society: A Nineteenth-Century American Utopia* (New York: Vintage, 1954), and Karn Arnt, *George Rapp's Harmony Society, 1785–1847* (Philadelphia: University of Pennsylvania Press, 1965). For Zoarites, see Brian J. C. Berry, *American Utopian Experiments* (Hanover, N.H.: University Press of New England, 1992), 41–55.

54. For Robert Owen, see J. F. C. Harrison, *Quest for the New Moral Order: Robert Owen and Owenites in Britain and America* (New York: Charles Scribner's Sons, 1969). For Fourier, see Raymond Lee Muncy, *Sex and Marriage in Utopian Communities in the Nineteenth Century* (Baltimore: Penguin Books, 1973), 64–78. For Transcendentalist communities, see Richard Francis, *Transcendental Utopias: Individual and Community at Brook Farm, Fruitlands and Walden* (Ithaca, N.Y.: Cornell University Press, 1997).

55. For the influence of Fourier on French institutional and apartment architecture, see *From the Fires of Revolution*, 404–13.

56. Rosemary R. Ruether, "Women in Utopian Communities," in *Women and Religion in America: The Nineteenth Century,* ed. Rosemary R. Ruether and Rosemary S. Keller (San Francisco: Harper and Row, 1981), 69–70. Mormon views on polygamy may also be found in Foster, *Women, Family and Utopia,* 123–201, and Muncy, *Sex and Marriage,* 122–59.

57. For the Oneida Perfectionists, see Muncy, *Sex and Marriage,* 160–79; also Foster, *Women, Family and Utopia,* 74–107; and Richard DeMaria, *Communal Love at Oneida: A Perfectionist Vision of Authority, Property and Sexual Order* (New York: E. Mellon Press, 1978).

58. Roger Wunderlich, *Low Living and High Thinking at Modern Times* (Syracuse, N.Y.: Syracuse University Press, 1992).

59. Ceclia Morris Eckhardt, *Fanny Wright: Rebel in America* (Cambridge, Mass.: Harvard University Press, 1984).

60. David J. Rothman, *The Discovery of Asylum: Social Order and Disorder in the New Republic* (Boston, Mass.: Little, Brown, 1971; rev. ed. 1990), 3–27.

61. Ibid., 79–108.

62. Ibid., 109–29.

63. Ibid., 155–79.

64. Ibid., 164–66.

65. Ibid., 191–92.

66. Daniel Burton, ed., *The Celling of America: An Inside Look at the U.S. Prison Industry* (Monroe, Maine: Common Courage Press, 1998).

67. Suffragists formed the National Women's Loyal League to work for the Union war effort so long as the federal government was pledged to free the slaves if and when it won the war; see Eleanor Flexner, *Century of Struggle: The Women's Rights Movement in the United States* (Cambridge, Mass.: Harvard University Press, 1959; rev. ed. 1996), 104–6.

68. Ibid., 100–1; also Mary Elizabeth Massey, *Bonnet Brigades: American Women and the Civil War* (New York: Alfred A. Knopf, 1966).

69. Flexner, *Century of Struggle,* 137–43.

70. Ibid., 143–48.

71. Aileen S. Kraditor, *The Ideas of the Women's Suffrage Movement* (New York: Columbia University Press, 1965), 163–218.

72. Angelina Grimké's appeal "To the Christian Women of the South" strove to arouse antislavery sentiments among southern women; see Catherine Clinton, *The Plantation Mistress: Women's Work in the Old South* (New York: Pantheon Books, 1982), 180–81. For the text of this treatise, see Larry Ceplair, ed., *The Public Years of Sarah and Angelina Grimké: Selected Writing, 1835–1839* (New York: Columbia University Press, 1989), 36–79.

73. Ceplair, *Public Years,* 182–98.

74. Ibid., 16–35.

75. Anne Firor Scott, *The Southern Lady from Pedestal to Politics, 1830–1930* (Chicago: University of Chicago Press, 1970), 80–102; Clarence Mohr, *On the Threshold of Freedom: Masters and Slaves in Civil War Georgia* (Athens, Ga.: University of Georgia Press, 1986); also Catherine Clinton and Nina Silber, eds., *Divided Houses: Gender and the Civil War* (New York: Oxford University Press, 1992), 171–212.

76. Clinton and Silber, *Divided Houses,* 199–222.

77. Ibid., 203.

78. Jacqueline Jones, *Labor of Love, Labor of Sorrow: Black Women, Work and the Family from Slavery to the Present* (New York: Basic Books, 1985), 11–43.

79. Herbert Gutman, *The Black Family in Slavery and Freedom, 1750–1975* (New

York: Pantheon Books, 1976), 363–431; also Woloch, *Women and the American Experience,* 226–30.

80. Jones, *Labor of Love,* 81–95.

81. Ibid., 18.

82. Ibid., 127–34.

83. Ibid., 113–14.

84. Ryan, *Cradle of the Middle Class,* 145–55; also Jeanne Boydston, *Home and Work: Housework, Wages and the Ideology of Labor in the Early Republic* (New York: Oxford University Press, 1990).

85. Ryan, *Cradle of the Middle Class,* 198–208.

86. For this view of the child and the mother as primary parent, see ibid., 158–61. For changing views of the child, see Philippe Aries, *Centuries of Childhood: The Social History of Family Life* (New York: Alfred A. Knopf, 1962).

87. Barbara Welter, "The Cult of True Womanhood," in *Dimity Convictions: The American Woman in the Nineteenth Century* (Athens, Ohio: Ohio University Press, 1976), 21–41.

88. Welter, "The Feminization of American Religion, 1800–1860," in ibid., 83–102; also Ann Douglas, *Feminization of American Culture* (New York: Alfred A. Knopf, 1977).

89. Horace Bushnell, *Women's Suffrage: The Reform against Nature* (New York: Charles Scribner's Sons, 1869).

90. Ryan, *Cradle of the Middle Class,* 156–57.

91. G. J. Barker-Benfield, *The Horrors of the Half-Known Life: Male Attitudes toward Women's Sexuality in Nineteenth-Century America* (New York: W. W. Norton, 1976). For parallel views in Britain, see Cynthia Eagle Russell, *Sexual Science: The Victorian Construction of Womanhood* (Cambridge, Mass.: Harvard University Press, 1986).

92. See Clinton, *The Other Civil War,* 153–56; also Linda Gordon, *Woman's Body, Woman's Right: A Social History of Birth Control in America* (New York: Vintage, 1976).

93. Flexner, *Century of Struggle,* 208–17, 241–314.

94. Ibid., 108–25.

95. Ibid., 126–35; also Frances E. Willard, *The Ideal of the "New Woman" according to the Women's Christian Temperance Union,* ed. Carolyn DeSwarte Gifford (New York: Garland Press, 1988).

96. Flexner, *Century of Struggle,* 126–35, 185–94, 233–40.

97. Social Gospel writers such as Walter Rauschenbusch generally supported the middle-class family pattern in which women should be full-time mothers, and hoped that workers would gain a "family wage" to make this possible: see his books

Christianity and the Social Crisis (New York: Macmillan, 1907), 276–77, and *Some Moral Aspects of the Woman's Movement* (Chicago: University of Chicago Press, 1913).

98. Ida B. Wells, *Crusade for Justice: The Autobiography of Isa B. Wells*, ed. Alfreda Duster (Chicago: University of Chicago Press, 1970).

5. **From the Progressive Era through the Great Depression: 1890–1940**

1. Lois Scharf, *To Work and to Wed: Female Employment, Feminism and the Great Depression* (Westport, Conn.: Greenwood Press, 1980), 4–5.

2. Margery Davis, *Women's Place Is at the Typewriter: Office Work and Office Workers, 1870–1930* (Philadelphia: Temple University Press, 1982).

3. Scharf, *To Work and to Wed,* 5–10.

4. Nancy Woloch, *Women and the American Experience* (New York: McGraw-Hill, 1994), 2:253–68. See also Eleanor Stebner, *The Women of Hull House: A Study in Spirituality, Vocation and Friendship* (Albany: SUNY Press, 1997), 75–76.

5. Woloch, *Women and the American Experience,* 261–63.

6. Stebner, *Women of Hull House,* 93.

7. Ibid., 123–24.

8. Ibid, 113–14.

9. Robyn Muncy, *Creating a Female Dominion in American Reform, 1890–1935* (New York: Oxford University Press, 1991), 66–92.

10. Ibid., 38–47.

11. Ibid., 47–65.

12. For the use of Watsonian behaviorism in the Children's Bureau's pamphlets and counseling of mothers, see ibid., 113; also Winifred Wandersee, *Women's Work and Family Values, 1920–40* (Cambridge, Mass.: Harvard University Press, 1981), 57–58. The behaviorist view of child-raising may be found in John B. Watson's *Psychological Care of Infant and Child* (New York: W. W. Norton, 1928). See also Molly Ladd, *Raising a Baby the Government Way: Mother's Letters to the Children's Bureau, 1915–1932* (New Brunswick, N.J.: Rutgers University Press, 1986).

13. Muncy, *Creating a Female Dominion,* 63–64.

14. Susan B. Anthony and Ida H. Harper, eds., *History of Women's Suffrage* (Rochester, N.Y.: Susan B. Anthony, 1902), 4:158–74; Carrie Chapman Catt and Nellie Rogers Shuler, *Woman Suffrage and Politics: The Inner Story of the Suffrage Movement* (New York: Charles Scribner's Sons, 1923), 267–69; also Woloch, *Women and the American Experience,* 334–36.

15. For the social programs of the WCTU, including suffrage, see *"Do Everything" Reform: The Oratory of Frances Willard* (Westport, Conn.: Greenwood Press, 1992).

16. For the Women's Educational and Industrial Union, see Karen J. Blair, *Club Woman as Feminist: True Womanhood Redefined, 1860–1914* (New York: Holmes and Meier, 1980), 73–91.

17. Ibid., 15–30, 93–110.

18. For the National Consumers' League, see Woloch, *Women and the American Experience,* 301.

19. For the Women's Trade Union League, see ibid., 207–9; also Nancy Schrom Dye, *As Equals and As Sisters: Feminism, the Labor Movement and the Women's Trade Union League of New York* (Columbia, Mo.: University of Missouri Press, 1980).

20. See Blair, *Club Woman as Feminist,* 111–14.

21. See Woloch, *Women and the American Experience,* 353. For Catt's politics, see Robert Booth Flower, *Carrie Catt: Feminist Politician* (Boston: Northeastern University Press, 1986), and Jacqueline Van Voris, *Carrie Chapman Catt: A Public Life* (New York: Feminist Press of the City University of New York, 1987).

22. For the links between feminism and temperance, see Barbara Leslie Epstein, *The Politics of Domesticity: Women, Evangelism and Temperance in Nineteenth-Century America* (Middletown, Conn.: Wesleyan University Press, 1981); also Joseph Gusfield, *Symbolic Crusade: Status Politics and the American Temperance Movement* (Urbana, Ill.: University of Illinois Press, 1963).

23. See Blair, *Club Woman as Feminist,* 108–10; for a biography of Josephine Ruffin, see *Notable American Women,* (Cambridge, Mass.: Harvard University Press, 1971), 3:206–8.

24. Catholic women founded a number of clubs in the late nineteenth and early twentieth centuries, ranging from ethnic-group clubs such as the Polish Women's Alliance to the women's auxiliary of the Knights of Columbus, the Daughters of Isabella. The main Catholic women's organization under the Catholic Bishops is the National Council of Catholic Women. The major Jewish woman's group is the National Council of Jewish Women, founded by Hannah Solomon in 1893. The major American Jewish Zionist organization is Hadassah, founded by Henrietta Szold in 1911. See Ann Braude, "Women and Religious Practice in American Judaism," in *In Our Own Voices: Four Centuries of American Women's Religious Writings,* ed. Rosemary R. Ruether and Rosemary S. Keller (San Francisco: Harper San Francisco, 1995), 120, 129–34.

25. James J. Kenneally, *The History of American Catholic Women* (New York: Crossroads, 1990), 131–44.

26. See Rosalyn Terborg-Penn, "Discontented Black Feminists and the Nineteenth Amendment," in Lois Scharf and Joan Jensen, *Decades of Discontent: The Women's Movement, 1920–1940* (Westport, Conn.: Greenwood Press, 1983), 261–78.

27. See Judith Schwartz, *Radical Feminists of Heterodoxy: Greenwich Village, 1912–1940* (Lebanon, N. H.: New Victoria, 1982).

28. For the meaning of the term *feminism* in the early twentieth century and its

claiming, see Nancy Cott, *The Grounding of Modern Feminism* (New Haven: Yale University Press, 1987), 3–10.

29. See Woloch, *Women and the American Experience*, 344–49. For Crystal Eastman, see Blanche Weisen Cook, ed., *Crystal Eastman on Women and Revolution* (New York: Oxford University Press, 1978).

30. For Emma Goldman, see her own writings, *Living My Life*, 2 vols. (New York: Alfred A. Knopf, 1931); also Joseph Drinnon, *Rebel in Paradise: A Biography of Emma Goldman* (New York: Harper, 1961); Alix Kates Shulman, ed., *Red Emma Speaks: An Emma Goldman Reader* (New York: Schocken Books, 1983); and Alice Wexler, *Emma Goldman: An Intimate Life* (New York: Pantheon Books, 1984).

31. For Margaret Sanger, see David M. Kennedy, *Birth Control in America: The Career of Margaret Sanger* (New Haven: Yale University Press, 1970); also Ellen Chesler, *Woman of Valor: Margaret Sanger and the Birth Control Movement in America* (New York: Simon and Schuster, 1992).

32. See Polly Wynn Allen, *Building Domestic Liberty: Charlotte Perkins Gilman's Architectural Feminism* (Amherst, Mass.: University of Massachusetts Press, 1988); also Delores Hayden, *The Grand Domestic Revolution: A History of Feminist Designs for American Homes, Neighborhoods and Cities* (Cambridge, Mass.: MIT Press, 1981), 182–205.

33. Hayden, *Grand Domestic Revolution*, 228–65.

34. Ibid., 206–27.

35. Ibid., 280–89.

36. Marie Louise Degan, *The History of the Women's Peace Party* (Baltimore: John Hopkins University Press, 1939).

37. The organizations named on the spider chart were the Women's Joint Congressional Committee, the National League of Women Voters, the General Federation of Women's Clubs, the Women's Christian Temperance Union, the National Congress of Mothers and the Parent-Teacher Association, the National Women's Trade Union, the American Women's Home Economic Association, the National Consumers' League, the National Association of University Women, the National Council of Jewish Women, the Girl's Friendly Society, the Young Women's Christian Association, the National Federation of Business and Professional Women, the Women's International League for Peace and Freedom, and the Women's Committee for World Disarmament. See Nancy Cott, *Grounding of Modern Feminism*, 242, 249–50; also Scharf and Jensen, *Decades of Discontent*, 213–14.

38. See Christine Lunardini, *From Equal Suffrage to Equal Rights: Alice Paul and the National Women's Party, 1912–1928* (New York: New York University Press, 1986).

39. Ibid.; also Susan D. Becker, *The Origins of the Equal Rights Amendment: Feminism between the Wars* (Westport, Conn.: Greenwood Press, 1981).

40. For protective legislation, see Alice Kessler-Harris, *Out to Work: The History of*

Wage-Earning Women in the United States (New York: Oxford University Press, 1982), 180–214; also Susan Lehrer, *The Origin of Protective Labor Legislation for Women, 1905–1925* (Albany: SUNY Press, 1987).

41. The ideological split between the League of Women Voters and the National Women's party is discussed in Woloch, *Women and the American Experience,* 383–88; and Cott, *Grounding of Modern Feminism,* 121–29.

42. For the flapper image, see Scharf and Jensen, *Decades of Discontent,* 5–6, 31, 33; and Woloch, *Women and the American Experience,* 392–412; also Paula S. Fass, *The Damned and the Beautiful: American Youth in the 1920s* (New York: Oxford University Press, 1977).

43. For the "new woman" in the movies, see Scharf and Jensen, *Decades of Discontent,* 116–28; also Susan Ware, *Holding Their Own: American Women in the 1930s* (Boston: Twayne, 1982), 171–96.

44. For the distaste of social feminists such as Catt and Gilman for birth control and sexual liberation, see Woloch, *Women and the American Experience,* 413–14; and Ware, *Holding Their Own,* 65.

45. For the major essay that began the exploration of female-female erotic relations in the nineteenth century, see Carroll Smith-Rosenberg, "The Female World of Love and Ritual: Relations between Women in Nineteenth-Century America," *Signs* 1, no. 1 (autumn 1975): 1–30.

46. For "Boston marriages," see Woloch, *Women and the American Experience,* 275; for the relation between Jane Addams and Mary Rozet Smith, see Stebner, *Women of Hull House,* 160–66. For Willard's relations as revealed in her diary, see Carolyn Gifford, ed., *Writing Out My Heart: Selections from the Journal of Frances E. Willard, 1855–1896* (Urbana, Ill.: University of Illinois Press, 1995).

47. See Lillian Faderman, *Odd Girls and Twilight Lovers: A History of Lesbian Life in Twentieth-Century America* (New York: Columbia University Press, 1991). For Freud's view of lesbianism, see his "The Sexual Aberration: Inversion," in *Three Essays on the Theory of Sexuality* (1905), vol. 7 of the *Complete Psychological Works of Sigmund Freud* (London: Hogarth, 1953), 135–48, and "The Psychogenesis of a Case of Homosexuality in a Woman" (1920), ibid., 18:145–72. For Havelock Ellis's views, see his *Studies in the Psychology of Sex: Sexual Inversion* (1897; reprint, Philadelphia: F. A. Davies, 1911).

48. For the private religious persuasion of Jane Addams, see Stebner, *Women of Hull House,* 20–23, 77–83.

49. Martin Marty argues that the United States followed a different path from Germany and England, remaining strongly religious in private and family life while secularizing public life. He sees the 1870s as the turning point for this secularization of public life. See his *The Modern Schism: Three Paths to the Secular* (New York: Harper and Row, 1969), 98–102, 140–41. While generally agreeing, I would argue that distinct subcultures on the Right and in the black community retained a public religious discourse. These were marginalized from mainline secular American society but became the basis for a revival of public religion from the 1960s to today.

50. For the National Council of Catholic Women, see Kenneally, *History of American Catholic Women*, 121–26.

51. Mrs. Francis Slattery, "The Catholic Woman in Modern Times," *The Catholic Mind* 28 (22 March 1930): 124–31. For an excerpt of the speech, see Ruether and Keller, *In Our Own Voices*, 45–47.

52. For the failure of the Social Gospel to address racism, see Ronald C. White, *Liberty and Justice for All: Racial Reform and the Social Gospel, 1877–1925* (San Francisco: Harper and Row, 1990). For the movement's views of women's place, see note 97, p. 256, above.

53. See Letha Dawson Scanzoni and Susan Setta, "Women in Evangelical Holiness and Pentecostal Traditions," in *Women and Religion in America, 1900–1968*, vol. 3, ed. Rosemary R. Ruether and Rosemary S. Keller, (San Francisco: Harper and Row, 1986), 223–34, 241–48.

54. For Alma White's autobiography, see her *The Story of My Life and the Pillar of Fire*, 4 vols. (Zarephath, N.J.: Pillar of Fire, 1938). For her connections with the Klan, see Kathleen M. Blee, *Women of the Klan: Racism and Gender in the 1920s* (Berkeley: University of California Press, 1991), 72–76.

55. Blee, *Women of the Klan, passim.*

56. See Muncy, *Creating a Female Dominion*, 96–101.

57. For the WJCC, see ibid., 103–6.

58. Ibid., 106–11.

59. See Woloch, *Women and the American Experience*, 387.

60. Ibid.

61. Muncy, *Creating a Female Dominion*, 124–25, 135–50.

62. See Jacqueline Jones, *Labor of Love, Labor of Sorrow: Black Women, Work and Family from Slavery to the Present* (New York: Basic Books, 1985), 160–62.

63. For new areas of women's work in the 1920s, see Woloch, *Women and the American Experience*, 391–92; also Kessler–Harris, *Out to Work*, 219–35.

64. For women in college teaching, see Woloch, *Women and the American Experience*, 393; also Barbara Harris, *Beyond Her Sphere: Women and the Professions in American History* (Westport, Conn.: Greenwood Press, 1978), 113–15, 138–39.

65. See Woloch, *Women and the American Experience*, 392.

66. For married women in the labor force in 1930, see Kessler-Harris, *Out to Work*, 228–30; and Wandersee, *Women's Work and Family Values*, 68.

67. For the consumer economy of the 1920s, see Cott, *Grounding of Modern Feminism*, 162–63, 172–74.

68. For studies of changes in women's housework, see Susan Strasser, *Never Done: A History of American Housework* (New York: Pantheon Books, 1982), and Ruth Schwartz Cowan, *More Work for Mother: The Ironies of Household Technology from the Open Hearth to the Microwave* (New York: Basic Books, 1983). For the changing role

of domestic servants in American homes, see David M. Katzman, *Seven Days a Week: Women and Domestic Service in Industrializing America, 1865–1895* (New York: Oxford University Press, 1978).

69. For the view that women are incapable of higher education, see Edward Clarke, *Sex in Education* (Boston: J. R. Osgood, 1873); for medical views of women, see G. J. Barker-Benfield, *The Horrors of the Half-Known Life: Male Attitudes toward Women and Sexuality in Nineteenth-Century America* (New York: Harper and Row, 1976).

70. For critics of working wives and mothers, see Cott, *Grounding of Modern Feminism,* 153–54, 179–211. Male psychiatrists of the 1920s developed a series of principles to reinforce the traditional separation of female natures and spheres and to characterize the working or politically active woman as sexually maladjusted; see Jill Morawski, "Not Quite New Worlds: Psychologists' Conception of the Ideal Family in the 1920s," in *In the Shadow of the Past: Psychology Portrays the Sexes,* ed. Miriam Lewis (New York: Columbia University Press, 1984), 97–125, and her "Measurement of Masculinity and Feministy: Engendering Categorical Realities", in *Journal of Personality* 53, no. 2 (June 1985): 196–223.

71. For the feminist defense of combining marriage and career, see Scharf, *To Work and to Wed,* 21–42; also Cott, *Grounding of Modern Feminism,* 175–209.

72. For 1920s women social historians of changing work-marriage relations for women, see Beatrice M. Hinkle, "Changing Marriage: A Product of Industrialization," *Survey* 57 (December 1926): 286–89; also Sophronisba Beckenridge, *Women in the Twentieth Century: A Study of Their Political, Social and Economic Activities* (New York: McGraw-Hill, 1933).

73. See Scharf, *To Work and to Wed,* 36.

74. For the Depression-era attack on the working wife, see ibid., 43–66; also Kessler-Harris, *Out to Work,* 251–55; Susan Ware, *Holding Their Own,* 24–29; and Cott, *Grounding of Modern Feminism,* 209–11.

75. For married women barred from teaching, see Scharf, *To Work and to Wed,* 66–85.

76. For section 213 of the Economic Recovery Act, see ibid., 46–48.

77. For the coalescing of women's groups in the struggle to repeal section 213 of the Economic Recovery Act, see ibid., 57–59.

78. Ibid., 62–61; for publications, see 185 nn. 56–59.

79. See Kessler-Harris, *Out of Work,* 250–72.

80. On the male takeover of the upper levels of teaching, librarianship, and social work, see Scharf, *To Work and to Wed,* 91.

81. Ibid., 92–93.

82. See Muncy, *Creating a Female Dominion,* xii–xiii.

83. See Susan Ware, *Beyond Suffrage: Women in the New Deal* (Cambridge, Mass.: Har-

vard University Press, 1987); also George W. Martin, *Madame Secretary: Frances Perkins* (Boston: Houghton Mifflin, 1976).

84. See Ware, *Beyond Suffrage,* 105–14; also Susan Ware, *Partner and I: Mollie Dewson, Feminism and New Deal Politics* (New Haven: Yale University Press, 1987).

85. See her autobiography: Rose Schneiderman, *All for One* (New York: P. S. Eriksson, 1967).

86. On the common backgrounds of New Deal women, see Woloch, *Women and the American Experience,* 452–55; also Ware, *Beyond Suffrage,* 18–42.

87. See Woloch, *Women and the American Experience,* 420–37. Biographies of Eleanor Roosevelt abound; see particularly Tamara K. Hareven, *Eleanor Roosevelt: An American Conscience* (Chicago: Quadrangle Books, 1968), and Joan Hoff-Wilson and Marjorie Lightman, eds., *Without Precedent: The Life and Career of Eleanor Roosevelt* (Bloomington, Ind.: Indiana University Press, 1984). Eleanor Roosevelt herself wrote two autobiographies, *This Is My Story* (New York: Harper and Brothers, 1937) and *This I Remember* (New York: Harper's, 1947). For her views on women's reforming work, see her *It's Up to the Women* (New York: Frederick A. Stokes, 1933).

88. For unemployed women and relief, see Scharf, *To Work and to Wed,* 119–24; also Ware, *Holding Their Own,* 40.

89. Scharf, *To Work and to Wed,* 123–29; Ware, *Holding Their Own,* 39–41.

90. Ware, *Holding Their Own,* 41; also Hilda W. Smith, "Educational Camps for Unemployed Girls," *New York Times Magazine,* 15 January 1936.

91. Scharf, *To Work and to Wed,* 110–13.

92. Ibid., 112: Scharf cites the U.S. Department of Labor, Women's Bureau, *Employed Women under the N. R. A. Codes,* Bulletin no. 122 (Washington, D.C.: Government Printing Office, 1934), 24–25, for this phrase in the codes (197 n. 5).

93. Kessler-Harris, *Out to Work,* 265.

94. Ibid., 162–63.

95. For the development of the welfare state and Aid to Dependent Children in the Social Security Act, see Linda Gordon, ed., *Women, the State and Welfare* (Madison, Wisc.: University of Wisconsin Press, 1990); also Theda Skocpol, *Protecting Soldiers and Mothers: Political Origins of Social Policy in the United States* (Cambridge, Mass.: Harvard University Press, 1992).

96. For Mexican women workers, see Rosalinda Gonzalez, "Chicana and Mexican Immigrant Families," in Scharf and Jensen, *Decades of Discontent,* 59–84; also Vicki L. Ruiz, *Cannery Women, Cannery Lives: Mexican Women, Unionization and the California Food Processing Industry, 1930–1950* (Albuquerque: University of New Mexico Press, 1987).

97. See Scharf, *To Work and to Wed,* 128–29.

98. Muncy, *Creating a Female Dominion*, 153 and 210 n. 105, citing Edith Abbott, "Child Welfare in Review: May 9, 1950," folder 9, Box 3, Addendum, Abbott papers.

99. Ibid., 153–157.

100. See Wandersee, *Women's Work and Family Values*, 68.

101. Black women in northern cities during the Depression resorted to what was called the slave market, standing on street corners to obtain occasional cleaning work; see Jones, *Labor of Love*, 205–6.

102. Several studies of the Depression years have noted that American families strove not simply to survive but to keep up the level of consumption to which they had become accustomed in the 1920s, and that middle-class wives sought a second income for these reasons: see Scharf, *To Work and to Wed*, 148–50; also Wandersee, *Women's Work and Family Values*, 1–6, 27–54.

103. Ware, *Holding Their Own*, 6–10.

104. Ibid., 55–56.

105. For the gradual legalization of contraceptive information, see Kennedy, *Birth Control in America*, 248–71.

6. Changing Ideologies and Realities: 1940–1975

1. Susan M. Hartmann, *The Home Front and Beyond: American Women in the 1940s* (Boston: Twayne, 1982), 53–55.

2. See Sherma Berger Gluck, *Rosie the Riveter Revisited: Women, the War and Social Change* (Boston: Twayne, 1987), 12. For war propaganda to recruit women, see Maureen Honey, *Creating Rosie the Riveter: Class, Gender and Propaganda During World War II* (Amherst, Mass.: University of Massachusetts Press, 1984); also Leila J. Rupp, *Mobilizing Women for War: German and American Propaganda, 1939–1941* (Princeton, N.J.: Princeton University Press, 1978).

3. Rupp, *Mobilizing Women for War*, 9: also Hartmann, *Home Front and Beyond*, 61.

4. Hartmann, *Home Front and Beyond*, 57; Gluck, *Rosie the Riveter Revisited*, 65; also Karen Anderson, *Wartime Women: Sex Roles, Family Relations and the Status of Women During World War II* (Westport, Conn.: Greenwood Press, 1981), 75–90.

5. Before 1940, a few women musicians played in major orchestras, but most performed in all-female orchestras or in amateur or community groups. The absence of men during the war allowed women to play in major orchestras such as the Chicago Symphony, the National Symphony, the New Orleans Symphony, the Boston Symphony, and the St. Louis Symphony. Some of these gains were lost again after the war, but women had found a foothold and were able to improve their access to major orchestras thereafter. See Hartmann, *Home Front and Beyond*, 89; also Carol Neuls-Bates, "Women's Orchestras, 1925–45," in *Women Making Music: The Western*

Art Tradition, 1150–1950, ed. Jane Bowers and Judith Tick (Urbana, Ill.: University of Illinois Press, 1985), 349–69.

6. Women earned as much as $50 a week in defense manufacturing, while in female production or clerical work they were paid about $25–29 a week; see Hartmann, *Home Front and Beyond,* 85–86, 92. The Women's Bureau surveyed former war workers in Baltimore and compiled data on their loss of income in postwar jobs; see ibid., 99 n. 34.

7. In a study of 135 women defense workers, Nancy Baker Wise and Christy Wise found that a number commented on harassment by male workers, though some also found helpful mentors; see their *A Mouthful of Rivets: Women at Work in World War II* (San Francisco: Josey-Bass, 1994), 88–107.

8. Hartmann, *Home Front and Beyond,* 64–66.

9. In their interviews of 135 war workers, Nancy Baker Wise and Christy Wise heard many comment on the greatly enhanced self-confidence they felt after succeeding in new "male" work. Although about twenty of the women happily stopped working after the war (to resumed working later), the rest continued in some kind of jobs. Some at first dropped down into work such as waitressing, only to go on to more prestigious work later in life, including becoming active in politics and in one case being elected mayor. Hotel and restaurant management, social work, teaching, librarianship, art, architecture, journalism, tax consulting, and nursing were among the fields these women entered after the war. See Wise and Wise, *Mouthful of Rivets, passim.*

10. Hartmann, *Home Front and Beyond,* 28.

11. Anderson, *Wartime Women,* 75–90.

12. Ibid., 122–153.

13. Ibid., 31–52.

14. Fanny Christine Hill was among the black women in Los Angeles who were able to find production work in manufacturing thanks to the local Negro Victory Committee, which campaigned against racial discrimination in war work. Hill worked at North American Aircraft in 1943. She was on maternity leave during the layoffs in 1945 but was rehired thereafter and worked at North American until her retirement, in 1980. See Gluck, *Rosie the Riveter Revisited,* 22–49.

15. Hartmann, *Home Front and Beyond,* 80–82; and Anderson, *Wartime Women,* 31–42. Also Jacqueline Jones, *Labor of Love, Labor of Sorrow: Black Women, Work and the Family from Slavery to the Present* (New York: Basic Books, 1985), 235–56.

16. Hartmann, *Home Front and Beyond,* 86.

17. The threatened march on Washington was preceded by the organization of a "Double-V" campaign in which blacks argued that Americans must defeat not only nazism abroad but racism at home. Roosevelt's Executive Order 8802 banning discrimination was followed up by the creation of the Fair Employment Practices

Commission, charged with monitoring its implementation. See Penny Colman, *Rosie the Riveter: Women Working on the Home Front in World War II* (New York: Crown, 1995), 27–28.

18. For the Japanese American internment, see Roger Daniels, *Concentration Camps, U.S.A.: Japanese Americans and World War II* (New York: Holt, Rinehart and Winston, 1972).

19. See Susan M. Hartmann, "Prescriptions for Penelope: Literature on Women's Obligations to Returning World War II Veterans," *Women's Studies* 5 (1978): 223–39.

20. Many unions kept separate seniority lists for men and women, so women were not rehired in their real order of seniority. Some unions also colluded in reclassifying the work women did to make them ineligible for reopened jobs. See Nancy Gabin, " 'They Have Placed a Penalty on Womanhood': The Protest Actions of Women Auto Workers in Detroit-Area UAW Locals, 1945–1947," *Feminist Studies* 8 (1982): 378–98; also Lynn Goldfarb et al., *Separated and Unequal: Discrimination against Women Workers after World War II: The UAW, 1944–1954* (Washington D. C.: URPE Education Project, n.d.); and D'Ann Campbell, *Women at War with America: Private Lives in a Patriotic Era* (Cambridge, Mass.: Harvard University Press, 1985).

21. The Women's Bureau did a study of women defense workers' work options after the war and found that 75 percent wanted to continue in their present jobs: *Women's Bureau Bulletin*, no. 209. This statistic caused a sensation when it was published under a banner headline in the *Wall Street Journal;* see Gluck, *Rosie the Riveter Revisited,* 16, 272 n. 30.

22. Hartmann, *Home Front and Beyond;* also Campbell, *Women at War with America.* For the falling ratio of female to male wages in the fifties, see Nancy Woloch, *Women and the American Experience* (New York: McGraw-Hill, 1994), 502.

23. The major expression of this view of women may be found in Marynia Farnham and Ferdinand Lundberg, *Modern Woman: The Lost Sex* (New York: Harper and Brothers, 1947). Popular misogyny was also expounded in Philip Wylie, *Generation of Vipers* (New York: Rinehart and Company, 1942).

24. A major exposition of the Freudian view of women is given in Helene Deutsch, *The Psychology of Women,* 2 vols. (New York: Grune and Stratton, 1944–45).

25. See Nancy Pottishman Weiss, "Mother, the Invention of Necessity: Dr. Benjamin Spock's Baby and Child Care," *American Quarterly* 29 (winter 1977): 519–46.

26. Edward A. Strecker, *Their Mothers' Sons: The Psychiatrist Examines an American Problem* (Philadelphia: J. B. Lippincott, 1946).

27. See Robert Griffith and Athan Theoharis, *The Specter: Original Essays on the Cold War and the Origins of McCarthyism* (New York: New Viewpoints, 1974). For the exploitation of homophobia in McCarthy's anti-Communist crusade, see Lillian Faderman, *Odd Girls and Twilight Lovers: A History of Lesbian Life in Twentieth-Century America* (New York: Columbia University Press, 1991), 139–58.

28. This incident took place in 1953. The retired naval officer (whose name I can't remember) complained to the high school president and sought to have the newspaper staff dismissed, but the principal simply called us in to report the incident to us and then affirmed his support of us.

29. See Leila J. Rupp and Verta Taylor, *Survival in the Doldrums: The American Women's Rights Movement, 1945 to the 1960s* (New York: Oxford University Press, 1987).

30. Ibid., 135–65.

31. Hartmann, *Home Front and Beyond,* 107.

32. Ibid., 108–10.

33. Lynn White, Jr., *Educating our Daughters* (New York: Harper and Brothers, 1950).

34. See Hartmann, *Home Front and Beyond,* 112–14.

35. Ibid., 165.

36. Steven Mintz and Susan Kellogg, *Domestic Revolutions: A Social History of American Family Life* (New York: The Free Press, 1988), 137.

37. See Lillian Faderman, *Surpassing the Love of Man: Romantic Friendship and Love between Women from the Renaissance to the Present* (New York: William Morrow, 1981), 314–31; also her *Odd Girls and Twilight Lovers,* 139–58.

38. For the rising divorce rate in the United States from 1890 to 1990, see Woloch, *Women and the American Experience,* 586.

39. Hartmann, *Home Front and Beyond,* 179.

40. Ibid., 213.

41. For graphs on women's work occupations and women in the professions, see Woloch, *Women and the American Experience,* 589–90.

42. Michael Harrington, *The Other America: Poverty in the United States* (New York: Macmillan, 1962).

43. Jack M. Bloom, *Class, Race and the Civil Rights Movement* (Bloomington, Ind.: Indiana University Press, 1987), 87–103.

44. Ibid., 137–43: also Peter B. Levy, *The Civil Rights Movement* (Westport, Conn.: Greenwood Press, 1998), 9–11, 106–8. See also Martin Luther King, Jr., *Stride toward Freedom* (New York: Harper and Row, 1958); David J. Garrow, ed., *The Montgomery Bus Boycott and the Women Who Started It: A Memoir of Jo Ann Gibson Robinson* (Knoxville: University of Tennessee Press, 1987); and Rosa Parks, *Rosa Parks: My Story* (New York: Dial Press, 1992).

45. Levy, *The Civil Rights Movement,* 11–13; also Bloom, *Class, Race and the Civil Rights Movement,* 111–13; and Daisy Bates, *The Long Shadow of Little Rock* (New York: David McKay Co., 1970).

46. Bloom, *Class, Race and the Civil Rights Movement,* 149-50. Also Martin Luther King, "Who Speaks for the South?," *Liberation* (1958), 13ff.

47. See Sara Evans, *Personal Politics: The Roots of Women's Liberation in the Civil Rights Movement and the New Left* (New York: Vintage, 1979), 29-33.

48. Levy, *The Civil Rights Movement,* 13; also William Chafe, *Civilities and Civil Rights: Greensboro, North Carolina, and the Black Struggle for Freedom* (New York: Oxford University Press, 1980).

49. For the SNCC Freedom Summer (1964) in Mississippi, see Levy, *The Civil Rights Movement,* 59-78; also Howard Zinn, *SNCC: The New Abolitionists,* 2d ed. (Boston: Beacon Press, 1979).

50. For the text of Martin Luther King's "I Have a Dream" speech, see Peter B. Levy, *Let Freedom Ring: A Documentary History of the Modern Civil Rights Movement* (Westport, Conn.: Praeger, 1992), 122-25.

51. For excerpts from the text of John F. Kennedy's June 11, 1963, speech on civil rights, see Peter B. Levy, *The Civil Rights Movement,* 172-75.

52. Evans, *Personal Politics,* 78-82; also see ibid., 238-40, for the 1977 reflections by Cynthia Washington on her experiences as a black woman SNCC organizer in 1963-65.

53. Cynthia Harrison, *On Account of Sex: The Politics of Women's Issues, 1945-1968* (Berkeley: University of California Press, 1988), 73-88.

54. Ibid., 89-105.

55. Ibid., 140-59.

56. Ibid., 109-37; also see Rupp and Taylor, *Survival in the Doldrums,* 166-74.

57. Harrison, *On Account of Sex,* 160-61, 172-74.

58. Rupp and Taylor, *Survival in the Doldrums,* 176-79.

59. Harrison, *On Account of Sex,* 176-82; also Pauli Murray and Mary Eastwood, "Jane Crow and the Law: Sex Discrimination and Title VII," *George Washington Law Review* 34 (December 1965): 232-56.

60. Harrison, *On account of Sex,* 187-91.

61. Ibid., 192-96; also Judith Hole and Ellen Levine, *Rebirth of Feminism* (New York: Quadrangle Books, 1971), 81-86. For Betty Friedan's account of the founding of NOW, see her *It Changed My Life: Writings on the Women's Movement* (New York: Random House, 1976), 75-86.

62. Maren Lockwood Carden, *The New Feminist Movement* (New York: Russell Sage, 1974), 104-6.

63. Harrison, *On Account of Sex,* 201-4; also Friedan's report on the first year of NOW (1967), in her *It Changed My Life,* 91-103.

64. See Friedan's announcement of a Bill of Rights for Women in her presidential

speech of 1967, *It Changed My Life,* 101–2; for the text of this Bill of Rights as subsequently formulated by NOW, see Hole and Levine, *Rebirth of Feminism,* 441–42.

65. Jo Freeman, *Politics of Women's Liberation* (New York: McKay Company, Inc., 1975), 152–54; also Carden, *New Feminist Movement,* 136–36.

66. Carden, *New Feminist Movement,* 139; Freeman, *Politics of Women's Liberation,* 160–-62; Myra Marx Ferree and Beth B. Hess, *Controversy and Coalition: The New Feminist Movement* (Boston: Twayne, 1985), 56–57.

67. For feminist publications in the late sixties and early seventies, see Ferree and Hess, *Controversy and Coalition,* 72–74.

68. A good example of this conflict of cultural styles comes from my own experience as a civil-rights worker with the Delta Ministry in Mississippi in the summer of 1965. Our group of students came from the Claremont colleges in California and was based in Beulah, at a former black college. The director of the project sternly advised the group to wear clean dress-up clothes when attending a black church as a sign of respect for the members of the local community, who, though poor, always wore their "Sunday best" to church. This advice also applied to other public occasions and demonstrations.

69. On the sexual revolutions in America in the 1920s, 1950s and 1960s, see Mintz and Kellogg, *Domestic Revolutions,* 115–16, 199, 201, 207–10.

70. Evans, *Personal Politics,* 85–88; see pages 233–35 for the text of the SNCC policy paper "On the Position of Women in the Movement."

71. Ibid., 107–25, 156–92; also Freeman, *Politics of Women's Liberation,* 57–60, 224; and Carden, *New Feminist Movement,* 60–62.

72. Evans, *Personal Politics,* 193–211.

73. Ibid., 214–15; also Freeman, *Politics of Women's Liberation,* 116–18; and Carden, *New Feminist Movement,* 33–37.

74. Carden, *New Feminist Movement,* 62–63; Freeman, *Politics of Women's Liberation,* 112; Evans, *Personal Politics,* 213–14.

75. Carden, *New Feminist Movement,* 73–87.

76. Freeman, *Politics of Women's Liberation,* 119–23. For Betty Friedan's objections to the radical, structureless style of women's liberation, see her *It Changed My Life,* 154–60.

77. Freeman, *Politics of Women's Liberation,* 137–39; Carden, *New Feminist Movement,* 53–59; also Lillian Faderman, *Odd Girls and Twilight Lovers,* 215–40.

78. Faderman, *Odd Girls and Twilight Lovers,* 148–50, 240–45; also Barry D. Adams, *The Rise of a Gay and Lesbian Movement* (Boston: Twayne, 1987), 62–101.

79. Freeman, *Politics of Women's Liberation,* 135; Faderman, *Odd Girls and Twilight Lovers,* 212; see also the quotation from Betty Friedan in Robin Morgan, *Going Too Far: The Personal Chronicle of a Feminist* (New York: Random House, 1976), 176.

80. Faderman, *Odd Girls and Twilight Lovers,* 176.

81. See Freeman, *Politics of Women's Liberation,* 230–37; Carden, *New Feminist Movement,* 93–99; Ferree and Hess, *Controversy and Coalition,* 67–68, 89–90. Black feminist groups included San Francisco's Black Women United for Action and the National Black Feminist Organization (1973) as well as the National Alliance for Black Feminists (1977): Ferree and Hess, 86.

82. Carden, *New Feminist Movement,* 112, 128–32.

83. Freeman, *Politics of Women's Liberation,* 202–5.

84. Marion Faux, *"Roe v. Wade": The Untold Story of the Landmark Supreme Court Decision That Made Abortion Legal* (New York: Macmillan, 1988), 92–94.

85. Freeman, *Politics of Women's Liberation,* 111–14, 148–49.

86. Ibid., 220–21.

87. James Cone, *Black Theology and Black Power* (New York: Seabury, 1969).

88. See Rosemary R. Ruether, *Women and Redemption: A Historical Theology* (Minneapolis: Fortress Press, 1998), 179–82.

89. My own first feminist article was written as a talk in 1968 and reflected the style of black power: "Male Chauvinist Theology and the Anger of Women," published in *Cross Currents* 21, no. 2 (spring 1971): 173–84. For the theological thought of Margaret Fell, the Grimké sisters, Lucretia Mott, and Elizabeth Cady Stanton, see my *Women and Redemption,* 138–40, 160–77.

90. See Rosemary R. Ruether, "Christianity and Women in the Modern World," in *Today's Woman in World Religions,* ed. Arvind Sharma (Albany: SUNY Press, 1994), 275–76.

91. See Norene Carter, "The Episcopal Story," in *Women of Spirit: Women's Leadership in the Jewish and Christian Traditions,* ed. Rosemary R. Ruether and Eleanor McLaughlin (New York: Simon and Schuster, 1979), 356–72.

92. See Ruether, "Christianity and Women in the Modern World," in *Today's Woman,* 276–82.

93. Ibid., 282–84.

94. For Troy Perry's autobiography, see his *The Lord Is My Shepherd and He Knows I'm Gay* (Los Angeles: Universal Fellowship Press, 1972); for the story of the Metropolitan Community Church, see Troy Perry, *Don't Be Afraid Anymore* (New York: St. Martin's, 1990).

95. For gay male theology and pastoral psychology, see the writings of former Jesuit priest and psychologist John J. McNeill: *The Church and the Homosexual* (Kansas City: Sheed, Andrews and McMeel, 1976); *Taking a Chance on God: Liberating Theology for Gays, Lesbians and Their Lovers, Families and Friends* (Boston: Beacon Press, 1988); and *Freedom, Glorious Freedom: The Spiritual Journey to the Fullness of Life for Gays, Lesbians and Everybody Else* (Boston: Beacon Press, 1995; also his autobiography, *Both Feet Firmly Planted in Midair: My Spiritual Journey* (Louisville: Westmin-

ster/John Knox, 1998). For writings of lesbian theologians, see, for example, Carter Heyward, *Touching Our Strength: The Erotic as the Power and Love of God* (San Francisco: Harper and Row, 1989), and Mary Hunt, *Fierce Tenderness: A Feminist Theology of Friendship* (New York: Crossroads, 1991).

7. The Family Agenda of the Christian Right

1. See Alan Crawford, *Thunder on the Right* (New York: Pantheon Books, 1980); also Lawrence R. Bruce, *Defenders of God: The Fundamentalist Revolt against the Modern Age* (San Francisco: Harper and Row, 1989); and Sara Diamond, *Roads to Dominion: Right Wing Movements and Political Power in the United States* (New York: Guilford Press, 1995), 19–108.

2. Diamond, *Roads to Dominion,* 178–202.

3. Ibid., 199–200.

4. Norman Podhoretz, "The New American Majority," *Commentary,* January 1981, 35.

5. See James D. Hunter, *Culture Wars: The Struggle to Define America* (New York: Basic Books, 1991), 67–86; also George Marsden, *Fundamentalism and American Culture: The Shaping of Twentieth-Century Evangelism, 1870–1925* (New York: Oxford University Press, 1980). For the fundamentalist story from an adherent's perspective, see David O. Beale, *In Pursuit of Purity: American Fundamentalism since 1850* (Greenville, N.C.: Unusual Publications, 1986).

6. For the Christian Right in the 1940s–'60s, see Diamond, *Roads to Dominion,* 92–106; also James D. Hunter, *American Evangelicals: Conservative Religion and the Quandary of Modernity* (New Brunswick, N.J.: Rutgers University Press, 1983). The evangelical magazine *Theology Today* is a major source for conservative Protestant views of this period.

7. For the history of the antifeminist backlash, see Susan Faludi, *Backlash: The Undeclared War against American Women* (New York: Crown, 1992), 46–72.

8. Jane J. Mansbridge, *Why We Lost the ERA* (Chicago: University of Chicago Press, 1986), 8–10; also Susan D. Becker, *The Origins of the Equal Rights Amendment: American Feminism between the Wars* (Westport, Conn.: Greenwood Press, 1981).

9. Mansbridge, *Why We Lost the ERA,* 11–12; also Jane K. Boles, *The Politics of the Equal Rights Amendment: Conflict and Decision Process* (New York: Longmans, 1979).

10. Mansbridge, *Why We Lost the ERA,* 29–35.

11. Carol Felsenthal, *The Sweetheart of the Silent Majority: The Biography of Phyllis Schlafly* (Garden City, N.Y.: Doubleday, 1981), 31–117.

12. See Phyllis Schlafly, *The Power of the Positive Woman* (New Rochelle, N.Y.: Arlington House, 1977); also Andrea Dworkin, *Right Wing Women* (New York: Coward, McCann, 1983).

13. Schlafly's *A Choice, Not an Echo* was self-published and self-distributed. She also wrote a series of books with retired Rear Admiral Chester Ward, accusing the East Coast political establishment of selling out American military preeminence; these were self-published as well, under the imprint of Père Marquette Press, Alton, Illinois: *The Gravediggers* (1964); *Strike from Space* (1965), and *The Betrayers* (1968). Schlafly and Ward also collaborated on *Kissinger on the Couch* (New Rochelle, N.Y.: Arlington House, 1975). See Felsenthal, *Sweetheart of the Silent Majority*, 215–31.

14. Felsenthal, *Sweetheart of the Silent Majority*, 231–41.

15. See Phyllis Schlafly, *The Phyllis Schlafly Report* 5, no. 7 (February 1972): 3, 4.

16. Mansbridge, *Why We Lost the ERA*, 45–59.

17. Ibid., 36–44, 60–66.

18. Ibid., 90–117.

19. For a study of the social dynamics of the pro- and anti-ERA campaigns in the state of North Carolina, see Donald G. Matthews and Jane Sherron DeHart, *Sex, Gender and the Politics of the ERA: A State and the Nation* (New York: Oxford University Press, 1990).

20. For Mormon involvement in the anti-ERA movement, see Diamond, *Roads to Dominion*, 167–68.

21. See Sara Diamond, *Spiritual Warfare: The Politics of the Christian Right* (Boston: South End Press, 1989), 1–22; also her *Not by Politics Alone: The Enduring Influence of the Christian Right* (New York: Guilford Press, 1998), 20–30, 57–71. For a critique of the Robertson media empire by a former insider, see Gerald Thomas Straub, *Salvation for Sale: An Insider's View of Pat Robertson* (Buffalo: Prometheus Press, 1988).

22. Diamond, *Spiritual Warfare*, 22–44.

23. Diamond, *Not by Politics Alone*, 21–22.

24. Ibid., 21; see also the National Religious Broadcasters' *1977 Directory of the Religious Media*, 34, 222.

25. Diamond, *Not by Politics Alone*, 30–36.

26. Among Pat Robertson's books are *Shout It from the Housetops* (Plainfield, N.J.: Logos International, 1972); *The New Millennium* (Dallas: Word, 1990); *The New World Order* (Dallas: Word, 1991); and *The Turning Tide: The Fall of Liberalism and the Rise of Common Sense* (Dallas: Word, 1993). Jerry Falwell's major book is *Listen, America* (Garden City, N.Y.: Doubleday, 1980).

27. Among the leading evangelical novels are Charles W. Colson, *Gideon's Torch* (Dallas: Word, 1995); Tim LaHaye, *Left Behind: A Novel about Earth's Last Days* (Wheaton, Ill.: Tyndale Press, 1995); and Frank Peretti, *The Oath* (Dallas: Word, 1995). See Diamond, *Not by Politics Alone*, 53–56.

28. Diamond, *Not by Politics Alone*, 45–53.

29. Diamond, *Spiritual Warfare*, 60–61.

30. Ibid., 62–63.

31. See Katherine S. Newman, "Winners and Losers in the '80s and '90s," in *Declining Fortunes: The Withering of the American Dream* (New York: Basic Books, 1993), 28–55. For patterns of economic downturn in the eighties, see Bennett Harrison and Barry Bluestone, *The Great U-Turn: Corporate Restructuring and the Polarization of America* (New York: Basic Books, 1988); and Frank Levy, *Dollars and Dreams: The Changing American Income Distribution* (New York: W. W. Norton, 1987).

32. See Diamond, *Spiritual Warfare*, 161–200.

33. Ibid., 200–4; also Ruth W. Mouly, *The Religious Right and Israel: The Politics of Armageddon* (Chicago: Midwest Research, 1985) and Grace Hadsell, *Prophecy and Politics: Militant Evangelicals on the Road to Nuclear War* (Westport, Conn.: Lawrence Hill, 1986). For popular evangelical writings on the Middle East and the coming Armageddon, see Mike Evans, *Israel: America's Key to Survival* (Plainfield, N.J.: Logos International, 1981); Hal Lindsay, *The Late Great Planet Earth* (Grand Rapids; Zondervan, 1970) and *The 1980s, Countdown to Armageddon* (New York: Bantam, 1981); and David Allen Lewis, *Magog 1982 Cancelled* (Harrison, Alaska: New Leaf Press, 1982). For the history of Christian Zionism, see Rosemary and Herman Ruether, *The Wrath of Jonah: The Crisis of Religious Nationalism in the Israeli-Palestinian Conflict* (San Francisco: Harper and Row, 1989), 86–90, 175–79.

34. Anti-Defamation League, *The Religious Right: The Assault on Tolerance* (New York: ADL, 1994), 70.

35. The Anti-Defamation League's study on the Christian Right (ibid.) profiles leaders such as Pat Robertson primarily in terms of their anti-Semitism, which it sees as being implicit in their pro-Zionism.

36. Diamond, *Not by Politics Alone*, 76–79; see also Ralph Reed, *Politically Incorrect: The Emerging Faith Factor in American Politics* (Dallas: Word, 1994). For stealth election tactics, see Rob Bisher, "Stealth Strategy," *Church and State*, October 1995, 64ff.

37. Diamond, *Not by Politics Alone*, 219–21, 231–37.

38. Ibid., 84–88. Also the American Center for Law and Justice newsletter, *Law and Justice*; and see the profile on the American Center for Law and Justice and its major attorney, Jay Sekulow, in the ADL publication *The Religious Right*, 47–52.

39. Diamond, *Spiritual Warfare*, 84–90. Also Sara Diamond, "School Days, Rule Days," in *Facing the Wrath: Confronting the Right in Dangerous Times* (Monroe, Maine: Common Courage Press, 1996), 57–64. A major examplar of the Christian Right's views on "secular humanism" is Tim LaHaye's *The Battle for the Mind* (Old Tappan, N.J.: Fleming H. Revell Co., 1979).

40. Diamond, *Not by Politics Alone*, 126–30.

41. New Right women leaders have written a number of books expounding the

evangelical view of women, sex, and marriage. See Marabel Morgan, *Total Woman* (Old Tappan, N.J.: Fleming H. Revell, 1975); also the numerous books by Beverly LaHaye, such as *The Act of Marriage: The Beauty of Sexual Love* (Grand Rapids: Zondervan, 1976); *The Spirit-Controlled Woman* (Eugene: Harvest House Publications, 1970); and *The Restless Woman* (Grand Rapids: Zondervan, 1989). For critiques, see Faludi, *Backlash*, 247–56; and Carol Flake, *Redemptorama* (New York: Penguin Books, 1984).

42. For the Family Protection Act, see John Dempsey, *The Family and Public Policy* (Baltimore: Brook Publications, 1981), 89–90; also Rosemary R. Ruether, "Feminism, Church and Family in the 1980s," *New Black Friars* (May 1989), 207–8.

43. Diamond, *Not by Politics Alone*, 102–3. The author cites articles in the *Washington Post* (18 May 1995) and the *Washington Times* (20 May 1995) on the Contract with the American Family; see page 254, notes 50 and 51.

44. Michele McKeegan, *Abortion Politics: Mutiny in the Ranks of the Right* (New York: Free Press, 1992), 147–76.

45. Diamond, *Not by Politics Alone*, 140–41. Also Karen O'Connor, *No Neutral Ground? Abortion Politics in an Age of Absolutes* (Boulder: Westview Press, 1996).

46. Faludi, *Backlash*, 400–53; also Diamond, *Not by Politics Alone*, 135–39.

47. A handbook for Christian Right clinic closings is Joseph M. Schleider's *Closed: 99 Ways to Stop Abortions* (Westchester, Ill.: Crossway Books, 1985). For antiabortion violence, see Tom Burghart, *Low-Intensity Warfare: An Anti-Abortion Strategy of Terror* (San Francisco: Bay Area Coalition for Reproductive Rights, 1989), and Dallas A. Blanchard and Terry Prewitt, *Religious Violence and Abortion* (Gainesville: University Press of Florida, 1993).

48. For justifications of murdering doctors, see Michael Bray, *A Time to Kill: A Study Concerning the Use of Force and Abortion* (Portland, Ore.: Advocates for Life, 1994). For the links between antiabortion groups and Christian militia, see John Kifner, "Abortion Foes Find Allies in Right-Wing Militant Groups," *San Francisco Examiner*, 6 December 1998).

49. For an assessment of the accessibility of abortion, see the National Abortion and Reproductive Rights Action League, *Who Decides? A State-by-State Review of Abortion and Reproductive Rights*, 6th ed. (Washington, D.C.: NARRAL, 1997).

50. See Anita Bryant, *The Anita Bryant Story: The Survival of Our Nation's Families and the Threat of Militant Homosexuality* (Old Tappan, N.J.: Fleming H. Revell, 1977). Both the Bryant and the Briggs campaigns became major opportunities for gay and lesbian political organizing. News of the anti-Briggs campaign appeared in the California magazine *Lesbian Tide* from July to December 1978: see Lillian Faderman, *Odd Girls and Twilight Lovers: A History of Lesbian Life in Twentieth-Century America* (New York: Columbia University Press, 1991), 199–200, 343–44 nn. 19, 20.

51. Chris Bull and John Gallagher, *Perfect Enemies: The Religious Right, the Gay Movement and the Politics of the 1990s* (New York: Crown, 1996), 40–60.

52. See Jean Hardisty, "Constructing Homophobia: Colorado's Right Wing Attack on Homosexuals," in *Eyes Right: Challenging the Right Wing Backlash* (Boston: South End Press, 1995), 86–104. Also Didi Herman, *The Anti-Gay Agenda: Orthodox Christianity and the Christian Right* (Chicago: The University of Chicago Press, 1997), 137–69. An insider's view may be found in Stephen Blansford, *Gay Politics vs. Colorado: The Inside Story of the Amendment* (Cascade, Colo.: Sardis, 1994).

53. Legal data on gay and lesbian rights are taken from March 1999 Fact Sheets on Hate Crimes, Sodomy Laws and Civil Rights, published on-line by the National Gay and Lesbian Task Force, www.ngltf.org. An earlier study is Richard D. Mohr, *Gay Justice: A Study of Ethics, Society and Law* (New York: Columbia University Press, 1988).

54. Gay and lesbian groups and researchers have published a number of books supporting gay and lesbian marriages and parenting; see Robert P. Cabaj and David W. Purcell, eds., *On the Road to Same-Sex Marriage: A Supportive Guide to Psychological, Political and Legal Issues* (San Francisco: Josey-Bass Publishers, 1998), April Martin, *The Lesbian and Gay Parenting Handbook: Creating and Raising Our Families* (New York: Harper Perennial, 1993), Kath Weston, *Families We Choose: Lesbians, Gays, Kinship* (New York: Columbia University Press, 1991); and Elizabeth Say and Mark R. Kowalewski, *Gays, Lesbians and Family Values* (Cleveland: Pilgrim Press, 1998).

55. Legal data are taken from March 1999 Fact Sheets on Marriage and on Family Issues, published on-line by the National Gay and Lesbian Task Force, www.ngltf.org.

56. Herman, *Anti-Gay Agenda,* 60–91; also Laura Flanders, "Hate on Tape," in *Eyes Right,* 105–8. A major Christian Right tract is Tim LaHaye, *What Everyone Should Know about Homosexuality* (Wheaton, Ill.: Tyndale House, 1978).

57. Herman, *Anti-Gay Agenda,* 92–106.

58. This statement by Robertson was reported by Maralee Schwartz and Kenneth J. Cooper in "Equal Rights Initiative in Iowa Attacked," *Washington Post,* 23 August 1992, A15.

59. See. Diamond, *Not by Politics Alone,* 164–65. People for the American Way has done major monitoring on the movement for "conversion" of homosexuals in the Christian Right: see the organization's *Hostile Climate 1995: A State-by-State Report on Anti-Gay Activity* (Washington, D.C.: People for the American Way, 1995). For Christian Right publications on this topic, see Darlene Bogle, *Strangers in a Christian Land: Reaching Out with Hope and Healing to the Homosexual* (Old Tappan, N.J.: Chosen Books, 1990), and Bob Davies and Lori Rentzel, *Coming Out of Homosexuality* (Downers Grove, Ill.: Intervarsity Press, 1971).

60. Diamond, *Not by Politics Alone,* 224–35; also Russ Bellant, "Promise Keepers: Christian Soldiers for Theocracy," in *Eyes Right,* 81–85; Joe Conason, Alfred Ross, and Lee Cokorinos, "The Promise Keepers Are Coming: The Third Wave of the Religious Right," *The Nation,* 7 October 1996, 11–19; Nancy Novosad, "God Squad: The Promise Keepers Fight for a Man's World," *The Progressive,* August 1996,

25-27. See also Promise Keepers Watch, Center for Democracy Studies, c/o The National Institute, 177 E. 87th Street, Suite 404, New York City, NY 10128; e-mail: CDSResearch@compuserve.com.

61. *Seven Promises of a Promise Keeper*, ed. Bill McCartney et al. (Dallas: Word, 1999).

62. Diamond, *Not by Politics Alone,* 123. The author cites the Barna Report 1, no. 1 (1996), which noted that while the average divorce rate for Americans was one in four (24 percent), born-again Christians averaged 27 percent, and Christian fundamentalists 30 percent.

63. Peggy Leslie, "A Woman at Promise Keepers," and "New Women's Organizations Patterned after PK," *Southern California Christian Times,* August 1996, 26, 27.

64. Among the recent books on Promise Keepers are Bryan W. Brickner, *The Promise Keepers: Politics and Promises* (Lanham, Md.: Lexington Books, 1999); Nancy Novosad, *Promise Keepers: Playing God* (New York: Prometheus, 1999); and Judith Newton, *The Promise Keepers: Postmodern Encounter with Men on the Right* (Cleveland: Pilgrim Press, 1999).

65. For a critique of the Million Man March by a black feminist, see Patricia J. Williams, "Different Drummer Please, Marchers," *The Nation,* 20 October 1995, 493. For a black Christian male perspective, see Garth Baker-Fletcher, ed., *Black Religion after the Million Man March* (Maryknoll, N.Y.: Orbis Press, 1998).

66. Joel Dyer, *Harvest of Rage: Why Oklahoma City Is Only the Beginning* (Boulder: Westview Press, 1997).

67. The Southern Poverty Law Center regularly monitors the Patriot, militia, and Christian Identity movements: see *Patriot Games,* Intelligence Report of the Southern Poverty Law Center, spring 1998. Numerous studies have been written about these movements; see James Coates, *Armed and Dangerous: The Rise of the Survivalist Right* (New York: Hill and Wang, 1987); Leonard Zeskin and James Corcoran, *Bitter Harvest: Gordon Kahl and the Posse Comitatus: Murder in the Heartland* (New York: Penguin Books, 1990); and Brian Levin and Brian Halpern, *Limits of Dissent: The Constitutional Status of Armed Civilian Militias* (Amherst, Mass.: Aletheia Press, 1996).

68. Sara Diamond has studied the far-Right Patriot and Identity groups; see her *Facing the Wrath,* 188-217, and *Roads to Dominion,* 257-273. She cautions against a liberal conflation of these groups with the mainline Christian Right in an article entitled, "It's Political, Stupid," in *Facing the Wrath,* 39-46.

69. See the "Vatican Declaration on the Question of Admission of Women to the Ministerial Priesthood" (1976), and the critical commentary in Leonard and Arlene Swidler, eds., *Women Priests: A Catholic Commentary on the Vatican Declaration* (New York: Paulist Press, 1977). For the Southern Baptist conflict over women's ordination, see Dina G. Mainrod, *The Voices among Us: An Exploration of the Meaning and Practice of Ministry for Ordained Southern Baptist Clergywomen* (D.Min. thesis, Garrett-Evangelical Theological Seminary, 1997), 47-64.

70. See Nancy J. Berneking and Pamela Carter Joern, eds., *Remembering and Reimagining* (Cleveland: Pilgrim Press, 1995).

71. The Reconciling Congregation Program can be contacted at 3801 N. Keeler Avenue, Chicago, IL 60641. Its Web site address is www.rcp.org.

72. Numerous articles appeared on the Greg Dell trial; see Steve Klohn, "God under the Collar," *Chicago Tribune Magazine*, 21 February 1999, 10–14; and Louis Weisberg, "Honoring Vows: Local Pastor Defies Methodists' Marriage Ban," *Windy City Times*, 1 October 1998.

73. The In All Things Charity movement of the United Methodist Church is based at the Broadway United Methodist Church, 3344 N. Broadway, Chicago, IL 60657; e-mail: IATC98@aol.com.

8. The Many Faces of American Families in the Year 2000

1. U.S. Census data are taken from the *1999 World Almanac and Book of Facts* (New York: World Almanac, 1999), 373. The census states that whites make up 83 percent of the American population, an unsupportable claim by its own figures unless Hispanics are counted as white. I have subtracted the percentages for African Americans, Hispanics, Asians and Pacific Islanders, and Native-Americans to reach the figure of 71 percent white.

2. See Cynthia B. Costello, Shari Miles, and Anne J. Stone, eds., *The American Woman, 1999–2000* (New York: W. W. Norton, 1998), 219.

3. See Steven Mintz and Susan Kellogg, *Domestic Revolutions: A Social History of American Family Life* (New York: The Free Press, 1988), 178–79; also Costello et al., *American Woman, 1999–2000*, 217.

4. Costello et al., *American Woman, 1999–2000*, 218; also *Monthly Vital Statistics Report* 45, no. 12 (17 July 1997), cited in Constance Ahron, *The Good Divorce: Keeping Your Family Together When Your Marriage Comes Apart* (New York: Harper Perennial, 1995), 279.

5. Ahron, *The Good Divorce*, 25, 205.

6. Mintz and Kellogg, in *Domestic Revolutions*, cite the figure that women lose 73 percent of income after divorce, while men gain 43 percent (page 227). These data are drawn from Lenore Weitzmann, *The Divorce Revolution: The Unexpected Social and Economic Consequences for Women and Children* (New York: The Free Press, 1985). This figure is generally seen as an exaggeration: women's economic loss from divorce is actually closer to 40 percent. See the critique of Weitzmann's research in Susan Faludi, *Backlash: The Undeclared War against American Women* (New York: Crown, 1991), 19–25.

7. Ahron, *The Good Divorce*, 217–18.

8. Ibid, 207–11. See also Judith Stacey, *Brave New Families: Stories of Domestic*

Upheaval in Late-Twentieth-Century America (New York: Basic Books, 1990). Stacey studied the complex forms of kinship being created by divorce and remarriage among working-class people in California's Silicon Valley during the mid-1980s.

9. These data are drawn from the studies of the Alan Guttmacher Institute, cited in *The State of America's Children: A Report from the Children's Defense Fund*, introduction by Marian Wright Edelman (Boston: Beacon Press, 1998), 96.

10. Ibid., 93.

11. Rebecca Blank, *It Takes a Nation: A New Agenda for Fighting Poverty* (New York and Princeton, N.J.: Russell Sage Foundation and Princeton University Press, 1997), 36–37.

12. *State of American's Children,* 97.

13. Rebecca Blank disputes the popular conservative view that AFDC encourages poor women to be sexually promiscuous and to have out-of-wedlock children; she sees the latter problem instead as primarily an effect of the lack of marriageable, employed males among the cohort of teens: see her *It Takes a Nation,* 33–39, 149. William Julius Wilson makes a similar argument, with a focus on black youth, in his *The Truly Disadvantaged* (Chicago: University of Chicago Press, 1987), 81–92.

14. For the use of contraception, see *The State of America's Children*, 96–97. Although three in four teens use contraception regularly, many are reluctant to go to health clinics to obtain information on birth control for fear of being stigmatized as sexually promiscuous.

15. See Andrew Hacker, "Post-Marital Economics," *Fortune,* 23 December 1985, 167–70; also Mintz and Kellogg, *Domestic Revolutions,* 305 n. 85.

16. I draw these remarks from personal observation over thirty years. In my experience, though men who divorce at the time of the empty nest seem more often to marry younger women and start new families, and women who divorce at this stage more often seem to enter into careers, these directions are not necessarily two sides of the same couple. Some men's first wives feel shocked and abandoned, unprepared for self-support; the women who enter into careers are generally those who have been preparing for such careers through education and employment during marriage.

17. See Mintz and Kellogg, *Domestic Revolutions,* 227.

18. Ahron, *The Good Divorce,* 152–53.

19. Judges in divorce courts often overestimate the ability of divorced wives to support themselves, failing to reckon with that group of wives which has not worked during marriage; see Mintz and Kellogg, *Domestic Revolutions,* 230.

20. A major study of housework and child care in two-earner families is Arlie Hochchild, *The Second Shift: Working Parents and the Revolution at Home* (New York: Viking Penguin, 1989).

21. For tables of life expectancy by decade, race, and gender, see Nancy Woloch, *Women and the American Experience* (New York: McGraw-Hill, 1994), 2:585.

22. See Blank, *It Takes a Nation,* 20–21.

23. Ahron, *The Good Divorce,* 280.

24. See note 62, chapter 7 above.

25. Ahron, *The Good Divorce,* 34–36, 92.

26. Ibid., 27–29, 185–187.

27. For Milton's treatise on divorce, see page 250, note 73, above.

28. *The State of America's Children,* 6.

29. Studies on the economic downturn in the United States since 1973 abound. See particularly Bennett Harrison and Barry Bluestone, *The Deindustrialization of America: Plant Closing, Community Abandonment and the Dismantling of Basic Industry* (New York: Basic Books, 1982). For a general evaluation of this trend, see Andrew J. Winnick, *Toward Two Societies: The Changing Distribution of Income and Wealth in the United States since 1960* (New York: Praeger, 1989), 35–49.

30. Blank, *It Takes a Nation,* 67–68.

31. Major series on economic downsizing in the United States appeared in the *Chicago Tribune* in August 1995 and in the *New York Times* in March 1996. The first of these, authored by R. C. Longworth and Sharman Stein, ran in five installments in the *Tribune* on August 20–24, 1995. The *New York Times* series of seven articles was authored by Louis Uchitelle, N. R. Kleinfield, Rick Bragg, Sara Rimer, Kirk Johnson, Elizabeth Kolbert, Adam Clymer, David E. Sanger, and Steve Lohr, and ran under the general title "The Downsizing of America" on March 3–9, 1996. In this same area, see Bennett Harrison and Barry Bluestone, *The Great U-Turn: Corporate Restructuring and the Polarization of America* (New York: Basic Books, 1988).

32. For job ladders and job segmentation for men and women, see Blank, *It Takes a Nation,* 64; also Harrison and Bluestone, *The Great U-Turn,* 44, 55.

33. See chapter 5, pages 107–8.

34. See Frank Levy, *The New Dollars and Dreams* (New York: Russell Sage Foundation, 1998), 191–93.

35. Katherine S. Newman, *Falling from Grace: The Experience of Downward Mobility of the American Middle Class* (New York: The Free Press, 1988), 20–41, and *Declining Fortunes: The Withering of the American Dream* (New York: Basic Books, 1993), 29–40.

36. For popular misconstruals of the causes of poverty, see Blank, *It Takes a Nation,* 3–6.

37. Newman, *Declining Fortunes,* 171–99.

38. See the *1999 World Almanac,* 242; also the *1999 Wall Street Journal Almanac* (New York: Ballantine Books, 1999), 607.

39. Newman, *Declining Fortunes,* 217–18; also *The State of America's Children,* 49, on the cost of education. Pell grants for low-income college students, which covered

77 percent of the tuition for public colleges in 1979, in 1993 covered only 35 percent of the tuition costs.

40. Newman, *Declining Fortunes,* 29–40.

41. Ibid., 22–23, 165–66.

42. Ibid., 30–31.

43. Ibid., 38–40, citing the United States National Commission on Children, *Beyond Rhetoric: A New American Agenda for Children and Families: Final Report of the National Commission on Children* (Washington, D.C.: The Commission, 1991), 228 n. 28.

44. A classic study of suburbanization in the 1950s and '60s is Herbert Gans, *The Levittowners: Ways of Life and Politics in a New Suburban Community* (New York: Vintage, 1967). For the relation between suburbanization and road building and the promotion of automobiles, see Kenneth T. Jackson, *Crabgrass Frontier: The Suburbanization of the United States* (New York: Oxford University Press, 1985). For a more recent study of the crisis in suburban life, see Mark Baldassare, *Trouble in Paradise: The Suburban Transformation in America* (New York: Columbia University Press, 1988).

45. Costello, *American Woman, 1999–2000,* 313.

46. Ibid., 310.

47. See Elizabeth Higginbotham, "Black Professional Women: Job Ceilings and Employment Sectors," in *Women of Color in U.S. Society,* ed. Maxine Baca Zinn and Bonnie Thornton Dill (Philadelphia: Temple University Press, 1944), 113–31. For the 1960s to '80s, see Natalie Sokoloff, *Black and White Women in the Professions: Occupational Segregation by Race and Gender, 1960–1980* (New York: Routledge, 1992).

48. These figures are drawn from two graphs provided in Blank, *It Takes a Nation,* 62–63.

49. Costello, *American Woman, 1999–2000,* 193–94.

50. Ibid., 193, 239.

51. Ibid., 243.

52. Ibid., 287.

53. Ibid., 306.

54. Ibid., 301, 307.

55. Ibid., 301, 303.

56. For a survey of changing wealth and poverty based on figures from the 1996 U.S. Census Report, see R. C. Longworth, "A Bottom-Line Blight on American Life," *Chicago Tribune,* 5 October 1997, sec. 2, 1.

57. Ibid.; also Winnick, *Toward Two Societies,* 180–88 and table 7–7.

58. Winnick, *Toward Two Societies,* 180–88 and table 7–7; see also Keith Bradstreet,

"The Rich Control More of U.S. Wealth, Study Says, as Debts Grow for the Poor," *New York Times*, 22 June 1996.

59. For the roots of welfare policy from the Progressive era to the New Deal, see Linda Gordon, *Pitied but Not Entitled: Single Mothers and the History of Welfare, 1890–1935* (New York: The Free Press, 1994).

60. For the National Welfare Rights Organization, see Frances Fox Piven and Richard Cloward, *Regulating the Poor: The Functions of Public Welfare* (New York: Pantheon Books, 1971), 320–30; also Guida West, *The National Welfare Rights Movement: The Social Protest of Poor Women* (New York: Praeger, 1981); and Jacqueline Pope, *Biting the Hand That Feeds Them: Organizing Women on Welfare at the Grass-Roots Level* (New York: Praeger, 1989).

61. For the shifting image of the black female welfare recipient from black matriarch to black teenager, see Nancy Fraser and Linda Gordon, "A Genealogy of Dependency: Tracing a Key Word of the U.S. Welfare State," in *Rethinking the Political: Gender, Resistance and the State*, ed. Barbara Laslett, Johanna Brenner, and Yesim Arat (Chicago: University of Chicago Press, 1995), 51.

62. The American welfare system is often referred to as "two-tiered," with one set of programs that are fully funded federally and that are seen as entitlements, particularly Social Security but now also SSI, and another set of programs that are seen as morally questionable and are funded at both federal and state levels: AFDC and General Assistance. See Warren R. Copeland, *And the Poor Get Welfare: The Ethics of Poverty in the United States* (Nashville: Abingdon, 1994), 48–53: also Barbara J. Nelson, "The Origins of the Two-Channel Welfare State: Workmen's Compensation and Mother's Aid," in *Women, the State and Welfare*, ed. Linda Gordon (Madison, Wisc.: University of Wisconsin Press, 1990), 123–51. I have spoken here of the system as three-tiered in order to bring corporate subsidies into the picture.

63. For the military-industrial complex as state capitalism, see Seymour Melman, *The Permanent War Economy: American Capitalism in Decline* (New York: Simon and Schuster, 1974), 27–73.

64. For a definition of the current complex of welfare subsidies, see Blank, *It Takes a Nation*, 84–88.

65. For the falling level of AFDC grants from 1970 to 1994, as well as a list of differences by state, see ibid., 100–1.

66. For the age distributions of the poor, see ibid., 16.

67. For the distribution of the poor by types of household, see ibid., 17.

68. For differences between whites and blacks in terms of years in poverty, for and the number of poor people who received AFDC in 1994, see ibid., 21, 24.

69. For differences between whites and blacks in years of receipt of welfare over a lifetime, see ibid., 153.

70. For the lack of social citizenship in the United States compared to other nations,

see Nancy Fraser and Linda Gordon, "Contract Versus Charity: Why Is There no Social Citizenship in the United States?," *Socialist Review* 22, no. 3, (1992): 45–68.

71. For a leading spokesman for the conservative view that blames welfare for perpetuating poverty, see Charles Murray, *Losing Ground: American Social Policy, 1950–1980* (New York: Basic Books, 1984).

72. See Blank, *It Takes a Nation,* 133–90, for an evaluation of the successs of the various government antipoverty programs.

73. For Nixon's rejection of the day-care bill, see page 150.

74. For time limits by state on the receipt of TANF, see the Children's Defense Fund Report, *The State of America's Children,* 9–10.

75. The drop in welfare caseloads from August 1996 to July 1998 was reported by the Administration for Children and Families, Department of Health and Human Services, 20 August 1998.

76. For a summary of the negative income tax plan that was proposed by Milton Friedman and almost passed under Nixon, see Friedman's book *Capitalism and Freedom* (Chicago: University of Chicago Press, 1962), 190–92. A summary may be found in Copeland, *And the Poor Get Welfare,* 56–59.

77. A two year-report on the effects of TANF may be is found in "Tracking Recipients after They Leave Welfare: Summaries of State Follow-up Studies," National Governors Association, National Conference of State Legislators, American Public Welfare Association, July 1998.

78. For the effects of TANF on recipients and former recipients of assistance in twenty states, as tracked through the Catholic charity system, see *Poverty amid Plenty: The Unfinished Business of Welfare Reform,* a study undertaken by the NET-WORK National Welfare Reform Watch Project (Washington, D.C.: NET-WORK, 1999), obtainable from NETWORK, a National Catholic Social Justice Lobby, 801 Pennsylvania Avenue SE, Suite 460, Washington, DC 20003–2167; e-mail: network@networklobby.org.

79. This study was done through the Children's Defense Fund Community Monitoring Project. The Children's Defense Fund's Web site is http://www.childrensdefense.org.

80. These remarks on the history of the concept of dependency are drawn from Fraser and Gordon, "A Genealogy of Dependency."

81. For a study of the time bind between expanding hours of work and home time, see Arlie Hochschild, *The Time Bind: When Work Becomes Home and Home Becomes Work* (New York: Metropolitan Books, 1997); also Juliet B. Schor, *The Overworked American: The Unexpected Decline of Leisure* (New York: Basic Books, 1991).

9. **Reimagining Families: Home, Work, Gender, and Faith**

1. For a study on sustainable community, see *One Creator, One People, One Place: A Statement of the Interreligious Sustainability Project of Metropolitan Chicago* (1999), pub-

lished by the Center for Neighborhood Technology, 2125 W. North Avenue, Chicago, IL 60647; Web site: www.cnt.org.

2. For the application of the Sabbath theme to contemporary spirituality and community in America, see Arthur Waskow, "A Temple in Time: The Jewish Vision of Shabbat," *The Other Side*, January–February, 1996, 18–19, and Tilden Edwards, *Sabbath Time* (Nashville: Upper Room, 1992).

3. For short biographical accounts of my parents, see "Solidly Rooted, Ready to Fly," *Witness* 11, no. 2 (Summer 1995): 34–38, and "A Wise Woman," *Christian Century*, 17 February 1993, 164–65.

4. For the definition of the term "postmodern family" as referring both to a diversity of forms of family and also to the loss of a normative model of family, see Judith Stacey, *In the Name of the Family: Rethinking Family Values in the Postmodern Age* (Boston: Beacon Press, 1996), 7–8.

5. Western Europe in the 1980s established a norm of a less-than-forty-hour (thirty-five to thirty-nine hours) full-time work week, plus four to six weeks of vacation, creating the equivalent of a four-day work week. See John D. Owen, *Reduced Working Hours: Cure for Unemployment or Economic Burden?* (Baltimore: John Hopkins University Press, 1989), 17–25. See also Juliet B. Schor, *The Overworked American: The Unexpected Decline of Leisure* (New York: Basic Books, 1991), 81–82.

6. See *The Swedish Experiment in Family Politics: The Myrdals and the Interwar Population Crisis* (New Brunswick, N.J.: Transaction Press, 1990).

7. See Leslie Mann, "Domesticated Dads," *Chicago Tribune*, 20 June 1999, sec. 13, p. 1. For manuals and support networks for full-time-parenting men, see athomedad@aol.com; also Dadtodad@aol.com; and www.parentcity.com.

8. A covenanted community of Jewish families that developed such a communitarian bar/bat mitzvah was described to me in May 1999 in an interview with lesbian parents in Chicago. For coming-of-age and leaving-home ceremonies, see Rosemary R. Ruether, *WomanChurch: Theory and Practice of Feminist Liturgical Communities* (San Francisco: Harper and Row, 1986), 188–92.

9. The repression by missionaries of puberty ceremonies that taught young people sexual enjoyment without pregnancy, and the consequent rise in teenage pregnancy, were described to me by Dr. Ephraim Mosethoane of the Department of Religion, University of the Transkei, South Africa, during a visit I paid there in 1989.

10. Ruether, *WomanChurch*, 163–73; see also Alternative Rituals Committee, Board of Discipleship, United Methodist Church, *Ritual in a New Day: An Invitation* (Nashville: Abingdon Press, 1976).

11. Sir Matthew Hale in circa 1678 formulated the English legal tradition that a man cannot rape his wife: "The husband cannot be guilty of rape committed by himself upon his lawful wife, for by their mutual matrimonial consent and contract the wife hath given up her self in this kind unto her husband which she cannot retract." See Rosemarie Tong, *Women, Sex and the Law* (Savage, Md.: Rowinan and Littlefield, 1989), 94–96.

12. For this debate, see Paula L. Ettelbrick, "Since When Is Marriage a Path to Liberation?," *OUT/LOOK* 2, no. 2 (1989): 9, 14–17, and Thomas B. Stoddard, "Why Gay People Should Seek the Right to Marry," *OUT/LOOK* 2, no. 2 (1989): 9–13.

13. See Janice G. Raymond, *Women as Wombs: Reproductive Technologies and the Battle over Women's Freedom* (San Francisco: Harper San Francisco, 1993).

14. On the population crisis and the impossibility of a just, sustainable life-style for six billion or more people, see David C. Korten, *When Corporations Rule the World* (San Francisco: Berrett-Koehler, 1995), 33–38.

15. See the publications put out by Catholics for Contraception, 1436 U Street NW, Washington, DC 20009.

16. Rebecca M. Blank, *It Takes a Nation: A New Agenda for Fighting Poverty* (Princeton, N.J.: Princeton University Press, 1997), 252–79.

17. Frances Fox Piven and Richard A. Cloward have argued that welfare and poor relief in America have represented a way of suppressing protest by the poor in times of instability; relief is then cut back in more stable times in order to force the poor to take low-wage jobs. See their *Regulating the Poor: The Functions of Public Welfare* (New York: Pantheon Books, 1971), 32–38.

18. For amended tables for Friedman's proposal for a negative income tax, based on a minimum grant at the poverty level and a 50 percent work incentive, see Warren R. Copeland, *And the Poor Get Welfare: The Ethics of Poverty in the United States* (Nashville, Tenn.: Abingdon Press, 1994), 58–59.

19. Korten, *When Corporations Rule the World*, 307–24.

20. For ecological ethics for a just, sustainable society, see particularly Daniel C. Maguire, "Population-Consumption-Ecology"; John B. Cobb, "Christianity, Economics and Ecology"; and Larry Rasmussen, "Global Ecojustice: The Church's Mission in Urban Society," in Rosemary R. Ruether and Dieter T. Hessel, eds., *Christianity and Ecology* (Cambridge, Mass.: Harvard University Press, 2000), 403–27, 497–511, 515–27.

21. The contact persons for Call to Action are Sheila and Dan Daley, 4419 W. Kedzie, Chicago, IL 60618. For the Witherspoon Society, contact Eugene TeSelle at the Divinity School, Vanderbilt University, Nashville TN 37240. Progressive Presbyterians have linked their reform movements into an umbrella group named Semper Reformanda, whose Web site is SemperReformanda.org. The address for the Methodist Federation for Social Action is 212 Capitol Street, Washington, DC 20003. The contact person for the Consultation is Canon Ed Rodman, Diocese of Massachusetts, 138 Tremont Street, Boston, MA 02111.

22. For the Jewish tradition of modeling holy sexual union after the union of God and his Shekinah, see Raphael Patai, *The Hebrew Goddess* (New York: Ktav Publishing, 1967), 258–69.

23. Bernard of Clairvaux, "On the Song of Songs," sermon I.3 in *The Works of Bernard of Clairvaux,* vol. 1, ed. Kilian Walsh (Spencer, Mass.: Cistercian Publishers, 1971), 2.